A THEOLOGY OF CREATION

CATHOLIC IDEAS FOR A SECULAR WORLD

O. Carter Snead, series editor

Under the sponsorship of the de Nicola Center for Ethics and Culture at the University of Notre Dame, the purpose of this interdisciplinary series is to feature authors from around the world who will expand the influence of Catholic thought on the most important conversations in academia and the public square. The series is "Catholic" in the sense that the books will emphasize and engage the enduring themes of human dignity and flourishing, the common good, truth, beauty, justice, and freedom in ways that reflect and deepen principles affirmed by the Catholic Church for millennia. It is not limited to Catholic authors or even works that explicitly take Catholic principles as a point of departure. Its books are intended to demonstrate the diversity and enhance the relevance of these enduring themes and principles in numerous subjects, ranging from the arts and humanities to the sciences.

A THEOLOGY OF CREATION

Ecology, Art, and Laudato Si'

THOMAS S. HIBBS

University of Notre Dame Press
Notre Dame, Indiana

University of Notre Dame Press
Notre Dame, Indiana 46556
undpress.nd.edu

All Rights Reserved

Copyright © 2023 by University of Notre Dame

Published in the United States of America

Paperback edition published in 2026

Library of Congress Control Number: 2023937440

ISBN: 978-0-268-20562-1 (Hardback)
ISBN: 978-0-268-20563-8 (Paperback)
ISBN: 978-0-268-20564-5 (WebPDF)
ISBN: 978-0-268-20561-4 (Epub3)

GPSR Compliance Inquiries:
Lightning Source France, 1 Av. Johannes Gutenberg, 78310 Maurepas, France
compliance@lightningsource.fr | Phone: +33 1 30 49 23 42

To Paulette and Buddy,
who have been dear friends for two decades,
I dedicate whatever there is here of a book

CONTENTS

Preface ix

Acknowledgments xv

ONE
Laudato Si', Technocracy, and the Renewal of Human Making 1

TWO
Jacques Maritain and the Twilight of Civilization 31

THREE
Nihilism and Modernity in Endless Crisis 51

FOUR
The Ecological Poetics of Robinson Jeffers 71

FIVE
The Sacramental Poetics of William Everson 83

SIX
Georges Rouault: Artist of Alienation and Transfiguration 109

SEVEN
Culture Care, Generativity, and the Calling of the Artist 139

Notes 155

Index 185

PREFACE

A young boy in Terrence Malick's film *The Tree of Life* asks his mother, "Tell us a story from before we can remember." Malick begins his film with *the* story from before we can remember. A lengthy opening sequence traces the history of the universe, from initial explosion and expansion through the formation of galaxies and planets to the development of life on a "poor little planet born of a catastrophe," as the philosopher Charles De-Koninck calls earth.[1] The film is an ambitious artistic exploration of questions rarely formulated by religious believers: How are we to think about cosmology, about the place of human existence in the capacious orders of time and space? What does or should it matter to us, to the universe, or to God that we occupy a speck of seemingly insignificant space in an incomprehensibly vast universe? What we know of modern cosmology and paleontology makes the Psalmist's question even more weighty: "What is man that you are mindful of him, the son of man that you care for him?" (Ps 8:4). As one character puts it to God, "What are we to you?" Malick's opening gives dramatic weight to the film's epigraph from Job: "Where were you when I laid the foundations of the earth? When the morning stars sang together and all the sons of God shouted for joy?" (38:4, 7). Those questions frame the story of a family in Waco, Texas, in the 1950s.

Not only does the film envelop the individual lives of the family members in a cosmic drama of creation, but it also continually interjects a vertical perspective into their linear story line. Emmanuel Lubezki's always stunning cinematography here takes the form of mildly disorienting vertical camera angles. The suggestion is that we need to look up and down in addition to before and after to get our bearings on events and persons. In Malick's hands, the violation of linear narrative unity is neither a postmodern repudiation of the possibility of meaning nor a celebration of the dissolution of personal identity and the absurdity of human life. It opens up the possibility of another perspective on the action, one descending from above, from the God who transcends the entire order of time and space and yet mysteriously intervenes.

Complementing the sparse dialogue between characters is their interior monologues. The characters' interior conversations occasionally contain comments on other characters, but more often than not, their intended audience is God, to whom they pose questions and express doubts or remorse. The story begins with catastrophe, with the parents receiving word of the death of a son. The loss prompts silent questioning of God: "Why? Where were you? Why should I be good if you aren't?"

Malick's film is a corrective to the contemporary Christian tendency to avoid nature and science altogether. In flight from the doctrine of evolution and in dread of what Pascal calls "the silence of these infinite spaces," many Christians have little to say about the physical cosmos or our bodies.[2] The danger is angelism, the temptation to think of ourselves as if we were not animals, as if we were not part of a grand, terrifying, and mysterious physical universe, crafted by the same God who created us. To be embodied is to be part of a complex and interconnected network of physical beings. The wonder inspired by encountering the vast power of nature should increase, rather than diminish, our awe of God.

What we most need is a reimagining of the place of human persons in the entirety of the created cosmos. This, I would argue, is precisely what Pope Francis offers in *Laudato Si': On Care for Our Common Home*, in which he discerns beneath contemporary ecological problems a metaphysical and existential affliction of the human person, who is now lost in the cosmos, increasingly alienated from self, others, nature, and God.[3] Pope Francis's encyclical *Laudato Si'* is a theologically rich document, containing an extensive analysis of the crisis of modernity, an analysis informed in surprising and fruitful ways by medieval sources—Francis of Assisi of course but also Aquinas. In fact, the juxtaposition of the mystic poet and the metaphysician of creation calls to mind Chesterton's brilliantly eccentric take on the two saints. It also suggests possibilities for rereading these medieval figures in ways that recognize them as important voices in contemporary conversations.

Both the analysis and the culling of resources from the past suggest a line of development that the document does not explicitly follow. To respond to the alienating features of modern thought and culture requires a renewed understanding of human making, of the place of human persons within the whole of creation, and a renewal of certain kinds of virtues: wonder, receptivity, gratitude, and generosity. *LS* explicitly calls for an "aesthetic education," but I have in mind something more ambitious. There has been a good deal of philosophical and theological work done on the relevant theological and philosophical topics in aesthetics, work that has not yet been brought fully into conversation with the broad ecological issues that *LS* raises. Moreover, many artists have addressed these topics, implicitly in their artistic work and explicitly in their occasional writings about art. Indeed, it is one of the contentions of this book that artists have much to teach us, that they are often wiser than philosophers and theologians.

Although the climate change sections of the document received, quite reasonably, a great deal of attention in the popular press, the larger philosophical and theological themes of the document continue to be neglected. Read as a unified whole, the document diagnoses an environmental manifestation of a deeper and more widespread crisis. Francis follows his immediate papal predecessors—and many modern Catholic thinkers—in tracing the roots of the crisis to radical anthropocentrism or technocracy. What is new in this document is not just a further development of the inherent links between human and natural ecology, especially of what the latter entails, but also and more profoundly the claim that the other great source of the crisis is biocentrism, which arises as a reaction to anthropocentrism. We vacillate between the two, Francis says.

If anthropocentrism finds a natural home in a certain strain of Enlightenment progressive rationalism, biocentrism has its roots in certain forms of Romanticism, with which it continues to share numerous family resemblances. In contrast to anthropocentrism, which has been subject to extensive critical engagement in contemporary Catholic thought, biocentrism is generally ignored. That's unfortunate, and not just because biocentrism is, as *LS* notes, influential in the environmental movement. Variants of Romanticism inform the most powerful contemporary views of nature, views that provide alternatives to technocracy. Catholic thinkers sometimes formulate the options concerning nature in a mutually exclusive manner, as if the contest were between anthropocentric technocracy and some version of natural law. But many contemporaries see the merit of the critique of the former without being moved by the latter. There are many reasons for this but one of them is that a compelling and pervasive narrative about nature, running through much of our culture, high and low and from film to music, is that of Romanticism.

In these two modern traditions, there is a preoccupation with the human person as maker, as scientific technician or as artistic creator. One way to sum up the crisis of late modernity is as a crisis of the human person as maker, in which our capacity to make and remake knows no limits and evacuates the natural world, even human life, of purpose and meaning.

One of the most important Catholic thinkers in this conversation is Jacques Maritain, who, along with other mid-twentieth-century thinkers, shares Francis's concerns about technocracy. In works such as *Education at the Crossroads*, Maritain worries about an ascendant technocracy that would divest civilization of properly human ends and capacities.[4] Very early on, Maritain was focused on the threat of nihilism and not in a merely academic mode. He and his wife, Raissa, began their time together with a suicide pact, an agreement that if they could not discover a purpose to human life they would end their lives instead of resigning themselves to an absurd existence.

Alone among influential Thomistic thinkers, Maritain was preoccupied with modern art, in which he detected both a playing out of some of the self-destructive tendencies in modern philosophy and lines of development that suggested ways of averting or overcoming the threat of nihilism. His writing on art often arises not just from theoretical questions, but from ongoing conversations with some of the most influential artists of the twentieth century, including Chagall, Cocteau, and Rouault. Maritain embraces positive developments in modern art. His genealogy of modern art is thus quite different from his standard, and standardly neo-Thomist, genealogy of the history of philosophy, a story of rise (up to Aquinas) and fall (from Scotus on).

This is not to say that Maritain's work is without flaw. Indeed, his work on art remains in some sense an unfinished project. And, as we shall see, it is vulnerable to critique. Like another contemporary French philosopher, Jean-Luc Marion, whose work I also consider, he may be too much under the influence of Romantic models of genius. Perhaps surprisingly for all his intimacy with working artists, his own analyses rarely attend in detail to the specific elements of particular works of art. That is something I attempt to remedy in the second half of this book.

Whatever its limitations, Maritain's writings on the creative process continue to be embraced by artists—from Flannery O'Connor to Seamus Heaney. Perhaps the most interesting contemporary example of his ongoing influence can be found in the work of the Japanese American painter Makoto Fujimura, who also includes Rouault among his sources of inspiration. Fujimura's accent on "culture care" resonates with a number of themes from *LS*. The title of his book on this topic, *Culture Care: Reconnecting with Beauty for Our Common Life*, calls to mind the themes, and even the title, of *LS*: common home, common life.[5] The implicit argument of *LS*, namely, that ecological imagination requires an aesthetic education, is made explicit in Fujimura's work. Culture care provides for "our culture's soul . . . so that reminders of beauty—both ephemeral and enduring—are present in even the harshest environments where survival is at stake."[6] Like Maritain, Fujimura discovers in Rouault an artist who was attuned to the threats of meaninglessness and the dislocations of human persons in the modern world, immersed in the currents and techniques of contemporary art, and able to draw on traditional theological and artistic resources in a way that could speak to, and in the language of, contemporary artistic culture.

In a quite different medium and in a quite different spirit, the poet William Everson produces a body of work that wrestles with the dislocation of the modern person, from self, other, cosmos, and God. Everson was a midcentury Beat poet, then—after his conversion to Catholicism and his entrance into the Dominican order—a religious poet. During his time at St. Albert's in Oakland, living under the name Brother Antoninus, he produced a remarkable body of poetry, the quality of which has led the literary scholar Albert Gelpi to call him the second greatest (behind T. S. Eliot) religious poet of the twentieth century.[7] The chief influence on his work is the California nature poet Robinson Jeffers, often called the poet laureate of the environmental movement.

It is the contention of this book that these artists have much to teach us about the sources of our dislocation and about how we might come to see and speak in a discourse that recovers a sense of our place within the whole. They avoid the mutually exclusive extremes of anthropocentrism and biocentrism. Even here they complicate matters; for they see that hitting and maintaining a clearly defined mean between the two is going to be elusive. What they often present or display in their art is the right sort of tension between the two.

They can also help us overcome certain limits to the standard Catholic genealogical critique of modernity. A fundamental problem with this standard story is that it fails to take note of what Pierre Manent calls the difference between the causality of ideas and the causality of motives.[8] It assumes that undesirable changes in modern life can be traced to the emergence of new, erroneous ideas or malformed theories: nominalism, mechanism, determinism, anthropocentrism, and so forth. But, as Manent notes, an idea by itself is not a motive. The standard Catholic genealogy fails to account for why the ideas were so readily embraced. In the case of *LS*, for example, it seems at times to fall prey to a naively Romantic conception of nature, as harmonious, pacific, and naturally calling forth the virtues of wonder and gratitude. But one reason anthropocentrism, with its promise of technological mastery, gained such traction is that nature is in many ways inhospitable to human desire and aspiration. As a number of theologians sympathetic to the project of *LS* have noted, the document itself seems too often to embrace a naively Romantic view of nature. It thus fails to reckon with the role of violence in nature. A related criticism of the document has to do with its relative neglect of the role in nature of contingency and chance, highlighted in modern evolutionary theory. Of course, there are theological and philosophical resources that can aid us in developing a more capacious theological account of the created universe. The artists to which I turn resisted the reductionistic accounts from the very start.

ACKNOWLEDGMENTS

This book arises from many years of research and conversations, almost all of which had their institutional home in Baylor University's Honor College during a time when I served as its inaugural dean. I have incurred many happy debts.

Some material in the current book is reworked from previous publications. Revised passages from three book reviews, originally published in *First Things*, appear in the present book: "Annihilating Nihilism," December 2008, review of William Desmond, *God and the Between*; "Whose Modernity? Which Revolution?," December 2009, review of David Walsh, *The Modern Philosophical Revolution: The Luminosity of Existence*; "A Place in the Cosmos," February 2009, review of *The Writings of Charles De Koninck*.

Also, as president of the American Catholic Philosophical Association in 2017, I delivered an address that was published as "Laudato Si', Modernity, and Catholic Aesthetics," *American Catholic Philosophical Quarterly* 91 (2017): 1–15.

In a previous book, *Aquinas, Ethics, and Philosophy of Religion: Metaphysics and Practice* (Indiana University Press, 2007), I developed an account of beauty in Aquinas and its relationship to the writings of James Joyce. That treatment is independent of but complementary to the work in the present volume.

In 2009, I was honored to write a lengthy expository essay for the guidebook and catalog of an exhibition held at the Dillon Gallery in Chelsea in New York City. The book, *Soliloquies*, included numerous works of Georges Rouault alongside new paintings by Makoto Fujimura, conversations with whom have stimulated my interest in, and understanding of, the art and artists, including Mako himself, who are discussed in the book.

A chapter of the book is devoted to the poetry and poetics of William Everson/Brother Antoninus, a Beat poet who converted to Catholicism and spent a decade as a Dominican at St. Albert's, the Dominican House in Oakland. A brief conversation about Everson with Dana Gioia during his visit to Baylor led me to take Everson seriously as a poet. During a trip to Northern California, Richard Schenk, OP, arranged for me to meet with Fr. Finbarr Hayes, OP, a friend of Everson's. I am ever grateful for Dominican hospitality.

During my time as dean of the Honors College at Baylor, I was fortunate to have the opportunity to organize two major art exhibitions. In 2010, the Honors College cosponsored an exhibition, with the Mark Foster Institute—which loaned the artworks—of Rouault's *Miserere* and Chagall's *Bible Series*. In 2012, the Honors College sponsored an exhibition, *Qu4rtets*, of the paintings of Bruce Hermann and Makoto Fujimura, works constructed in dialogue with T. S. Eliot's *Four Quartets*. Each of these events provided an occasion for me to reflect on, and deepen, my understanding of the art and artists covered in this book.

The initial research and writing for the book occurred during a sabbatical in the fall of 2018 at the Institute for Human Ecology (IHE) at the Catholic University of America (CUA). A trial run of some of the chapters also occurred at CUA, in the summer of 2021, as part of a seminar, Art, Meaning, and the Public Square, cosponsored by IHE and the Dominican House of Studies. I am grateful to the organizers of that conference, Joe Capizzi and Fr. Reginald, OP. I am especially grateful to the large group of student participants from universities far and wide for questions, comments, and stimulating conversations.

I have been blessed with fabulous colleagues at Baylor. Those with whom I have discussed material in the book include Josh King, Richard Russell, Jonathan Tran, Robert Miner, and Matthew Whelan. I am especially indebted to David Jeffrey, who hired me at Baylor, for numerous conversations about Maritain, Rouault, and Everson. The book was vastly improved in light of helpful comments offered by Natalie Carnes, from whose own work in theological aesthetics I have learned a great deal. Beyond Baylor, the Maritain scholar John Trapani and the Rouault scholar Soo Kang provided helpful comments on early drafts of chapters.

My first book, on Aquinas's *Summa Contra Gentiles*, was published in the Revisions Series, edited by Alasdair MacIntyre and Stanley Hauerwas, by the University of Notre Dame Press. Some years later, I am grateful to be working with the press again, now under the leadership of Stephen Wrinn. I would like to express my gratitude to Stephen and Rachel Kindler for their encouragement and guidance throughout the process. I would also like to thank Sheila Berg for her careful editing of the manuscript.

I am honored that this book is appearing in the series of publications sponsored by the de Nicola Center for Ethics and Culture. I have been involved in the center since its founding under my former teacher W. David Solomon and have been honored to work with the current director, Carter Snead.

As philosophy graduate assistants, Burke Rea, Trinity O'Neill, and Harrison Jennings helped with proofreading. Michael Bailey prepared the index. I am fortunate to be able to call on the assistance of Shannon Koehler, office manager in the Philosophy Department, where I now hold the J. Newton Rayzor Sr. Professor of Philosophy chair. Funds from the chair helped defray the cost of permissions for and reproduction of artwork in the book. During my time as dean at Baylor, I was blessed to work with Paulette Edwards, the finest administrative assistant I have encountered anywhere. Her work made it possible for me to continue to teach and write even as I spent many years on the dark side of academic life. She and her husband, Buddy Edwards, took an avid interest in all exhibitions and other events that in one way or another contributed to the thinking that went into this work.

ONE

Laudato Si', Technocracy, and the Renewal of Human Making

In the encyclical *Laudato Si'*, Pope Francis discerns beneath contemporary ecological problems a metaphysical and existential affliction of the human person, who is now lost in the cosmos. The source of the crisis is a misconception of human freedom as radical autonomy. We have forgotten that "man is not only a freedom which he creates for himself. Man does not create himself. He is spirit and will, but also nature" (6). Francis echoes Benedict, his immediate papal predecessor: creation is harmed "where we ourselves have the final word, where everything is simply our property and we use it for ourselves alone. The misuse of creation begins when we no longer recognize any higher instance than ourselves, when we see nothing else but ourselves" (6). Francis calls this the anthropocentric or technocratic paradigm, which sees "no intrinsic value in lower beings." Reacting against this view is biocentrism, which accords "no special value to human beings" (118). Our predicament would be dire enough were we simply opting for one or the other of these two deficient understandings. It is exacerbated by the fact that we vacillate, in a "constant schizophrenia" (118), between the two with little awareness of alternatives.

2 A THEOLOGY OF CREATION

THE TECHNOCRATIC PARADIGM AND ITS CATHOLIC DISCONTENTS

Heralded as groundbreaking because of its attention to the issue of environmental devastation, the document's roots in the Catholic philosophical and theological tradition and in recent papal writing have been all but ignored in the popular press. The American media focused almost exclusively on the climate change portion of the document. Francis could not be clearer about the depth and breadth of the crisis. Ecological threats are symptoms of a much broader predicament: "If the present ecological crisis is one small sign of the ethical, cultural and spiritual crisis of modernity, we cannot presume to heal our relationship with nature and the environment without healing all fundamental human relationships" (119). The most audacious claim in the encyclical is not the affirmation of the reality of climate change but the insistence that to have a coherent and effective environmental philosophy requires an anthropology *and* a cosmology.

The argument of the encyclical is even more complicated than that, however, since it (a) provides a kind of genealogy of the origins of the "spiritual crisis of modernity"; (b) considers, if at times only briefly, rival genealogies; and (c) offers a metaphysics of creation that has its roots in Thomas Aquinas and is open to modern evolutionary biology. In the midst of these matters, it makes a case for a distinctively theological understanding of the human person as maker (*homo faber*). The need for a renewal of human making is one of the little noticed features of the encyclical; another has to do with the dispositions that need to be fostered in the human soul if we are to avert the crisis. Again, these dispositions are fundamentally theological; they reach their culmination in acts of praise, as the very title, *Laudato Si'*, indicates.

Yet questions persist about the coherence of the argument of *LS*. I am not thinking primarily of objections to the climate change portion of the encyclical or to its economic theory. I am thinking instead of its account of nature, which has seemed to some to downplay the presence of chance, discord, and violence in the cosmos. As critics have pointed out, this defect may be connected to the relative neglect of modern evolutionary theory, which the encyclical affirms but on which it rarely reflects. Such concerns have been raised not by unsympathetic secular critics but by theologians in fundamental agreement with the teaching of the encyclical. Dennis Edwards, for example, worries that *LS* "portrays God's creation as a harmonious ordered cosmos without acknowledging the violence, pain, and death of the natural world." But he does not suppose that Francis is bereft of theological resources: "In my view, a theology of the cross, a theology of God with suffering creation, is needed to speak in some way to this violence."[1] Further reflection on evolution would in turn prompt questions about the compatibility of that theory with the metaphysics of the created order that the encyclical articulates.

Whatever we make of these criticisms, we need to begin by noting that a careful reading of the encyclical belies easy categorization. Replete with paradox, it affirms the scientific consensus on climate change even as it casts a wary eye on the notion of unqualified technological progress. Francis's views on technology are complex. He is no Luddite. He observes, "Technology has remedied countless evils." He celebrates its genuine contributions, "especially in the fields of medicine, engineering and communications" (102). It is natural and appropriate for the human species to modify "nature for useful purposes" (102). The Christian insistence on divine transcendence "demythologized nature" (78) and paved the way for modern science's investigation of the intelligibility of the natural order.[2]

The crisis of modernity has much to do with the shift from a conception of the human person as receptive of the order and beauty of the cosmos to one that accentuates the human capacity to transform nature. Yet the corrective is not to eliminate or chastise the creative aspirations of human persons. Francis underscores the intrinsic and distinctive dignity of human persons (65), who in their interaction with the natural world are co-creators with God. It is a mark of the "nobility of the human vocation" that persons can "participate in God's creative action" (131). He calls for an "aesthetic education." On this view, *poesis*, or art, arises from, and fosters in viewers or readers, the ecological virtues of receptivity, wonder, humility, and gratitude (220–32).[3] Francis's corrective points in the direction of the recovery of a notion of artistic and human stewardship and a corresponding aesthetics of wonder and praise.

In all this, Francis is in continuity with his immediate papal predecessors, John Paul II and Benedict XVI. None of them castigates the scientific or artistic impulse. The target lies elsewhere. The primary worry has to do with the rise of technocracy, or what Naomi Oreskes calls "technofideism."[4] A professor of the history of science at Harvard, Oreskes rightly highlights Francis's insistence on the moral dimensions of ecology and technology, on the interconnectedness of persons with one another and with the environment, and on the problematic features of modern life that would deny these two claims.[5] The conundrum of modern technology, as Francis and Oreskes both see it, is that our ability to "direct" it in an ethical way has not kept up with our capacity to deploy its vast resources (112).

At times, Francis's rhetoric, influenced by Romano Guardini's *End of the Modern World*, approaches the sort of nightmare vision of humanity found in many science fiction films. The typical plot features human ingenuity giving rise to a technology that operates by its own logic, liberates itself from human control, and returns to plague the inventor. Francis writes, "Technology tends to absorb everything into its ironclad logic"; "in the most radical sense of the term, power is its motive—a lordship over all" (108). On this narrative, the unfettered Enlightenment pursuit of illumination, power, and freedom backfires and leads to darkness, enfeeblement, and enslavement. History, as the narrator in Ralph Ellison's *Invisible Man* puts it, is not so much a linear progressive march as a "boomerang" that recoils on mankind.[6] The very popularity of this science fiction plot indicates that suspicions and fears about technology lie just beneath the surface of everyday life.

Although the Catholic critique of the technocratic paradigm is now at least a century old, official Catholic teaching has only recently fully embraced it. As Michael Hanby notes, *LS* constitutes a significant development of recent Catholic thought in its critique of this paradigm.[7] Francis's worries about progressive technocracy echo those articulated by early to mid-twentieth-century Catholic authors like Guardini and Maritain. Francis's plea for integral ecology calls to mind Maritain's notion of integral humanism.[8] As I show in the next chapter, Maritain was deeply concerned about the rise of technocracy and sought to foster a renewal of the arts of human making, both in his own extensive writings in aesthetics and in his lifelong friendships with some of the most influential artists of the century.

For both Francis and Maritain, the distinguishing features of the Catholic view of making oppose both anthropocentrism and biocentrism. Woven into the analysis of contemporary ecological problems is a diagnosis of the metaphysical and existential affliction of the human person, who is now lost in the cosmos, increasingly alienated from self, others, nature, and God. As Walker Percy writes in *Lost in the Cosmos*, "We live in a deranged age—more deranged than usual, because despite great scientific and technological advances, man has not the faintest idea of who he is or what he is doing."[9] We face a very broad crisis indeed: "If the present ecological crisis is one small sign of the ethical, cultural and spiritual crisis of modernity, we cannot presume to heal our relationship with nature and the environment without healing all fundamental human relationships" (119). What is needed is a kind of reconciliation.

MODERN DILEMMAS, MEDIEVAL RESOURCES

As much as any recent encyclical, *LS* seems quite contemporary, and yet it draws richly on premodern sources. Of course, the pope is not reviving an outmoded astronomy. Rather, his focus is on the way resources in the Catholic tradition can help us articulate the place of persons in relation to one another and the natural world. There is something surprisingly Chestertonian about the image of Saint Francis that Pope Francis revives. Even more striking is the way Pope Francis calls to mind G. K. Chesterton in his yoking together of Saint Francis and Saint Thomas Aquinas. Nowhere is this more evident than in sections 86 and 87, in which Francis cites, first, Thomas Aquinas and, second, Saint Francis. Appealing to Thomas on the appropriateness of the creation of many and varied creatures, Francis writes:

> The universe as a whole, in all its manifold relationships, shows forth the inexhaustible riches of God. Saint Thomas Aquinas wisely noted that multiplicity and variety "come from the intention of the first agent" who willed that "what was wanting to one in the representation of the divine goodness might be supplied by another" inasmuch as God's goodness "could not be represented fittingly by any one creature." Hence, we need to grasp the variety of things in their multiple relationships. (*LS*, 86)[10]

He then quotes at length from Saint Francis's "Canticle." Here is an excerpt.

> Praised be you, my Lord, with all your creatures,
> especially Sir Brother Sun,
> who is the day and through whom you give us light.

And he is beautiful and radiant with great splendour;
and bears a likeness of you, Most High.
Praised be you, my Lord, through Sister Moon and the stars,
in heaven you formed them clear and precious and beautiful. (*LS*, 87)

Pope Francis's juxtaposition calls to mind the chapter, "Two Friars," in Chesterton's book on Thomas Aquinas, in which Chesterton suggests that a comparison with the life of Saint Francis of Assisi "brings us most rapidly to the real question of the life and work of St. Thomas."[11] They approached the same problem from different angles. The presence of such Chestertonian insights further underscores what a deeply philosophical and theological document *LS* is. Its working assumption is that what we most need today is a theologically informed reimagining of the place of human persons in the entirety of the created cosmos. Pope Francis finds in two friars a metaphysics and poetics of creation that supply a remedy for what ails the contemporary world. In fact, the passage from Aquinas might be said to contain the theory behind Saint Francis's poem of praise. It is helpful to have in mind the two sides of Thomas's account of creation, the first concerning the order of creation itself and the second concerning the nature and order of human knowing.

Concerning created nature, Thomas holds that God creates in order to manifest his power, goodness, and wisdom. Because God's goodness is infinite, no single created thing, indeed no sum of created things, can fully reflect the divine. A vast multiplicity of beings is the most fitting way for the created order to reflect God. Moreover, God gives to creatures their own proper powers to act. These ends are internal to the creatures; they are not raw material whose purpose is to be determined or refashioned by human whim. In actualizing these powers, creatures become like God. In so doing, they seek and imitate God. Thus the capaciousness of created being offers a panorama of the divine wisdom. As Elizabeth Johnson states in *Ask the Beasts*, "Biodiversity in its own natural way manifests the goodness of God which goes beyond our imagination."[12]

Concerning the human intellect, Thomas holds that there is an affinity between all knowable beings and the capacity of the intellect to know. The soul is potentially all things (*potens omnia*). Because the human intellect is a potency that is actualized by encountering and knowing natural things outside of it, the intellect reaches perfection, not by separating itself from the external world; rather, it is made actual and perfected only by knowing what is other than itself. It is thus naturally ordered to being fulfilled by knowing the order of created substances.

Aquinas rejects the notion that the human intellect has any direct, unmediated access to the divine. Instead, it must travel an indirect route, through created things, as effects, to God, as cause. In this life, we never transcend the effects, which are the exclusive means through which we know the creator. For Aquinas, as Johnson puts it in *Ask the Beasts*, "the ontological relationship whereby various creatures participate in the goodness of God is the basis for any speech about transcendent mystery at all, for in knowing the excellence of the world we may speak analogically about the One in whose being it participates."[13]

The teachings on creation and human knowing inform Aquinas's teaching that human beings have dominion over the rest of creation. He interprets Adam's naming of the animals not as a license to use creation for whatever preferences and desires humans happen to have. Instead, dominion has first a contemplative dimension. By knowing and naming created things, human persons come to know the creator who has fashioned all created things.[14] As Willis Jenkins observes in *Ecologies of Grace* about Aquinas's interpretation, "The garden scene reveals two general models of practice: contemplative charity for the sake of communion with God and prudential providence, superintending the good order of earthly communion."[15]

Contemplative and providential dominion over the order of created things is what Saint Francis expresses in song. In deploying these medieval topoi from Saints Thomas and Francis, Pope Francis seems to share Chesterton's view that the great friars were the opposite of benighted representatives of the so-called dark ages. Instead, they were responsible for a reformation of the church, a renaissance of learning, and a renewal in the appreciation of the natural world. Chesterton calls this a "movement of enlargement, a development of doctrine."[16] Each in his own way had a "liberating and humanizing effect on religion," one in the order of imagination and the other in the order of intellect.

The renewed appreciation of nature has nothing to do with pagan nature worship. Instead, it is rooted in their affirmation of the Incarnation—what Chesterton calls "the whole staggering story of the God-man in the Gospels."[17] Something like this logic is present in Pope Francis's presentation of the two friars. Contrary to the view that Christianity allows for or encourages treating the natural world as raw material at the hands of human preference, Francis argues that orthodox theology provides a foundation for a sound ecology, one in which natural and human ecology are inseparable.

Chesterton detects a congruence between Christian and Aristotelian themes in the accent in both Francis and Aquinas on the reality and goodness of the human body. In his humility, Francis regarded himself as an animal, referring to his body as a donkey. Thomas provided doctrinal clarity in his claim that the soul without a body is not a human person. The anthropocentric paradigm, as Francis refers to it in *LS*, reduces nature, including the human body, to raw material that can be used for whatever purposes human persons might have. Human choice is reduced to consumer preference. Such a model of human choice generates the "throwaway culture" about which Pope Francis has much to say. To counter such a culture, we need a renewed appreciation of embodiment.

The accent on the dignity of the human body and the goodness of the material world revives medieval themes. The intellectual origin of our alienation from nature can be traced to the loss of the Aristotelian and Thomist language of the soul as the form of the body. Whether early modern conceptions of human nature are materialist or dualist, they agree in repudiating an understanding of soul and body as a unity. Both are tempted to see the physical world, even the human body itself, as raw material to be manipulated and disposed of according to the will of the human agent. Percy calls this the modern heresy of angelism, the denial that our bodies are shot through with moral and spiritual significance. This is of course a prominent theme in Chesterton's writing on Aquinas; an entire chapter is devoted to the topic of Aquinas's refutation of the dualism of the Manichaeans. It is also there in Chesterton's depiction of Francis as a kind of hyper-realist concerning particular existing beings. Francis, he insists, was not a lover of mankind but a lover of individual human persons; he was not a lover of nature but a lover of this bird and that wolf.

Aristotle's insistence on the reality, intelligibility, and perfection of individually existing beings, his repudiation of the Platonist celebration of universals rather than particulars, is, for Chesterton, a philosophical revolution that matches perfectly the revolution wrought in history by the Incarnation of the Son of God. To Luther's query, who put Aristotle in my scripture?, Chesterton would respond Aristotle's philosophy helps us understand and articulate the distinctively Christian conception of the intelligibility and perfection of created beings, in their concrete materiality. Both embrace the lowest of things out of humility and out of a confidence that the "humblest fact leads to the highest things."[18]

The humblest things lead to the highest because they, no less than noble beings, are gifts of God. Chesterton writes at one point, "All goods look better when they look like gifts."[19] And this has implications for how we understand the human body. It is not just that, as Aristotle was able to see, the human body has an integrity befitting the rational soul; it is further that we are to understand our very bodies as gifts of the divine creator.

One important theme, common to Pope Francis and Saint Thomas, has to do with the understanding of divine creation as a kind of artistic activity. Eager to defend divine freedom and to avoid sheer arbitrariness in creation, Thomas crafts an analogy between creation and art. In a key passage in *LS*, Francis quotes Thomas on precisely this point: "Nature is nothing other than a certain kind of art, namely God's art, impressed upon things, whereby those things are moved to a determinate end. It is as if a shipbuilder were able to give timbers the wherewithal to move themselves to take the form of a ship" (80). But the builder in this case is the causal source not only of the original creation of the artifact, but of its ongoing existence. God's ongoing presence in creation, his divine presence, "which ensures the subsistence and growth of each being, 'continues the work of creation' (*ST*, I, q. 104, art. 1 ad 4)" (80).

As Denis Edwards notes, Francis articulates the received Catholic teaching on natural ecology by proposing a threefold relationship.[20] Beyond the relationship to God and neighbor, there is a relationship to nature. Francis puts it this way:

> Human life is grounded in three fundamental and closely intertwined relationships: with God, with our neighbour and with the earth itself. According to the Bible, these three vital relationships have been broken, both outwardly and within us. This rupture is sin. The harmony between the Creator, humanity and creation as a whole was disrupted by our presuming to take the place of God and refusing to acknowledge our creaturely limitations. (66)

Francis describes in various ways the role and place of the natural world in the divine providential plan. The natural world is the locus of divine presence (88); it is included within God's saving plan and in the world to come

(76); it is destined to participate in the fullness of God's transformation of all of creation (83). The last point—an eschatological point—bears amplification. Here is how Francis beautifully puts it toward the very end of *LS*:

> At the end, we will find ourselves face to face with the infinite beauty of God (cf. 1 Cor 13:12), and be able to read with admiration and happiness the mystery of the universe, which with us will share in unending plenitude. Even now we are journeying towards the sabbath of eternity, the new Jerusalem, towards our common home in heaven. Jesus says: "I make all things new" (Rev 21:5). Eternal life will be a shared experience of awe, in which each creature, resplendently transfigured, will take its rightful place and have something to give those poor men and women who will have been liberated once and for all. (243)

The poem of Saint Francis anticipates this eschatological vision. Aquinas's emphasis on creatures as having God-given natures that are both independent of human will and the indispensable source of human knowledge of God provides the primitive metaphysical and epistemological basis for the eschatology. What is Saint Francis's entire "Canticle" but a song of praise, an anticipation of the praise of the eternal Sabbath, responding to the beauty and artistry of the transcendent creator of all beautiful things? As Hopkins would later write, "He fathers forth whose beauty knows no change. Praise Him."[21]

Thomas's metaphysics of creation provides the philosophical foundations for rethinking the natural world as a contingent gift. For Chesterton, that metaphysical teaching finds mystical embodiment in the life of Saint Francis: "The mystic who passes through the moment when there is nothing but God does in some sense behold the beginningless beginnings in which there was really nothing else. He not only appreciates everything but the nothing of which everything was made."[22] That the whole of creation is brought into being from no antecedent subject and for the sake of manifesting God to other beings means that creation is sheer gift—what some medieval authors call the first grace. As is true for Pope Francis, so too for Chesterton: Saint Francis is the exemplar of cosmic reconciliation. In one of his most remarkable observations about Saint Francis, Chesterton writes, "St. Francis walked the world like the Pardon of God. . . . [H]is appearance marked the moment when men could be reconciled not only to

God but to nature and, most difficult of all, to themselves."[23] Here is precisely the reconciliation with God, nature, others, and self that *LS* calls for.

CULTURE CARE

Both Chesterton and Pope Francis find in the medieval saint an articulation of the cosmic significance of the dramatic encounter of God and human persons. With few exceptions, contemporary Christian thought and art have focused on the human drama without attending to the shape of the created cosmos or to the way in which we are to perceive and praise God through the created world. The pope's encyclical calls for a renewal of human life within the whole of the natural order. There is a remarkable affinity between the document and that of the contemporary artist and writer Makoto Fujimura, whose notion of "culture care" provides for an aesthetic ecology, at once natural and human. Influenced by the thought of Maritain and the painting of Maritain's friend Georges Rouault, Fujimura advocates for an ecological art. For him, the link between natural and human ecology is culture. I have already noted the overlap between the title and themes of his book and the key motifs of *LS*.[24] Moreover, his own art—a syncretism of East and West, traditional and contemporary, secular and sacred—involves a fusion of the art of Rouault with the so-called tradition of abstraction in Mark Rothko.

Fujimura's work addresses the crisis of *homo faber* directly. We should note first of all that he places the crisis of art and the artist at the center of the problem of meaninglessness in our time. He sees various forces, including reductionism and hyperspecialization, as depleting the cultural soil. These are features of technofideism already familiar to us. He also sees sources of alienation in a laissez-faire economic system and a consumerist approach to art. Moreover, our view of culture war indicates how far removed we are from inhabiting a shared, living culture. As Fujimura observes, "Culture is not a territory to be won but a resource to steward with care. Culture is a garden to be cultivated."[25] Once again, the language of *LS*, in this case, the vocabulary of stewardship, is prominent.

The comprehensive vision that informs *LS* is equally operative here: "Individuals exist in community, in economies and ecologies." Fujimura repudiates the dualism that infects so much of modern philosophy and is at the root of the anthropocentric ideal: "Our multifaceted interaction with our physical and cultural environment directly affects our bodies, our minds, our spirits, and ultimately our souls." As a basis for thinking about the conditions of a healthy human ecology, he turns to the ingredients of "thriving ecosystems."[26]

Culture care accentuates stewardship and the inseparability of tradition and creativity. Ecology, whether natural or aesthetic, is in some measure about conservation. But the point, especially in the aesthetic sphere, is not simply to conserve or preserve, but to become "fruitful," capable of "originating new life or producing offspring."[27] His word for this practice is *generativity*. One of the goals of generativity is to "make our culture more humane and welcoming and inspire us to be more fully human."[28] Generativity is the capacity in the present to build on the past in such a way that we create the conditions for an ever more hopeful future. The ecological imagery of soil and the fruitful growth of plants underscores the need for deep roots as well as expansion, growth, and development.

Fujimura thus develops analogies between natural and human ecology. He implicitly affirms the mutual influence, indeed the inseparability, of the two ecological orders. While artistic freedom is indispensable and no theory of art can anticipate in advance the creative direction of artists in particular times and places, Fujimura sees a role for art in reflecting and cultivating healthy ecologies. His work thus bridges the modern divide between the fine and the useful arts in ways many modern theorists and artists have not. In a refreshing and surprising way, his accent on generativity echoes the work of the early Nietzsche. The crisis of advanced Western society is a kind of decadence; civilization seems doomed to either stale repetition or novelty for its own sake.

As Fujimura observes, in some artistic circles beauty is taboo; it is said to be tainted by association with cultural hegemony, imperialist power, oppressive practices of the past, and the "cosmetic sheen of superficial contemporary culture."[29] Now, Fujimura agrees in some measure with this critique of modern culture. He speaks of the "pollutants" of "the river of culture" and identifies its two principal sources as the "overcommodification of art and utilitarian pragmatism."[30] In such a social context, the soul is deprived of indispensable nourishment. Fujimura writes, "Appreciation of the depth of beauty is a condition of our physical, mental, and spiritual health."[31] His artistic roots in Japanese methods of painting connect his own making to natural materials and to the enveloping world of nature. Yet Fujimura does not advocate a naive Romantic return to pristine nature. In fact, current cultural conditions make it difficult for the beautiful to be directly accessed and presented. Fujimura thus insists that the "hell of the artistic imagination" is the "only real point of departure" for artistic creation today.[32] His art is thus both an example of ecological art and a corrective to certain tendencies in modern Christian approaches to nature.

CATHOLIC GENEALOGY AND MODERNITY

As I have already noted, *LS*, the most recent "official" Catholic statement on the place of human persons in the cosmos, touches regularly on large issues concerning the threat of meaninglessness that plagues denizens of advanced modern societies. Following John Paul II and Benedict XVI, Francis argues that the roots of the modern crisis have to do with anthropocentrism, which he calls both an epistemological and an ethical model. The document moves back and forth between secular and theological evidence and argument. Francis reflects on the way the teachings of faith offer believers "motivation to care for nature and for the most vulnerable of their brothers and sisters" (64). But Francis is not simply saying that Christians have additional motives to care for creation. Given his critique of a certain strain of modernity, he is implicitly posing the question whether contemporary environmentalists can sustain their vision without the sort of philosophical and/or theological vision of the cosmos and the human person that *LS* articulates.

The strategy here resembles that of John Paul II in *Fides et Ratio*, a document that attempts to rescue reason from its contemporary dissolution. The encyclical poses the question whether modernity, which veers back and forth between boasting of the powers of pure reason and succumbing to pervasive skeptical doubts, can sustain a commitment to reason. In *LS*, the question is whether the crisis of ecology can be resolved without reference to something like the Christian vision of the created order. However, as I have intimated already, that vision is open to certain criticisms and has certainly been marred by confused accounts. First, there is the question of the interpretation of the motives for the origins of the technocratic turn in early modernity. Even if the critique is on the mark in its assessment of the implications of this turn, that leaves untouched the question of the motives for the turn, or at least it leaves open the question of the extent to which those motives were reasonable. Second, in reaction to anthropocentrism, many moderns embrace some version of biocentrism or Romanticism. Thus it is crucial to clarify the key differences between standard forms of Romanticism and the Catholic position. Third and finally, both Enlightenment constructivism and Romanticism are obsessed with the question of human making. It is necessary in this context to clarify the Catholic understanding of divine and human making and to show how the account of nature might accord with the conception of nature found in evolutionary biology.

The contemporary political philosopher Pierre Manent has raised questions about the standard critique, particularly in Catholic circles, of early modern thought. Manent has in mind the thesis that modernity as a social, political, and cultural phenomenon arises from philosophical ideas such as nominalism or voluntarism or mechanism. Manent distinguishes between the causality of ideas and the causality of motives. He objects to the assumption that ideas have causal force all by themselves. As he puts it, "An idea as such is not a motive." Ideas "enter into historical argument only in relation to a political situation or problem that they formulate and seek to resolve."[33] So the political thought of Hobbes might well be inconceivable without, or at least most convincingly articulated in terms of, nominalism, voluntarism, and mechanism. But that does not explain why so many took some version of the *Leviathan*'s vision of the human condition seriously. That has to do rather, as Manent sees it, with a particular configuration of human imagination and desire about power, violence, and death in the early modern period.

Catholic narratives of modernity do indeed tend to conflate the causality of ideas with the causality of motives. For example, the ideas of autonomy, anthropocentrism, and biocentrism are often introduced as if the mere identification of faulty ideas is sufficient to explain the wayward course of modern culture. Francis claims that our relationship with nature has in the modern period become "confrontational" (106). But were the motives that gave rise in the early modern period to the project of conquering nature entirely unnatural or even peculiarly modern? It was not just the absence of rational politics and the threat of civil war that made premodern life "poor, nasty, brutish, and short."[34] Nature itself is often inhospitable to the deepest human longings. *LS*, moreover, proposes that what has been lost are dispositions toward nature characterized by wonder and humility, gratitude and awe. The project of technological control diminishes both the appreciation and the practice of these dispositions. But these are not the only attitudes nature inspires. One might ask, does not nature also inspire fear, dread, even horror and the reasonable urge to want to temper nature's ill effects?

These possibilities are rarely probed deeply in the modern Catholic critique of anthropocentric technofideism. One wonders whether *LS*, despite explicitly distancing its teaching from that of "naïve romanticism" (11), does not come precariously close to such naïveté at certain points. I have already noted criticisms of *LS* for its naive conception of nature. Edwards draws our attention to the theme of "universal communion," of the cosmos as a family that "excludes nothing and no one" (92). As *LS* puts it, "Everything is related and we human beings are united as brothers and sisters on a wonderful pilgrimage, woven together by the love God has for each of his creatures and which also unites us in fond affection with brother sun, sister moon, brother river and mother earth" (92). As Edwards and others have noted, it remains unclear what precise obligations such a familial notion of created beings imposes on human beings. Moreover, it seems almost as if nature itself in *LS* is pacific and harmonious and only accidentally and rarely characterized by violence, chaos, and waste. But is this accurate?

Edwards thinks not. The flaw in the document is not necessarily fatal to its underlying argument, however. Edwards himself thinks that a richer theology accommodates, indeed calls for, a more complex account of nature. He reflects on a quotation in *LS* from John of the Cross, who says of the mountain, valleys, islands, rivers, and breezes that "in each of these sublime realities is God" (*LS* 234). He proceeds to note that "something can be spoken of as sublime when it throws our notions of reason, order, and proportion into utter confusion, when it points to what is totally beyond us, to the incomprehensible. The sublime can be shocking and disorienting."[35] He continues:

> This line of thought suggests that "sublime communion" could be developed to embrace what is not taken up in *Laudato Si'*, the pain, the deaths, the chaos, the randomness, the ugliness of so much of the natural world. It could include what cosmology tells us of the 13.8 billion

year history of the observable universe, the more than a hundred billion galaxies that make it up, and the possibility of multiverses. A theology of the sublime communion of creation could engage with the strange otherness and counterintuitive nature of what we have discovered about our world at the quantum level of reality. And it could embrace the costs of evolution as well as the beauty and rich diversity of life around us.[36]

I address the question of evolution, chance, and cosmic violence later. Even before human beings became aware of the vastness of the cosmos or of the duration of time required for the development of life, they were cognizant of the tension between nature's ways and human longing. Even if common Catholic genealogies admit the important role technology has played in doing just that, the standard story tends to be forgetful of the underlying motivation.

Another way to come at this issue is to consider carefully the notion of earth as our common home, which appears in the subtitle of *LS*. There is certainly some truth in the claim, but the full truth about the human abode on earth is more complicated and deeply paradoxical. A corollary to nature's inhospitality is the human person's restlessness in the face of all created goods. Such restlessness has both natural and unnatural or disordered sources. The disordered soul can find rest nowhere. Abandoning rest in God or in the natural order, the slothful or avaricious soul moves from one object or activity to another in flight from the good and in a futile quest for rest in evanescent pleasures.

But a rightly ordered soul is not one that is fully satisfied with finite, temporal goods. We are open-ended creatures, endlessly capable of conceiving ways of transcending and altering whatever place we happen to inhabit. Foundational modern thinkers such as Hobbes see in this restlessness an aimlessness, a serial pursuit of one thing after another without ultimate end or unifying purpose. At least one earlier tradition, traceable to Augustine, marks in the disquiet a longing for God. As he puts it in the opening page of his *Confessions*, "Our hearts are restless until they rest in thee."[37]

For Augustine, restlessness is not finally an aimless wandering in search of we know not what. When we lose the sense of creatureliness, then the material world can easily become raw material for our use. Thomas's accent on the contemplative and prudential dimensions of dominion counter that tendency. If instead created things have God-given natures that reflect God, then there is a path from this home to the next, a "journey towards the sabbath of eternity, the new Jerusalem, towards our common home in heaven" (243). There is further scriptural warrant for this claim. We have here, Saint Paul reminds us, no lasting city. We are, as medieval thinkers were fond of saying, wanderers or pilgrims on the earth. Each of us is a *homo viator*.[38] An authentic Catholic cosmology would account for the ordered restlessness of the human heart. The ordination of the soul to transcendence should not, however, be seen as a refusal or denial of this world. We await "a new heavens and a new earth," the transfiguration of this very world, in which "each creature, resplendently transfigured, will take its rightful place" (243). The Christian account of earth as a home is then quite complex.

In the classical tradition, ordered restlessness is understood in terms of human *eros*, the love of the beautiful. Eros marks the natural longing of the human soul to behold and be completed by what is true, good, and beautiful. Desire for beauty is partially satisfied by finite objects, either natural things or artifacts. The encounter with the beautiful, Maritain explains, "has the savor of the terrestrial paradise, because it restores, for a moment, the peace and the simultaneous delight of the intellect and the senses."[39] But if the beholding of the beautiful marks a kind of return to natural origins and provides an occasion for rest, it also moves us forward, by fostering a longing for complete beauty. Saint Francis again embodies this paradox, since he could behold, befriend, and appreciate the beauty of created, finite beings while simultaneously seeing them as signs and gifts of a transcendent beauty. That transcendent source is a personal creator who fashions human persons within the whole of creation, bestows on them the task of stewardship, and finally calls them home to communion with the triune God. As Matthew Croasmun and Miroslav Volf put it, "The hunger for home is return and advent intertwined. It is memory and imagination. Restoration and transformation. Creation and consummation."[40]

The paradoxes of the human animal, the only animal that can survey the whole of the cosmos and pose questions about the meaning of its presence within that whole, underscore the fact that we will never be fully at home in the natural world. Anthropocentrism and biocentrism miss the paradoxes. They suppose that the task is either to liberate us from embodiment and the limits of our earthly existence or to render us tame animals by subduing human longing. Each grasps part of the paradox and thus a portion of the truth.[41]

Veering from one to another conception of the place of the human within the cosmos, we are apt to exaggerate either the evils of the natural order or its pacific harmony. As Jenkins observes, Thomas acknowledges a "significant ecological role for natural evils"; but these are natural accompaniments of natural, physical beings; moreover, the presence of natural evils is necessary for, and subordinate to, the natural goods that God and nature primarily aim to maintain and cultivate. But "by denying" natural evils any "ontological finality, he still locates creation's integrity in God's goodness."[42] While Thomas can make sense of the natural evils, he does not reason from these evils to the "infamy in creatureliness." Thus he "disallows Christian enmity toward creation."[43] Moreover, the Christian account, in its acknowledgment of violence, does not treat it as coextensive with being itself. Maritain's comments are germane: "The philosopher's experience itself has been revitalized by Christianity. He is offered as a *datum* a world that is the handiwork of the Word, wherein everything bespeaks the Infinite Spirit to finite spirits who know themselves as spirits. Here is, as it were, a fraternal attitude towards things and reality."[44]

Such a fraternal attitude need not be naively Romantic. It includes an account of the alienation of human persons from nature through sin. It has as its centerpiece the transformation of the entire cosmos through the crucifixion of Christ, not through a return to some lost state of innocence. The same saint celebrated for his affirmation of nature is also honored for bearing the marks of the stigmata. The one who accentuated the multiform ways in which God is present in and through nature simultaneously embraced the natural discomforts and afflictions, as well as human evil, as instruments of grace, means of redemptive suffering. Created nature falls within the design of divine providence. These are elements of the Christian narrative that need to be recovered in order to spell out an alternative to Romanticism.

BIOCENTRISM AND/AS ROMANTICISM

One way to begin to articulate that alternative is to reflect on the different conceptions of Saint Francis that are operative in the Catholic tradition and in that of environmentalism, for Francis is a hero of the latter movement. The very title of the third chapter of *LS*, "The Human Roots of the Ecological Crisis," calls to mind an influential essay by Lynn White, titled "The Historical Roots of Our Ecological Crisis."[45] White's thesis is that the roots of the current crisis can be found in the Christian teaching that it is "God's will that man exploit nature for his proper ends." Yet for an alternative, healthy model of religious ecology, White turns to Francis of Assisi, whom he celebrates as a heretic who departs from the "orthodox Christian arrogance toward nature." Pope Francis offers a rejoinder to White. To the accusation that Christianity is the source of our ecological crisis, Francis provides a twofold response: (a) the origins consist rather in a certain strain of modernity; and (b) a proper understanding of Saint Francis suggests a thoroughly orthodox alternative to the modern model of autonomous control over nature. He explicitly addresses the thesis that scripture countenances "tyrannical anthropocentrism" (68). Pope Francis is committed to a very different genealogy of modernity than that which is prominent in the most influential narratives of modernity.

But one might object that the view espoused by Francis and by his Catholic predecessors, including Thomas Aquinas, is still a version of anthropocentrism. If the only alternative is biocentrism or ecocentrism, then the position is certainly going to appear anthropocentric. The discussions of Thomas in the contemporary literature on ecology have done a pretty good job of showing that his account cannot be easily assimilated to contemporary categories. In *Ecologies of Grace*, Jenkins recognizes that Thomas is not offering an ecocentric or biocentric view. Thomas's account, he explains, "escapes facile categorization by cosmological centrisms. Instead, he harmonizes (or resists the use of) anthropocentrism, theocentrism, and ecocentrism, precisely because he sees that God chooses to move creation to Godself by inviting humans into a friendship shaped by their intimacy with all creation."[46] Because of the peculiar status and role of humans in the natural order, an ethics of nature "needs to include not just how we treat the natural world around us, our particular environment, but also who we are as persons, our human nature."[47] This is the task of *LS*.

The source of the ecological crisis is, as I have noted, a misconception of human freedom as autonomy. If we consider how certain early modern thinkers interpret Genesis, we can see in their writings a basis for White's claim that scripture has been read as buttressing a doctrine of unfettered mastery of nature. As Rémi Brague notes, such an interpretation can be found in the writings of John Locke, who

> conceives of work as the self-creation of man. He emphasizes a verse that the church fathers had neglected to interpret literally enough: God gave man the entire earth and commanded him to master it. We appropriate what we work on, because work introduces something of us into the object. In truth, the products of the earth are almost without value, and it is only human labor and industry that confers it. Property, itself founded upon work, in turn founds political society, which only exists to safeguard it.[48]

A similar reading underlies Francis's critique of the rapaciousness so often prominent in global capitalism.[49] The critique of the calculative, control-over-nature model of Enlightenment reason is a staple of environmental literature.[50] Romanticism, which has been the preeminent intellectual influence on environmentalism, sometimes envisions human persons as enemies of nature. As *LS* observes, we vacillate between, on the one hand, an Enlightenment view that exalts human beings above nature as raw material at our disposal and, on the other, a view that engulfs humans within nature. In recent Catholic writing, the former is sometimes called a Promethean view, while the latter is often identified as an egalitarian form of pantheism. The contrast is between the "amoral language of libertarian technocracy" and the "morally infused and often pantheistic language of environmentalism."[51] In *LS*, Francis identifies the two opposed positions as anthropocentrism and biocentrism.

If *LS* aims most of its animosity at the former view, it nonetheless stresses the limitations to environmental biocentrism, which has deep roots within Romanticism. Especially in America, according to William Cronon, the standard Romantic accentuation of the sublime, combined with the notion of the frontier, engenders a dualistic account of person and nature. It opposes "malign civilization" to "benign nature." It constructs an artificial notion of wilderness as pristine, as if before Europeans arrived there were no Indigenous peoples inhabiting the so-called wilderness.[52] Without some acknowledgment of the peculiar status and role of human persons in the natural order, environmentalists cannot make sense of their moral pleading to the human animal to reform its behavior so as to avoid the destruction of nature. Cronon notes that the experience of the sublime can counter human arrogance and foster virtues of "remembrance and gratitude."[53] But he urges environmentalism to articulate a human ecology whose task would be to find a home for human beings in nature and to preserve elements of wilderness within spheres of human domesticity.[54]

The gap between *LS* and Romanticism is most dramatically evident from a comparison of *LS* with Leonardo Boff's *Cry of the Earth, Cry of the Poor*, a piece of liberation theology that unites environmental concerns and antipoverty efforts. Boff too celebrates Saint Francis, as the embodiment of "all the cardinal ecological virtues" and of an "ecological wisdom of living well with all beings." But he sees Saint Francis as restoring elements of pagan polytheism and thus as correcting the monotheistic error of separating nature from the divine. He rightly highlights Saint Francis's articulation of the erotic attraction of beauty but then inexplicably associates that with the teaching of Sigmund Freud. While not strictly pantheistic, the thinking about God is muddled. For example, Boff writes, "God is the name we give to the experience of enveloping mystery." God certainly can be encountered in mystery, but "enveloping mystery" can have numerous sources short of the experience of God.

At one point in *LS*, Pope Francis urges that the "best way" to secure an ecological understanding of the cosmos is to recognize divine omnipotence in the "figure of the Father who creates" all things and "alone owns the world" (75). In this way, we cannot help but recognize creation as a gift, not as the result of mere chance or arbitrary whim, but as an expression of divine love. The protean diversity of the created order is itself an expression of divine wisdom and a reflection of divine goodness and beauty (75–80). At this juncture in the encyclical, Francis pairs the philosophical reflections on creation from Thomas Aquinas with the poetic expression of ecstatic union with God through created things from Francis of Assisi. Without mentioning Saint Francis, Maritain makes the same point. Misconceptions of divine transcendence occlude the "personality of the true God":

> Clearly the god of immanence, be it the naïve immanence of the old pantheists or the rehashed and senile immanence of modern idealism, cannot be a personal God, lost as he is either in things or in the thought of philosophers and scholars. On the other hand, the idea of Divine Transcendence, if too humanly understood, and insufficiently

transcendent, seems at first sight equally incompatible with personality. How could an immense God, high above all things and all the concepts we use to name Him, be a person, one who says "I" as we do?⁵⁵

To escape from misleading conceptions of divine personality, we need to return to Thomas Aquinas's understanding of God as pure act, in whom there is "absolute unity, absolute integrity of nature, absolute individuality."⁵⁶ The consequences are palpable. Maritain lists them. First, "since God is sovereignly personal, the notion of creation makes sense: He is the absolute cause, by His intelligence and His liberty, of the entire being of that which is not Himself." Second, "sin makes sense." To "mar" the created order "is to wound God Himself in what He wills and loves." Third, "revelation makes sense: He can speak to us by the human instruments of His choice." And fourth, "grace makes sense: He can bring us into a participation of His very deity and His personal life, and make of us His friends."⁵⁷

The implicit theological genealogy of *LS* is in competition with other accounts. If Romanticism engages in a kind of dialectic with the Enlightenment, Francis is engaged in a dialectic with both. Now, modern Catholic thought has devoted a great deal of attention to Enlightenment rationalism but, by comparison at least, little attention to Romanticism.⁵⁸ Yet Romanticism permeates our contemporary world. There is, moreover, a close connection between Romanticism and what *LS* calls environmental biocentrism. As I have noted, the environmental movement is in some sense the "grandchild of romanticism."⁵⁹ But Romanticism is much more complicated and much more interesting than is biocentrism; in fact, the former is not so much a doctrine as a complex array of movements, thinkers, authors, and stances toward modernity. In its origins a reaction against certain strains of Enlightenment rationalism, Romanticism is about shifting the balance from the artificial to the organic and from the rational to the emotive and the imaginative. In its project of recovering what has been lost, Romanticism enlists the assistance and guidance of the arts—paradoxically mimicking what it opposes. It proposes a rival, vivifying techne to counter a sterile techne. *LS* is important in part because it reminds us how powerful that alternative, modern movement is. In its allusion to the way in which we vacillate between the two dominant modern paradigms, it may also hint at an important and now generally accepted truth, namely, that Enlightenment anthropocentrism and Romantic biocentrism are not as opposed as they may seem.⁶⁰

Take, for example, the Romantic accent on the sublime. Romantic aesthetics, going back at least to Kant, distinguishes between the beautiful, rooted in an experience proportionate to the human capacities, and the sublime, prompted by an experience of that which exceeds, overwhelms, and dwarfs human capacities. The latter is sometimes seen as especially useful in moving the viewer or reader beyond the self and into a larger world. It would seem to undermine the Enlightenment supposition of objectivity and mastery, of the human ability to stand apart from and control nature. Yet, as David Jeffrey shows in his treatment of the sublime in Romanticism, Romantic poets and theorists often trace the roots of the sublime to the human capacity of imagination. What might seem to lead beyond the self and into what Maritain calls the infinite richness of being becomes yet another occasion for anthropocentric affirmation.[61]

The interconnections between Enlightenment rationalism and Romanticism help explain why the Catholic critique of the Enlightenment has gained so little traction in contemporary discussions. Many see technocracy and radical anthropocentrism as problematic, if not deeply misleading; many sense the need for a recovery of the human connection to, and place within, nature. But they do not immediately, if ever, take the Catholic alternative seriously in part because influential alternative accounts of nature and the supernatural abound. If contemporary persons sense their alienation from nature, they most naturally recur to some form of Romanticism.[62] The supposition that the fundamental alternatives or options are anthropocentrism and natural law or some version of natural human teleology is a misleading oversimplification.

The realization that modernity is less a finished product than a dialectic of intertwined oppositions coincides with a growing skepticism about unifying syntheses or grand narratives. If this means a loss of continuity in tradition, it might allow for the recovery of what modernity has attempted to suppress. Particularly in its secularizing mode, modernity seeks uniformity through "similar beliefs," a consensus or concurrence on "plainer, more instrumental truths," and the monitoring of human persons through "better surveillance."[63] The result would be to make us at home in the world by creating docile creatures, souls without longing. In this context, as Colin Jager notes, one of the functions of Romanticism is to re-call to our attention matters that exceed or violate "the spaces marked out for them" in modernity's attempt to control human life and make it rational.[64] It highlights the "unquiet things."

As some modern Catholic authors have seen, fragmentation can provide an occasion for recovery of lost elements of traditions. Once the overarching narratives, including the narrative of Romanticism itself, lose their hold on the culture, artists can go in virtually any direction, drawing on fragments, often from premodern culture and from marginalized religious traditions.

GENEALOGY, NIHILISM, AND ARTISTIC PATHS FORWARD

Any genealogy of modernity must reckon with Nietzsche. Indeed, the supposition of White's environmental critique of Christianity, namely, that it alienates human persons from the natural world, sounds a Nietzschean theme. But Nietzsche is equally critical of the modern alternatives to Christianity; he envisions both the Enlightenment and Romanticism as secular versions of Christianity. Famous for prophesying (it is not Nietzsche himself but a fictional character in *The Gay Science* who makes the announcement) that God is dead, Nietzsche writes in detail about nihilism, particularly in an extended set of aphorisms that would be posthumously published as *Will to Power*. Nietzsche's account focuses on the roots of nihilism in the "Christian-moral interpretation" of existence, on the modern, democratic war of the least common denominator against the singular and the great, and on the possible overcoming of nihilism. If many agree that our age courts meaninglessness, they disagree sharply with Nietzsche—and often with one another—over the diagnosis of the sources of our present predicament and its purported cure.

Whatever difficulties—and some are insuperable—there are in Nietzsche's thought, his work has nonetheless prompted some of the most perceptive writings in contemporary philosophy. Some recent philosophers find in Nietzsche promising paths that he either started down before retreating or might have taken but never actually did. One might even speak of a positive legacy from Nietzsche, along with a set of problems arising out of that legacy. These can inform constructive philosophical thinking in our time. I begin with Nietzsche's genealogy of nihilism, his account of its sources, its distinctive features, and its legacy. It is important to see that Nietzsche offers a series of responses to the crisis of modern civilization.

For most contemporary commentators, the late Nietzsche's focus on creative will only serves to immerse humanity more fully in nihilism. It is not clear, however, that Nietzsche is utterly bereft of resources.

His early works are preoccupied with art and religion as remedies. They suggest paths that might be pursued in our time. Internal tensions can be found even in the early works, yet these works suggest possible paths around the extremes of anthropocentrism and Romanticism. On these matters, Nietzsche glimpses the fact that artists are often wiser than philosophers. He also understands the need for a healthy relationship to nature and to the past as conditions for generativity in the present. He would concur with David Walsh that there is "something irreducible in art and religion that philosophy can apprehend but not replace."[65]

Nietzsche trained as a philologist and had a remarkable gift for language. Unfortunately, he did not fully make use of philological resources. He is surprisingly inattentive to the many ways in which nihilism can be expressed. What Aristotle says of "being" is equally true of "nothing"; it can be said in many ways. Attention to these matters suggests that the overcoming of nihilism is built into our very modes of signifying.

Our awareness of modes of signifying is often enhanced by reflection on the work of great poets. Among the best poets who have sought to refine our language about nature and the place of the human person within the cosmos is Robinson Jeffers. Called the "poet of Nietzschean philosophy," he develops a genealogy of modern poetry that recapitulates insights of Nietzsche and anticipates some of those of Maritain.[66] Jeffers diagnoses the sources of nihilism and suggests a poetic overcoming. The plumbing of the depths of nihilism, rooted in an anthropocentric conception of the cosmos, ends not in despair but in poetic revelation. As Jeffers puts it in "The Beauty of Things," the "sole business of poetry," the chief task of the poet, is "to feel / Greatly, and understand greatly, and express greatly, the natural / Beauty."[67] The beautiful, in Nietzschean language, is beyond good and evil; for "justice and mercy" are but "human dreams." The imposition of exclusively human categories onto the natural cosmos falsifies and deludes. The misinterpretation of nature results from, and deepens, anthropocentrism, the correction to which involves the decentering of the human subject. Jeffers urges us to "uncenter" our minds. His is a radically biocentric vision, which he calls "inhumanism." Yet, as we shall see, Jeffers acknowledges a certain surprising and wondrous affinity between human consciousness and the cosmos. If he begins from a biocentric standpoint, he eventually recognizes the peculiar status of the human animal, the beast that appreciates and articulates the natural beauty.

Jeffers's work had a decisive influence on the work of William Everson, a Beat poet who converted to Catholicism and joined the Dominican order, taking the name Brother Antoninus. The literary scholar Albert Gelpi calls Everson (along with T. S. Eliot) one of the two great religious poets of the twentieth century. In Everson's early, preconversion poetry, there is an accent on beleaguered humanity, lost in the universe. He speaks of the "nameless galaxies," whose indifference embodies a kind of "vast, universal enmity against the human heart."[68]

Everson shares Jeffers's focus on natural beauty. But at least during the period in which he writes as Brother Antoninus, he recasts the poetic vision in theological language. In contrast to Jeffers's biocentric point of departure, Everson begins with persons, indeed often with his own self. He does not, however, affirm anthropocentrism. What he discovers within the human psyche is its porousness to what is outside it and, indeed, the impossibility of drawing clear lines of demarcation between self and other. The project of mastery is an illusion, predicated on the failure to see how fragile the self is and how incapable it is of establishing a firm ground on which to refashion the external world. His poetry moves back and forth between the natural and the human, as it seeks mutual illumination and discovers surprising points of intersection between the two orders. Everson wrestles with polarities that reflect the paradoxes of the human condition. If the self is open to hidden depths both within and outside it, it is also open to encounters with the divine, whose presence haunts both the natural world and the human soul. Recrafting scriptural language, Everson constructs a sacramental poetics. His poetry provides a vision of a world transformed in which the beautiful counters idolatrous consumerism. It arrests without giving rest; it renders suffering redemptive, even as it directs our longing to that which exceeds our grasp and can only be realized in the open receptivity to a gift. Everson's postconversion poetry seeks to trace the points of intersection between the human and the cosmic, as well as the presence in both of "serene agonization." It supplies in poetic form what Edwards calls "a theology of the cross, a theology of God with suffering creation" that speaks to natural "violence."[69]

Rethinking the relationship of art to nature is at the heart of the artistic corpus of Maritain's friend, the great artist Georges Rouault. For him, the "continual observation of nature" was "as necessary as breathing."[70] Against the modern artistic tendency to wallow in an endless critique of conventional society, Rouault had a need "to affirm, not deny or criticize[,] ... in the presence of life and nature."[71] "Imbued with nature," he nonetheless insisted that his goal was "expressiveness."[72] Although he was deeply influenced by artistic predecessors, especially Rembrandt, he warned against being "bewitched by the old masters" and sought his own artistic path.[73] Rouault, who was trained in the arts of stained glass and who always admired the anonymous craftsmen of the medieval cathedrals, was nonetheless decidedly modern both in the subject matters of his art and in his stylistic methods.

Early on in his career, he is preoccupied with human debasement, with the ways in which the exaltation of the self, a version of anthropocentrism, leads to misery, presumption, and despair. Human pollution degrades the natural environment, as is evident in some of his landscapes. Rouault's sustained focus on the human form, especially on the human face, sets him apart from most twentieth-century painters. In the human form, he detects both the distortions and the glory of natural beauty. In some of his later landscapes, he manages simultaneously to humble human persons, who occupy tiny, barely recognizable positions within the natural order, and to acknowledge their cosmic significance, as they are the portion of the natural order capable of acknowledging the beauty manifest in it. He thus wrestles with but never settles for the anthropocentrism/biocentrism dichotomy.

Despite their many differences, Rouault and Everson share an appreciation for neglected traditions. They repudiate both an overly intellectualized art and any conception of art as the mere release of subjective emotion. Their art includes an indictment of the degradation wrought, in nature and human society, by modern anthropocentrism. Rather than succumb to or avoid the threat of nihilism, both artists travel through the twilight of civilization. Their art does not reflect self-indulgent despair. They see and exhibit in their art the luminosity of being that paradoxically makes possible our judgments concerning, indeed our very awareness of, disorder. For philosophers like Maritain and artists such as Rouault and Everson, the realm of unquiet things is the province of the artists. Refusing any offer of facile transcendence, they offer a path through the hell of the modern imagination. They do so by reconstructing a sacramental art that reflects and draws out the implications of the embodied character of human creatures, indeed of human making itself. They craft a poetics and painting of praise, twentieth-century versions of the song "Laudato Si'."

In our time, the art and writing of Makoto Fujimura, whom I have already invoked, provides a telling example of the way in which modern methods and styles can continue to speak the traditional language of beauty and move viewers to an experience of transcendence. Fujimura's art, often called abstract, presents an instructive test case for the surprising continuities of tradition in contemporary culture. His art stands in relationship to that of Mark Rothko in manner akin to that of the relationship of Everson to Jeffers. In fact, both Rothko and Jeffers are deeply influenced by Nietzsche, whereas Everson and Fujimura craft a sacramental art that engages the threats of nihilism while avoiding the flaws of the typical Catholic genealogy of modernity.

The artists reflect a wisdom about the cosmos and the human place within it that is wiser and more comprehensive than that of many philosophers and theologians. They provide pedagogies in seeing, feeling, and describing the rich contours, the mysterious depths, and the illuminating paradoxes of the human condition. They thus open fresh paths in the recovery of natural and human ecologies. There is no claim here that these artistic responses to the crisis of modernity, responses that draw deeply on theological resources and that avoid the vices of anthropocentrism and biocentrism, are the only ways of advancing the teaching of *LS* on human and natural ecology. Indeed, part of the claim here is that these artists help us correct some of the weaknesses in *LS* and other Catholic approaches to these questions. Given the atrophying of the human imagination and the impoverishment of our vocabulary, the guidance of artists such as the ones I study below is indispensable.

Before turning to the art and artistry of Everson, Rouault, and Fujimura, I shall consider in more detail the aesthetic thought of Maritain, the threat of nihilism, and the contested genealogies of modernity. I shall consider an alternative, theological genealogy of modernity, the broad outlines of which have been traced with introductory brevity above, in the reflections on the thought of Pope Francis and Maritain. The broadly Catholic account of the origins and development of modernity contends with Enlightenment, Romantic, and Nietzschean accounts. While defending key elements of the theological view, I shall also probe some of the weaknesses in what has become—from Maritain to Pope Francis—the most prevalent Catholic genealogy of modernity. That account too often suffers from forgetfulness of the motives for modern anthropocentrism and from a naively Romantic conception of nature. A more authentically Catholic understanding, or so I shall argue, turns out to be capacious rather than defensive or reactionary.[74] The position is open to the fragmentary, dislocated discourses that have come to dominate the postmodern or very late modern period.

TWO

Jacques Maritain and the Twilight of Civilization

Concerning the influence of Maritain's reflections on art and beauty on twentieth-century European artists,[1] Maritain's student Yves Simon comments, "That an artist should be interested in scholasticism, . . . and should use the principles of this philosophy to understand and explain what is going on in the vanguard of painting, music, and poetry in the twentieth century, will remain one of the best surprises that ever confronted historians of philosophy."[2] Here we face one of the great paradoxes of Maritain's life and thought; deeply traditional, he was also immersed in the currents of his time. *Anti-Moderne* is the title of one of his books. Yet he was at the center of a Catholic movement in Paris that sought a fusion of traditional philosophy and religious practice with contemporary cultural movements. He had a direct impact on Georges Rouault, Igor Stravinsky, and Jean Cocteau.[3]

Maritain's work belies the assumption that traditional conceptions of metaphysics, art, and anthropology are inherently antithetical to modern art. Just as Pope Francis eschews their incompatibility with modern environmental science, so too does Maritain repudiate their incompatibility with modern art. Such an assertion by itself would not mean much. Reasons for taking Maritain's claim seriously arise not just from his numerous, lengthy treatments of these matters but also from the fact that his work grows out of his encounter with modern artists.[4] His wife, Raïssa, observes, "It was with [the great French painter] Rouault in mind that Jacques wrote *Art and Scholasticism*."[5]

In his biography of Maritain, Ralph McInerny says that that early book was "far from being a reconstruction of a possible medieval aesthetics. Maritain was seeking in Thomas principles that could be applied to contemporary art and thus link the effort of the artist to his effort as a Thomist.... This little book was destined to have a tremendous impact throughout the century on working artists."[6] As Aidan Nichols, OP, has shown, the work had an immediate impact in England, on the craftsman Eric Gill and the painter David Jones, the latter of whom was instructed in the Catholic faith by John O'Connor, who was at the time working on an English translation of *Art and Scholasticism* and who had recently received Chesterton into the church. The English artists emphasized different features of Maritain's work, but both found in it a corrective to modern afflictions. For Gill, Maritain's accent on art as the good of the work provides a way of countering the corruption of the virtues of ordinary productive work under the capitalist factory system. Meanwhile, Jones detects in Maritain's teaching on artwork as sign a counter to "contemporary technocracy," in which the technician, void of cultural memory, replaces the artist. For Gill, the human animal is the creative beast, whose crafting of signs gives access to the richness of being and God, to whose gratuitous generosity beautiful signs ultimately point.[7]

Maritain's appeal has endured through the twentieth century and into our own. Thomas Merton, an aspiring poet writing a thesis on William Blake at Columbia University, discovered Maritain's *Art and Scholasticism*, in which he found a traditional account of art that accommodated modern poets such as Blake and demonstrated how art could remain open to the spiritual order.[8] His writings had an even more profound effect on Flannery O'Connor, who found Maritain's articulation of the distinction between art and ethics liberating.[9] More recently, the poet Dana Gioia and the painter Makoto Fujimura have found in Maritain's writing a language that helps them articulate their experience of the artistic process and mediate between the traditional goals of art and contemporary means and modes of expression. Perhaps most impressive is Seamus Heaney's appeal to Maritain's notion of creative intuition in his own account of poetic inspiration.[10]

I do not want to make more of Maritain's achievement than it is due. Questions about the internal coherence of his thought and about its fidelity to Catholic tradition endure.[11] While most of these questions transcend the scope of the present book, which is not an exegetical project, some have merit. I consider them and suggest ways around deficiencies in Maritain's thought later in this chapter. The most penetrating criticisms of Maritain fault him for an excessively subjectivist view of artistic creation, one that focuses too much on the sources of art in the psyche of the artist and not enough on the particular shape and distinctive features of specific works of art. In this respect, Maritain's weaknesses as a theorist anticipate those of another French Catholic philosopher, Jean-Luc Marion, who has had a great deal to say about the conditions of modern art. Like Marion, Maritain, despite his flaws, opens paths for the recovery of forgotten elements in the Catholic tradition, elements that can help us craft a much-needed language of human making. It is significant that Maritain does so in conversation with art and artists. In his occasional references to the similarities between the artist and the mystic, he also hints at the connections between art and the language and practice of praise.

TECHNOCRACY, NIHILISM, AND ART

In language crafted in response to his own historical setting, Maritain spells out a critique of technocracy that anticipates many of the themes of *LS*. For him, the crisis of our time concerns the reign of technocratic thinking and its exaltation of means over ends. The means have become so impressive that we lose sight of the ends to which technology should be ordered. As was true of many European intellectuals in the first half of the twentieth century, Maritain's life, imagination, and thought were informed by a deep sense of loss and of the tenuous status of civilized society. World wars fought in the heart of Europe shattered what seemed after the fact to have been deeply naive assumptions about the validity of progressive, enlightened modernity. World War I was a traumatic shock to the system of modern Western civilization, casting doubt on modernity, whose promises of progress seemed empty in the face of the rise of a barbarism unknown in previous epochs.[12] The issue of progress in the second Great War was quite different, however. Maritain's reflection can be found in a text with an unlikely topic and title for such ruminations. In 1943, Maritain was provoked by war to compose *Education at the Crossroads*, a book that scatters references to the Nazis and World War II throughout.[13]

Writing at a time when the West was calling on its technological prowess and a cohort of technocratic experts to defeat Nazism, Maritain worried, as did C. S. Lewis, Hannah Arendt, and numerous others, that the West might lose by winning.[14] That is to say, the means of victory, namely, superior technology and technical expertise, might undermine the very things for which the West was fighting. If the danger in Germany is fanatical group identity, the threat for the West is "technocratic pragmatics." The menace of the former is palpable, while the peril of the latter is more subtle. As many intimated at the time, subjection to technofideism could itself lead to a form of totalitarianism.[15]

With its reduction of knowledge to calculable phenomena, technocracy "leaves in human life nothing but relationships of force, or at best those of pleasure." It ignores or repudiates the "spiritual dignity of man" and rests on "the assumption that merely material or biological standards rule human life and morality."[16] It is striking how much of the argument of *LS* recapitulates these mid-twentieth-century themes from Maritain. Francis writes, "The idea of promoting a different cultural paradigm and employing technology as a mere instrument is nowadays inconceivable" (108). Thus we stand naked and exposed in the face of our ever-increasing power, lacking the wherewithal to control it. Nihilism, the loss of any sense of order, purpose, or meaning, haunts the modern, technocratic project.[17]

In the preface to the English edition of *The Twilight of Civilization*, Maritain writes:

> If twilight ushers in night, night itself precedes the day. And in human history it often happens that the first rays of a dawn are mingled with the twilight. In my mind the notion of the present trials endured by civilization was inseparable from that of a new humanism, which is in preparation in the present death struggle of the world, and which at the same time is preparing the renewal of civilization, even if it be only for the time that St. Paul predicts as a resurrection from among the dead.[18]

Here we find encapsulated Maritain's sense of the threats to civilization, alongside his lingering hope that through confronting these threats civilization can be reborn. Maritain thinks that we shall have to reckon with nihilism rather than simply circumvent it with quick, dismissive arguments. But, according to the Maritain of this period, renewal is coming. He was not always so hopeful.

In a famous passage in her memoir, *We Have Been Friends Together*, Raïssa Maritain describes the threat of nihilism that she and Jacques confronted during their early days at the Sorbonne. Raïssa traces nihilism to its roots in skepticism, to the denial of "the objectivity of our knowledge, our very ability to grasp the real."[19] The form of skepticism reduces all knowledge to "works of art and the imagination—and with even less reference than art to reality."[20] She does not hesitate to draw out the implications: "relativism, intellectual skepticism, and—if one was logical—moral nihilism."[21] There are cultural and political consequences. Raïssa sees a parallel to philosophical skepticism in the rise of the "new barbarism" that was to "deck itself out in the prestige of a culture already worn thin, already hypocritical, already prepared for the worship of force."[22] Epistemological skepticism and ethical relativism create the conditions for the fascist politics of raw power. Driven by integrity of spirit, the pair confronted the problem directly.

> On this particular day ... we had just said to one another that if our nature was so unhappy as to possess only a pseudo-intelligence capable of everything but the truth, if, sitting in judgment on itself, it had to debase itself to such a point, then we could neither think nor act with any dignity. In that case everything became absurd—and impossible to accept.[23]

Refusing to take part in such a comedy, they made what was in effect a suicide pact. If they did not discover a truth worthy of devotion, they would end their lives in a year's time. During that year, they would "extend credit to existence, look upon it as an experiment to be made, in the hope that to our ardent plea, the meaning of life would reveal itself."[24] Otherwise, the only option would be freely elected suicide. Raïssa goes on to describe their encounter with the philosopher Henri Bergson, who would introduce them to his philosophy of the Absolute. Although they would eventually part ways with Bergson, his teaching put them on a path toward a truth both knowable and livable.

Raïssa draws attention to the worrying trend of reducing knowledge to a kind of artifice, a construction that risks severing the link between the mind and anything external to it. In the classical conception of knowledge, the mind, in its pursuit of theoretical truth, is measured by things and must conform itself to the real in order to achieve knowledge; in the order of art, by contrast, the artist's mind takes external matter and refashions it according to some ideal. A certain strain of modern philosophy conflates the two, equating the known with the made or constructed.[25]

Now, a certain degree of freedom from fixed external standards is an element intrinsic to art. Precisely because artistic creativity is never mere passivity in relation to the world of things, Maritain emphasizes the freedom of the artist in relation to antecedent material conditions. Yet in its inordinate desire for freedom, modern art risks duplicating the idealism of modern philosophy. A certain strain of modern art seeks to free itself from nature, language, and intelligibility.[26] Art thus renounces "seeing into the inner depths of the world of nature, of visible and corporeal being"; it "cuts itself off from its connection with sense perception."[27] In both mainstream philosophy and contemporary art, Maritain sees the danger of succumbing to a kind of idealism, in which thought and art would be "walled in." Thus art would fail to illuminate or communicate. Severed from nature, our modes of knowing, acting, and making would court nihilism, the notion that there are no standards by which to distinguish true from false, better from worse, or noble from base. Maritain sees the crisis of advanced modernity as a crisis of *homo faber*, of the human person as maker. But Maritain is careful to distinguish between different types or movements of modern art. In one guise at least, modern art is wiser than modern philosophy. As David Walsh puts it, a certain strain of modern art serves to liberate us from the "epistemological straightjacket" in which modern idealism would trap the mind.[28]

The problem of the mind entrapped within itself is a feature of a distinctively modern construal of the relationship of mind and world. That construal involves a reconstruction of the classical understanding of the relationships among three distinctive human activities: *techne*, the human capacity for refashioning the physical world in light of the ends of crafts; *phronesis*, the capacity for practical wisdom, matching means to the ends of the good life for human beings; and *theoria*, the contemplative and receptive encounter with the cosmos that is rooted in wonder.

Now, these Aristotelian 16 ways of construing the operations of the mind have undergone notable transformations in modernity. Science edges out contemplation; in fact, knowledge becomes a kind of techne, intent on mapping and mastering the material world. The standard critique is that true knowledge of causes would provide the capacity to produce the effects. But ancient knowledge of causes bears no such fruit; therefore, its claim to knowledge is spurious. Once the productive paradigm is in place, prudence loses its role as the architectonic virtue of the practical order discerning the concrete means by which the good for human beings can be realized. It becomes a technique of manipulating means to whatever goals happen to be desired. In the succinct phrasing of Thomas Hobbes, science is not about the why but the how. Knowledge "comes into our power" and enables us to "see how to make" something.[29] Thoughts become the "scouts and spies" of the passions, finding the most efficient means for the realization of desire.[30] Techne, understood as the marshaling of increasingly refined techniques to the realization of whatever ends happen to be desired, expands its scope and invades the other two orders.

One way to articulate a persistent twentieth-century Catholic worry about our current situation is to say that the first capacity has come to overshadow and occlude from view the other two. Thus the source of the crisis is the misunderstanding and abusive practices of the human person as maker (*homo faber*). Without contemplation, which is rooted in dispositions of receptive wonder, and without practical wisdom, which orders means to the ends of human flourishing, the human intellect can easily be reduced to its calculating and constructing capacities.

Maritain will argue that the fine arts suggest ways of curbing the excesses and correcting the faulty suppositions of the empire of technology. Indeed, art itself enjoys an expansion in modernity. As Walsh observes, "We no longer instruct artists what to create; we simply await their instruction of us through art. Such is the extraordinary stature acquired by art in the modern period that we might well regard it as a parallel to the astonishing independence gained by science."[31] In its dominance of culture, high and low, and in its remarkable impact on our politics, art takes on increasing authority: "Modern society is the first thoroughly artistic civilization."[32] There is in fact more than a mere parallel between the authoritative independence of technological science and that of art. Both are rooted in a kind of awe in the face of human making.[33] The connection between the products of human artifice and the philosophical disposition of wonder goes back to Plato and Aristotle, the latter of whom notes in the opening of his *Metaphysics* that the philosopher and the poet are both concerned with wonder. The connection is important because it helps account for the willingness of both expert elite culture and ordinary citizens to remain silent in the face of technology's advances. We hesitate to raise ethical questions about technology's use not just because it promises to alleviate evils but also because we are stupefied by its continuously astonishing products.

As David Lachterman shows in his book on early modern science and mathematics, the balance shifts in modern mathematics from contemplation to productivity as the mark of knowledge. There is a tendency here to limit, or redefine, the knowable to that which can be constructed. Lachterman writes, "Objects owe their intelligibility to their mode of genesis." The distinction between the natural and the artificial nearly vanishes, and we are tempted "to regard the natural as a result of the artificial."[34] Consequently, the "*topos* of wonder," characteristic of the life of the philosopher, "now has a new home": "the artistry of the technician."[35]

The question for human making is whether it can enhance rather than foreclose the discovery of the natural and the human, that is, whether, in addition to inspiring awe at technical artistry itself, it can return us to the natural world as a source of wonder and gratitude.

ART, CONTEMPLATION, AND EROS

Maritain's response is complex, but I am going to try to offer a brief summary of it here. He concurs with Walsh that art takes on a novel status in the modern period. In *Art and Scholasticism*, Maritain initially invokes the classical scholastic distinction between art and prudence, the latter of which perfects the human agent while the former achieves perfection in the work produced. He notes that making in a certain sense "stands therefore outside the human sphere; it has an end, rules, values, which are not those of man, but those of the work to be produced. This work is everything for Art; there is for Art but one law—the exigencies and the good of the work." In words that anticipate those of Walsh, he writes, "Hence the tyrannical and absorbing power of Art, and also its astonishing power of soothing; it delivers one from the human; it establishes the *Artifex*—artist or artisan—in a world apart, closed, limited, absolute, in which he puts the energy and intelligence of his manhood at the service of a thing which he makes."[36]

Art and contemplation are alike in that neither is directly informed by moral virtue. For Aristotle and Thomas, practical reason cannot operate without the assistance and guidance of the moral virtues. Without the formation of the passions in virtue, prudence will go awry and be disabled by excessive desire for pleasure or by inordinate fear. This is not the case for art or contemplation. It is undoubtedly the case that some degree of moral virtue is instrumentally necessary for art and philosophy. Without the tempering of certain passions, one will be distracted from the activities necessary to pursue philosophy or create art. Without courage, one might simply give up or succumb to despair when matters become difficult. But it remains the case that one can be a bad person in many respects and still be a good painter or metaphysician.

Although it is impossible to sever completely the connection between art and morality, that is, between art and the human, Maritain is aware of the potential for serious division between the two. As he observes, "The Prudent Man and the Artist have difficulty in understanding one another."[37]

It is important to note that Maritain is using the term "prudence" in a specific and somewhat eccentric manner: to refer to the guardian of public morality, invested with a legal power of enforcement. Maritain thinks the gulf between prudence as legal guardian of morality, on the one hand, and art, on the other, is likely to lead to open conflict. Sensing that art might be disruptive of the morally good, "the Prudent man, if he has to intervene[,] . . . will brandish the moral law against this artist, and summon him to change his work, whatever his inner state of mind and his artistic conscience may be."[38] But Maritain thinks this is actually unwise. As he goes on to say, "The Wise man, I think, will not" intervene in such a manner.[39] Continuing with his somewhat eccentric use of terminology, Maritain distinguishes prudence and wisdom. Wisdom here, I would argue, is in fact prudence as the classical tradition understands it. That is, it is a wisdom about all things human and an ability to discern what ought to be done in particular circumstances. What Maritain goes on to say about how the wise person will approach these matters involves precisely the sort of deliberations involved in prudential judgment. Maritain resists peremptory calls for censorship, but he does not rule it out. Even in cases where it is unwarranted, he does not think that artists are above reproof for the impact of their art on the mores of the society. Criticism and open debate about particular works of art and about the role of art in the public sphere are not just fair game. They are to be encouraged.

Whatever we make of Maritain's thoughts about censorship, it is clear that what he has to say about the autonomy of art has nothing to do with the standard modern affirmation of techne, according to which technical expertise transforms prudence into calculation and contemplative wonder is forced to the margins. Techne itself, understood simply as the tailoring of means or processes or capacities to ends, remains for Maritain fully under the purview of prudence; the dangers of modernity, as Maritain makes clear in the writings on education discussed above, have much to do with the false liberation of techne from practical wisdom. Beyond his continued resistance to technocracy, Maritain seeks to recover and develop further the affinities between contemplation and art. Precisely both are rooted in wonder; the contemplative and the artist, "the one bound to wisdom, the other to beauty, are naturally close."[40] He elaborates:

> There is a curious analogy between the fine arts and wisdom. Like wisdom, they are ordered to an object which transcends man and which is of value in itself, and whose amplitude is limitless, for beauty, like being, is infinite. They are disinterested, desired for themselves, truly noble because their work taken in itself is not made in order that one may use it as a means.[41]

The alliance between art and contemplation allows Maritain to affirm the freedom of art even as it suggests an alternative to the exaltation of techne in modernity. Like contemplation, art fosters virtues of wonder, silent receptivity, humility, gratitude, and awe. It thus inculcates dispositions that counter the vices attendant on technocracy. Because in the encounter with art we experience the pull of the beautiful, drawing us out of ourselves, it suggests a corrective to anthropocentric idealism.

Maritain is interested in recovering a premodern account of the erotic encounter with the beautiful. He seeks to revive a classical account or emotion or desire as open to participation in reason and as having a kind of telos toward the beautiful. Now, Maritain's persistent claim that the encounter with the beautiful satisfies a natural human desire might seem to instrumentalize beauty and to violate his claim that the appreciation of beauty is "disinterested." To understand Maritain's position on this matter, we need to turn to the premodern understanding of ends and means. Some things are desirable only as instruments; other things are desirable both for their own sake and for what comes of them; finally, some things (the classical example from Aristotle's *Ethics* is happiness) are only ends and never a means to some further end. One can imagine some usefulness to the experience of the beautiful. It could offer relaxation and renewal that might aid one in returning to work. What Maritain has in mind when he calls the encounter with the beautiful disinterested has to do with the fact that during the time we are engaged by beauty, we are attracted to it for its own sake.

In her fine treatment of the vanishing (perhaps banishment would be a better word) of beauty and eros from modern art, Natalie Carnes focuses on the role of the museum in altering the relationship of viewer to the work of visual art. The creation of the museum was in part designed to disengage works of art from their original political or religious associations and thus to neutralize their nonaesthetic impact on viewers. The evolution of the notion of the fine arts plays a similar role; to the fine arts, viewers are expected to bring a peculiar mode of response, namely, the disposition of disinterestedness. Such an attitude of appreciation is "distinct from any benefit it might confer on the individual beholder."[42] Of course, the museum is the archetypal location for the experience of the fine arts and thus for the cultivation of disinterestedness.

Disinterestedness supplants the erotic relationship to the beautiful that dominates in classical and premodern Christian accounts. To recover eros, Carnes proposes, we need to move from modern conceptions of theory to the classical contemplative notion of *theoria*. The latter "opens up the reality of what is contemplated" and brings about a "transformation of the contemplator." It highlights not disinterestedness but participation in, or union with, the object contemplated. It underscores the "dynamism between the knower and knowledge, the seer and the seen, the way contemplating realities makes demands on the one contemplating."[43] In place of eros, critique and consumption come to the fore. The model of critical distance denies the erotic, while the model of total consumption literalizes it. Both express anxieties about how desire threatens our sovereignty, with each offering divergent strategies for containing it.[44]

For Maritain, beauty draws us into an experience of being as a gift. There is a connection here between Maritain's writing on art and his work in metaphysics. "Now if being is superabundant and communicative of itself," Maritain writes, "if it gives itself, love is thereby justified."[45] To understand existence as contingent allows for the possibility of seeing it either as the result of merely random processes or as a gift. In his metaphysics, Maritain makes arguments for the intelligibility of being, for the distinction between essence and existence, for priority of existence to essence, and for the dependence of each concretely existing thing on an act of existence. On the basis of sustained argumentation, Maritain concludes that being is indeed a gift, something distinct from and not owed to essences or to any individually existing thing.

Many of the properly metaphysical matters are beyond the scope of this book. I should note the following. It should not be surprising that there are points of overlap between Maritain's account of art and his metaphysics. The metaphysical arguments in some measure undergird claims about beauty. Readers of Maritain (and of Aquinas) often assume that one has to do metaphysics in order to do ethics or aesthetics. But there is a sense in which reflection on beauty is not only independent of metaphysics but also a prelude to it. There is no doubt that there are metaphysical assumptions and implications in ethics and aesthetics. But these need not be teased out and explicitly defended prior to other studies. Moreover, those who encounter the beautiful do not need instruction in metaphysics in order to sense the truth of what Maritain says about beauty as a gift. In fact, the experience could prompt metaphysical reflection on the givenness of beauty in the natural world and perhaps even initiate the sort of investigation of essence and existence that Maritain formulates in great detail. The pull of beauty can be a path into metaphysics. For Maritain, philosophy is "devoted to the mystery of the act of existing." It contemplates the means "by which an essence *which was nothing* is posited *extra nihil*, outside of nothingness; this is the assertion of an irreducible absolute, a kind of miracle of nature (which in reality supposes the action of God the Creator Who gives being to everything that is)."[46]

In fact, Maritain thinks that the logic of our experience of the beautiful draws us into the infinite richness, mystery, and gratuitousness of being. Maritain highlights what Aquinas calls splendor as an attribute of the beautiful. He writes that the beautiful has the splendor of intelligibility: *splendor veri*, said the Platonists; *splendor ordinis*, said Saint Augustine, adding that "unity is the form of all beauty"; *splendor formae*, said Saint Thomas in his precise metaphysician's language: for the form, that is to say, the principle which constitutes the proper perfection of all that is, which constitutes and achieves things in their essences and qualities, which is, finally, if one may so put it, the ontological secret that they bear within them, their spiritual being, their operating mystery.[47]

The question of being is the mystery of existence itself. Receptivity to being as a gift counters the anthropocentric assumption that the external world is raw material to be manipulated.

There is another paradox here of which we need to take note. If the encounter with the beautiful gives rest, it also incites greater desire. It leads us into a more comprehensive encounter with being. There is a parallel here with contemplative knowledge afforded in the philosophical disciplines. Knowledge of this or that matter gives momentary rest to the human intellect. Eventually, however, the resting in a part of knowledge gives way to a desire to understand the relationships and orders among the particular causes or disciplines. As I explain further below, even the highest of the philosophical disciplines, metaphysics, ends in wonder, in an avowal of what exceeds its grasp. From its inception to its culmination, philosophy is erotic. So too is our experience of the beautiful.

Now there is a question that needs to be addressed concerning the splendor of form. Maritain's reading bestows on beauty an objectivity that some interpreters have supposed Thomas does not. What are we to make of the objection that Maritain's objective account is incompatible with Aquinas's purportedly subjective one?

Thomas's description of the beautiful as that which pleases when seen seems to accent the subjective experience; as Umberto Eco points out in his criticism of Maritain, Thomas's own prefatory language to the description ("people call things beautiful") further tilts interpretation in the subjective direction.[48] It seems right to say that Thomas's language of the beautiful intends to eclipse entirely any supposed gulf between subject and object. Yet, there is no doubt that the appellation of beauty is fittingly applied to a set of attributes (the well-known marks of proportion, integrity, and splendor) discerned in an object. In terms of works of art, there is no predetermined way of saying precisely how these marks will or ought to surface within them. Thus does Maritain resist the temptation to settle in a peremptory way what counts for art or even what counts for religious art. This does not mean that one cannot offer an articulation, after the appearance of a work of art, of what makes it beautiful or what makes it religious.

FLAWS IN MARITAIN'S ACCOUNT

Maritain's analysis of the erotic encounter with beauty can be seen as a continuation of the thought of his medieval forebears, particularly that of Thomas Aquinas. Where his account of beauty is truly innovative is in its embrace of modern conceptions of the freedom of the artist. But this is where some have urged that his account goes awry. The accentuation of the autonomy of the artist might seem to be predicated on an overly Romantic conception of art and the artist.

One critic, C. A. Tsakiridou, goes so far as to attribute to Maritain a "solipsistic and messianic" conception of the artist.[49] She argues that Maritain "paid too little attention to the expressive integrity of the art object and allowed his aesthetics to be overdetermined by the creative aspects of art."[50] He focuses inordinately on the internal struggles of the artist for expression and ignores the independence of the artistic object. He thus fails to "allow the work of art to take full possession of itself."[51] So long as the work of art is tied principally to the expression of the artist, its meaning and intelligibility remain "a function of subjective and intersubjective agencies and powers."[52] She notes that, in keeping with his fundamentally subjective orientation to art, Maritain often pays more attention to what artists say about their art than to what they actually produce.

Another way to state this objection is to say that Maritain is insufficiently concerned with the ontology of the work of art as an independent object.[53] The work is understood less as an object in its own right, with its own peculiar form and matter, and more as an expression of the subjective intention of the artist.[54] For Tsakiridou, such an approach downplays the "depth and complexity" of the "aesthetic qualities and dynamics" of the work of art itself. The greater these characteristics, the "more the work resonates with its own peculiar personhood."[55] What sort of response might Maritain offer?

The first thing to be said is that the accusation of solipsism seems misplaced. In the section of *The Responsibility of the Artist* in which he criticizes art for art's sake, he credits Romanticism with bringing to fruition the revelation of the self in the artistic sphere.[56] Maritain writes, "Poetic activity is, of itself, essentially disinterested. It engages the human self in its deepest recesses—but in no way for the sake of the human Ego. The self is both revealing itself and sacrificing itself, . . . it dies to itself in order to live in the work."[57] The passage captures some of what worries Tsakiridou. Maritain's focus is on the interior struggle and transformation of the artist, who lives on in the work of art. Yet it is important to see that interiority is neither narcissistic nor epistemically self-enclosed. It involves a revelation of some feature of being, self-sacrifice on the part of the artist, and is ordered to the making of an external work.

It is true that the accent in this passage is on the artist's ongoing existence in the work of art. But the passage needs to be understood in the context of Maritain's overarching approach to modern art. Maritain finds in certain strains of modern art a genuine development. His insights about the sources of poetic creativity are what draw the attention and approval of so many contemporary artists, whom we have already mentioned, and these artists are certainly not Romantic artists. He describes the double awakening of the self, to itself and to nature, as an "invaluable advance" and a great "adventure."[58] Yet he does not uncritically embrace Romantic art or even Romanticism. His position contains both praise and blame, criticism of what he takes to be its self-destructive tendencies and affirmation of its genuine advances.

As we have seen, he is particularly critical of the strain of modern art that is about mere self-expression. Such art is, like idealism, "walled in."[59] That is to say, such art is solipsistic. Conversely, alongside his affirmation of the creative freedom of the artist, he asserts that the modern artistic awakening to its own sphere of freedom is "inseparable from—is one with another requirement—the grasping of the objective reality of the inner and outer world."[60] The wisdom he detects in modern art, a wisdom lacking in most of modern philosophy, has to do with what Heidegger calls the being-in-the-world of the person and of the artist. In *Creative Intuition*, Maritain speaks of the "mutual entanglement of nature and man" or of "the World and the Self."[61] As is so often the case for Maritain, Rouault is the exemplar:

It is true to say of the pictures of Rouault, as of those of the other great modern painters, that each one is an ideogram of himself. But each one is also, and by the same token, an ideogram of the mystery of things—of some interior aspect and meaning caught in the reality of the visible world, whose forms and appearances, before being recast in a new fabric on his canvas, are scrutinized by his eye implacably attentive to the most fleeting signs and nuances.[62]

Here we might agree with Tsakiridou that Maritain fails to explore sufficiently the "ideogram of the mystery of things" in the artists to which he is most drawn. There are, however, occasions, as Tsikiridou herself concedes, in which Maritain attends to content in detail.[63] Still, he is too often willing to substitute oracular observations about the mystery of things for careful reflection on the specific form and content of works of art. The second half of this book is intended to remedy that defect in Maritain's writing.

If Maritain's conception of art and the artist is not solipsistic, it seems nonetheless that he tends to want to quarantine the internal act of artistic creativity from the taint of outside influences. This is one of the reasons for his resistance to censorship. He also resists the notion that art must or should conform to ideological, social ends. Totalitarian politics seeks to control art and make it an instrument of propaganda. Art for the "social group makes the social value, social significance, or social impact of the work into an aesthetic or artistic value, even the supreme aesthetic or artistic value."[64]

Maritain is perhaps also to be faulted for an ambiguity concerning artistic integrity. He highlights the absolute demand on the artist of the artistic vision, a demand that is akin to the requirement of conscience in the moral sphere. Yet he does not want to say that the artist operates in a vacuum or that the artist cannot or should not fall under the sway of external influences. One might be tempted to think that the ideal would be an artist operating with minimal influence from outside. That for Maritain is perhaps true at the moment of artistic creation itself. At that moment, the artist needs to obey the demand of the vision. But what the artist has internalized from the external world prior to that moment is all fair game as it enters into the shaping of the internal vision. He elaborates on this point: "In the case of the idea or passion fully integrated in creative emotion, . . . it is in from the start. . . . Thus the autonomy of art is not impaired; it is, on the contrary, increased and fortified."[65]

Now Maritain is aware that there can be a complex interplay between external and internal impulses and motives, as in the case, for example, of commissioned art.⁶⁶ But it is a deficiency of his account that he does not develop the possibilities further. It seems to me that artists can properly exercise their freedom while being in conversation with a host of others who might suggest specific projects or novel ways forward in the production of works already under production. This is not to say that questions about the integrity of the artist, the artist's faithfulness to a certain vision, are unimportant. But one cannot in advance and in a peremptory way stipulate that this or that sort of external influence will necessarily constitute corruption or an abrogation of the artist's responsibility to the work. Indeed, artists often do their work in conversation not just with other artists, but with the public, with audiences, actual or potential, and with those who hire them to produce works of art. In some circles the creation of art is a highly social matter, with what is created being the result of the collaboration of many artists or of a conversation between the artist and the audience.⁶⁷ There is no reason, I think, that Maritain's account cannot be expanded in this way.

The objection concerning the individualism of the artist can be reformulated as an accusation that Maritain artificially servers the fine arts from the so-called useful arts. The elevation of the fine arts underscores the freedom of the artist, but it can also fall prey to a kind of gnostic or Romantic celebration of artistic genius. Maritain's position on this matter is not easy to determine. Various works contain different formulations. The gap is not as pronounced in the early work, *Art and Scholasticism*, as it seems to be in the later work, *Creative Intuition*. Indeed, as I have noted, Eric Gill discerns in *Art and Scholasticism* a basis for recovering an understanding of craft and thus for reforming the role of productive work in the lives of ordinary citizens. Even in *Creative Intuition*, Maritain sometimes expresses the contrast between the useful and fine arts in terms of relative emphasis.

> The good of the work, which is the aim of every art, depends more, in certain arts, on its relations to the needs of human life, and on the fact of the work being good for something else; and that, in certain other arts, the good of the work succeeds more in being a good in itself and for itself, a world of its own—whatever the relations it can and must continue to have with the concerns of human life may be.⁶⁸

Much hinges here on how we construe the notion of the "needs of human life." There is a danger of separating human needs from beauty as if the world of beauty had nothing to do with the human world. The instrumentalization of art for the sake of human needs as in the case of works that are mostly functional may indeed lack the freedom of the so-called fine arts. But Maritain does not equate this freedom with necessary indifference to human needs. Indeed, he consistently argues that there is a human need for beauty. The best of the fine arts, those whose influence endures over time, are those that manage to address the greatest and highest of human needs, the need to probe the great mysteries of human life and to feed the soul's longing for beauty. Unless we are willing to settle for a complete cleavage between the spheres of the useful and the beautiful, we will want to resist any impenetrable barriers between the two. The same soul that seeks rest in the beautiful also seeks to inhabit a built world, in which there is an easy commerce between form and function, between beauty and utility. As Gill intimates, there is need for the beautiful to be cultivated in the realm of the so-called useful arts. It is crucial for human civilization that there be no chasm between the so-called fine and useful arts.

The weaknesses in Maritain's account are clear, as is their root in an overly enthusiastic embrace of certain elements of Romanticism. It is important, however, to note the ways in which Maritain is critical of Romanticism. In his account of creative intuition, he is at pains to distance himself both from an overly intellectualized conception of art and from the Romantic emphasis on sheer emotion. His account of the beautiful seeks to restore the connection between desire and beauty. Maritain seeks a restoration of classical eros as that element in the human soul that is aroused by beauty—a notion to which modernity in its anthropocentric and biocentric modes is allergic.

There are advantages to Maritain's revival of the erotic encounter with beauty, an encounter that can affect the viewer in a variety of unpredictable ways. Maritain can make sense of the complicated rhetorical relationships among modern artists, their art, and their intended audiences. Modern artists often seek to undermine precisely the disinterested, purportedly objective, posture of audiences toward art. They seek to engage, sometimes to invite or implicate, to unsettle or even accuse, viewers. The assumption is that viewers will not see what is presented unless they recognize certain obstacles in their antecedent habits or dispositions. In other cases, the subject matter itself may demand that "disinterestedness" be put into question. Maritain himself objects to depictions of Christ's suffering that locate him as an object of contemplation in isolation from human suffering. Instead, Christ should be depicted in a way that fosters the participation of the viewer.[69]

MODERN ART AND LIMITED REVELATIONS

Artists, particularly in the modern period, often resort to indirect modes of communication, to images that accuse or implicate viewers, even to the obscure and offensive, because of assumptions they hold about the obstacles and distortions built into the dominant modern modes of communication or even into the souls and capacities of their audiences. Some of Maritain's favorite artists, for example, Baudelaire and Rouault, are preoccupied with these obstacles and distortions.

If Maritain retains much of the medieval vision of the arts of the beautiful, he is acutely aware that the condition of art in modernity is in many ways not fortuitous. Maritain's penchant for contrasting the ambient conditions of Dante's art to those of Baudelaire or Rouault is perhaps the strongest indication that the autonomy of art does not mean that artists create in a social or cultural vacuum. They inevitably draw from their own experiences (their upbringing, personal relationships, and education) and from the resources afforded them in the ambient culture.

Maritain's reflection on the limitations of modern art calls to mind a passage from Flannery O'Connor: "Unless we are willing to accept our artists as they are, the answer to the question, 'Who speaks for America today?' will have to be: the advertising agencies.... Where the artist is still trusted, he will not be looked to for assurance." We will need to take what the artist offers "as a revelation, not of what we ought to be but of what we are at a given time and under given circumstances; that is, as a limited revelation but revelation nevertheless."[70] O'Connor's assessment, which is more pessimistic than that of Maritain, is sobering and instructive. Her own preferred art form, the short story, underscores the fragmentary and partial expression of artistic vision. Artists can still communicate deep truths about beauty and the human condition, but the mode of communication is indirect and often violent.

Maritain's nuanced account of what we have to hope and fear from modern art should prompt us to rethink what has in many quarters become the standard Catholic genealogy of modernity.[71] In his more philosophical writings, Maritain sometimes writes in a way that assumes a grand narrative, with the rise of Western civilization from antiquity to Christianity peaking in the High Middle Ages, followed by a long decline. His genealogy of modern art complicates that narrative considerably. We have already noted that Maritain sees in modern art both a recapitulation of the self-destructive tendencies of modern philosophy and a corrective to those very tendencies.

If modern artists like Baudelaire lack the comprehensive vision of Dante, they are not to be dismissed. They may supply us with what no one else in our current cultural climate can. For his ability to perceive and describe "what kind of hell is our modern universe," Baudelaire is to be praised. Into that inferno, he descended and "looked at everything from there." Maritain concludes, "In distortion and cruelty, his vision of human love was the most profound—I do not say true—that the corrupt eye of a lost epoch was capable of."[72] He explains, "In the place where he [Baudelaire] was, and from which he looked at things," what was needed was "not to perceive the adjustment, but to feel the split and derangement." Baudelaire drew inspiration from the "unquiet things" in his culture. In such circumstances, there can be no facile recovery of tradition. The partial revelation often seems negative; it consists in helping us to name what is missing, to mark out and reflect on the absences and disorders of our time. But that in itself can be salutary and can prompt a quest to discover and recover what has been lost.

THREE

Nihilism and Modernity in Endless Crisis

In *The Twilight of Civilization*, Maritain cites Nietzsche in the context of a discussion of the "anthropocentric concept of man," which envisions "human nature as closed in upon itself or absolutely self-sufficient."[1] He adds that this conception cuts the human off not only from what is outside and above reason (nature and God) but also from the "infra-rational," from the "instincts, obscure tendencies and the unconscious, with all its malicious and even demonic, as well as fertile, implications." The result is an "opposition between life and intellect."[2] Reacting against the rationalism of modernity, Nietzsche should be seen as defending the whole of human nature against the dominance by one part, reason.[3] Particularly in his early writings on art, Nietzsche's concerns overlap in some important respects with those of Maritain, who in his own writings on art pursues a healing of the modern breach between passion and reason. As Maritain puts it in *Creative Intuition*, "Poetry is born in the root life of the artist, where the powers of the soul are active in common." Its source is not the abstract concept but knowledge "through affective union."[4] Similarly, Nietzsche counters the notion of the artist as autonomous creator. In *Birth of Tragedy*, he insists that the artist is as much artwork as creator.[5]

At various points in his career, Nietzsche turns to art as a source for the renewal of civilization and the overcoming of nihilism. In this chapter, I begin by examining Nietzsche's genealogy of nihilism and some of the most cogent criticisms of his diagnosis. Following the lead of a number of contemporary philosophers, the constructive engagement with Nietzsche's thought allows for the articulation of a positive account of artistic creativity. I make use of (a) William Desmond's philological diagnosis of nihilism, according to which "nothing" is said in many ways; (b) Desmond's and Jean-Luc Marion's suggestion that the recovery from nihilism consists, not in some confrontation with the abyss, but in the receptivity to being as gift, one manifestation of which is in the openness to being as beautiful; and (c) Charles De Koninck's brilliant analysis, in his unfinished work, *The Cosmos*, of the compatibility between Aquinas and evolutionary biology, a compatibility that accounts for the temptations of both anthropocentrism and biocentrism while showing the defects of each.

NIETZSCHE ON NIHILISM: GENEALOGY, DIAGNOSIS, PROGNOSIS

For Nietzsche, nihilism is a natural result of the decline in the credibility of comprehensive worldviews. Without some sense of being part of a larger, purposive whole, the human sense of meaning vanishes: "Man has lost faith in his own value when no infinitely valuable whole works through him."[6] Nihilism means that the "aim is lacking," and that "'why?' finds no answer."[7] In an instructive comment, Nietzsche observes that nihilism surfaces at the point when "the highest values devalue themselves." The values include all large-scale beliefs in an objective order of truth—whether they are philosophical, religious, scientific, or political. In its varying forms, belief in an overarching order "was the great antidote against ... nihilism."[8]

Judaism to some extent and Christianity to a great extent provide a further antidote. They teach that there is an objective truth, but they recognize that truth, goodness, and happiness elude us in our current condition. So, according to Nietzsche, they provide "an escape." They pass "judgment on the world of becoming as a deception and assert the existence of another world, either a world in history, a promised land, or—what is even better—a world beyond this one, a true world."[9] Not even philosophers have been immune to this sort of escape.

In popular thought, Nietzsche is most known for proclaiming the death of God. It was not in fact Nietzsche but a character, the madman, in Nietzsche's *Gay Science*, who issues the proclamation. But it is important to see that Nietzsche's scathing critique of objective morality is equally applicable to those who hold to science or secular, progressive morality. He writes, "Those who have abandoned God cling that much more firmly to the faith in morality." It is not just for Nietzsche that faith in morality is a substitute for the decline of Christianity. The very commitment to truth that has liberated some from Christianity is itself an offshoot of the will to truth that is at the heart of Christianity. All share a commitment to what Nietzsche calls the "ascetic ideal," the notion that we must conform ourselves to what is true or right—again, whether this is scientific or political truth.[10] Once the Christian impulse dissipates, it is only a matter of time until other highest values devalue themselves.

The result of such compounding acknowledgments of the loss of meaning is what Nietzsche calls "pessimism." This is but a "preliminary form of nihilism."[11] The disappointment that attends such pessimism is a direct result of having taken Christianity and its secular descendants seriously in the first place. Nietzsche states, "It is in one particular interpretation, the Christian-moral one, that nihilism is rooted."[12] The accentuation of truth and truthfulness in Christianity, whose remnants linger in modern science and politics, leads inquirers to recognize that Christianity is itself at best a partial truth and perhaps a distorting one. He writes, "Among the forces cultivated by morality was truthfulness: this eventually turned against morality, discovered its teleology, its partial perspective."[13] Pursuing truth to its logical extreme leads ultimately to the realization that there is no truth, at least not in any sense in which the tradition had promoted it. But the despair that results from this acknowledgment is parasitic on the very assumption that generated the need for truth in the first place. As Nietzsche writes, "The philosophical nihilist is convinced that all that happens is meaningless and in vain; and that there ought not to be anything meaningless and in vain. But whence this 'there ought not to be'?"[14]

That there must be such purpose presupposes that the Christian-moral interpretation of existence, or some version of it, is the only viable way of approaching human life. Nietzsche wants us to question this. Of course, questioning, not just the existence of God or the value of religion, but the very foundations of modern science and politics, would require a kind of philosophical courage that is exceedingly rare. The vast majority of human beings are simply incapable of it. Pessimistic nihilism breeds what Nietzsche calls the "last man." The leveling instincts of modern democracy are exacerbated by the threat of nihilism. Purpose is now found in the communal abdication of any longing for greatness. In *The Will to Power*, he writes, "What has been deified? The value instincts in the community. What has been slandered? That which sets apart the highest men from the lowest, the desires that create clefts."[15]

The imperative of the herd is that there should "one day be nothing anymore to be afraid of."[16] In the prologue to *Thus Spake Zarathustra*, the narrator describes the reign of the last man:

> Alas, the time of the most despicable man is coming, he that is no longer able to despise himself. Behold, I show you the last man. What is love? What is creation? What is longing? What is a star? Thus asks the last man and blinks. The earth has become small, and on it hops the last man who makes everything small.[17]

The great quests and questions that have animated human life at least since the time human beings became storytelling animals no longer register in the human soul. The blinking is an indication that the passions for anything beyond the satisfaction of one's petty and immediate desires have dissipated. As Robert Pippin puts it, nihilism is a "failure of desire, the flickering out of some erotic flame."[18] What might seem a horrifying vision of humanity sapped of all longing and knowledge is for Zarathustra's modern audience a welcome prospect. The crowd clamors, "Turn us into these last men." The inability to recognize one's debased condition is a sign of complete debasement. As Shakespeare puts it in *King Lear*, "This is not the worst, so long as we are able to say, 'this is the worst.'" The judgment that something is base presupposes a recognition of some other, better order of things. The vanishing of such standards might be said to mark the completion of nihilism.

Of course, the very notion of a better order might seem to point us back to traditional morality. Nietzsche himself is clear that he does not intend to sacrifice all standards or hierarchies. What appears to be amoralism from one perspective is from another a basis for ranking souls on the basis of their vigor, health, power, and creativity. Nietzsche simultaneously insists that there is a rank of value and that at the top of that scale resides radical self-creation. Pippin sums up the fundamental problem for Nietzsche's project. The very notion of an overcoming of nihilism, once it has been invited to destroy all existing foundations, is unlikely. Pippin remarks, "It is as if he thinks by defeating this legacy, or hastening its internal collapse, a new one could be created. We are not part of anything that could be continued, that is worth continuing and so are nowhere, not even at any time, given the eternal sameness of such moments."[19] This is Pippin's critique of eternal recurrence: it deprives us of the capacity to judge better and worse in our experience. All is equally to be affirmed. The ironic result is precisely the leveling that Nietzsche criticized.

Instead of providing a way to overcome nihilism, Nietzsche's remedy seems only to immerse us more fully in it. By exalting the confrontation of the creative will with nothingness, Nietzsche hoped to revive the grandeur of the tragic hero. But the absence of any goal or standard in light of which we might appraise the hero's life as noble opens the possibility of a comic reversal in our perception of the hero, whose longings now seem silly and farcical. Comic nihilism is the result. Pippin proposes an alternative: "The right diagnosis...would have to involve a re-engagement with the Socratic question that he so powerfully reintroduced: what are the conditions for the possibility of a 'life' now; what makes leading a life possible?"[20] As we shall see, Nietzsche did in fact devote a good deal of attention to this question. Moreover, his formulation of the question is more genuinely Socratic and less Kantian ("conditions for the possibility") than is Pippin's.

SPONTANEITY OR RECEPTIVITY

Pippin's view is that the Kantian framework is indispensable not just for understanding modernity but also for understanding any proposed solution to its perceived problems: "Spontaneous subjectivity, completely determining for itself what to accept as evidence about the nature of things, and legislating to itself its proper course of action, is, if nothing else, the appropriate image of modernity's understanding of itself as revolutionary and 'self-grounding.'" He insists that "being modern demands...being radically critical," the modern subject "relying only on itself, its own spontaneous self-legislation."[21] Of course, this is precisely the Kantian turn that Nietzsche thought invited another turn, toward aesthetic self-crafting.

Pippin writes, "Whatever ends up being the historically decisive result of the modern revolution, it will, from this Kantian perspective, still be a self-determined result, one we shall end up imposing on ourselves, rather than simply discovering it."[22] Of course, realists and idealists of various stripes would agree with some version of the last, modest formulation, namely, that morality is not a matter of "simply discovering it." The difficulty comes in the question of priority and in the precise articulation of the relationship between the knowing, purposive agent and the world in which the agent operates.[23]

The more radical version ("spontaneous subjectivity, completely determining for itself . . . and legislating for itself") seems to return us to the Nietzschean dilemma and to exacerbate, rather than alleviate, the crisis of *homo faber*. As Jean-Luc Marion notes, Nietzsche radicalizes Kantian self-legislation by describing the human person as value-creating, as an esteemer: "Every evaluation is performed by a will to power that attests to and thus recognizes this or that evaluation."[24] One might quibble with the language of will to power, but the phenomenon Nietzsche describes is precisely the result of the elevation of the spontaneous self-determination of the self-legislating subject. We should recall that this was the understanding of human knowledge that Raïssa Maritain thought led directly to skepticism and nihilism.

It is not surprising, then, that Pippin does not really take us back to Socrates. His Kantian-sounding language ("conditions for the possibility") betrays a quite different agenda. Another influential contemporary philosopher, Stanley Rosen, shares Pippin's worries about Nietzsche, his interest in salvaging what is worthwhile in modernity, and his appreciation of Socrates. Yet Rosen insists that the nihilistic crisis of modernity requires "the recovery of ordinary experience," which provides the "starting points of philosophical investigation."[25]

The primacy of ordinary experience neither establishes common sense as an infallible guide nor discounts the revolutionary impact of philosophy. Philosophy involves a disruption of ordinary life, but it aims to answer questions that arise in ordinary experience. Philosophy is at work in the making of sound judgments about ordinary experience and in the deliberative and reflective capacity to distinguish better and worse ways of life.[26] Everyone has desires and pursues goals. Among these desires and goals, agents incline to one good or another and deliberate about which goods to pursue and in what way. Every human being makes judgments about better and worse and thus, at least implicitly, engages in philosophy. As Rosen puts it, "Philosophy depends upon the ordinary language of everyday life, as deepened and articulated by poetic imagination. But this in turn is rooted firmly in the silence of the given."[27]

The Socratic understanding of eros further underscores the primacy of receptivity: "Erotic desire . . . is not the will, that is, not a projection from the intellect outward or the constitution of a world, but a force from above and outside the soul that comes down into it and raises it to the heavens."[28] For Rosen, what Plato offers to modernity is the possibility of reestablishing the intrinsic connection between reason and the good. Socrates does not so much reduce the good to what is rationally accessible as he inscribes reason itself within the good. That is the context for a Socratic response to Nietzsche's question concerning the value of truth. Rosen thinks there are important and positive anticipations of modernity in Plato, who pairs the contemplative activity of the intellect with a "practico-productive" activity, which involves fashioning or constructing the political and cultural conditions of human life in light of an antecedent apprehension of the good. Rosen and Pippin both see *homo faber* as the focus point of nihilism and its overcoming. Beyond this point, they differ sharply. For Pippin, what is needed is a dialectic within but never transcending spontaneous subjectivity. For Rosen, subjectivity is initially at least a matter of receptivity rather than creativity. Knowing is a matter of apprehending the other. Moreover, desires to act and to make are provoked and aroused by ordinary experience, by the pull of the good.

Recovering receptivity to what is given has been an abiding theme in post-Kantian continental philosophy. The task German phenomenologists and some French thinkers set for themselves is the recovery of the world—the reinsertion of the mind into the real. One commentator, Kevin Hart, expresses the project in terms of three reductions. The first, accomplished by Husserl, involves a reduction that leads back from immediate self-consciousness to phenomena as objects; the second, by Heidegger, involves the reduction from beings to Being; and the third, in the work of Marion, involves the reduction to an original receptivity, in the self-givenness of phenomena, that exceeds and overwhelms any human intentionality.[29] Marion's writings must be understood, in the wake of Husserl and Heidegger, as yet another response to Descartes's founding of modern philosophy in the isolated *cogito*, and the attendant retreat from the external world into the immediate certitude of interiority. Cut off from the external world, the mind loses its purchase on the real.

In dialogue with Husserl's account of intentionality, Marion proposes a "counter-intentionality," the shock of exteriority, grounded in the experience of the saturated phenomena, the experience of being drawn into what our intentionality does not anticipate and cannot comprehend. Marion stresses the overwhelming and destabilizing experience of the bedazzled phenomena. An important question here is whether the accent on the "bedazzlement" of the saturated phenomena risks entirely undermining intelligibility. How are we to distinguish between the blindness of intuitive excess and that of intuitive lack?[30] Put somewhat differently, we might ask: What basis is there for prudential distinctions between divine and demonic revelations? Or again, what sort of sublime are we encountering in the experience of bedazzlement?

In her book *Degrees of Givenness: On Saturation in Jean-Luc Marion*, Christina Gschwandtner offers a critique of Marion's failure to offer "nuanced distinctions between different kinds of blindness and excess."[31] Gschwandtner notes that for Marion painting is a privileged example of visible givenness and is thus an exemplary subject for phenomenological investigation. Yet in his specific reflections on painting and in his more general account of saturation, Marion fails to do justice to the complexity of our experience. Gschwandtner argues:

> There must be a way of depicting phenomenologically a whole range of aesthetic works and experiences that are saturated in different ways and in an endless variety of degrees with many types of mediocrity and mastery, without these degrees depending only on a failure to see adequately. There should be a way of depicting phenomenologically how a painting impacts the average mortal and not just the artistic genius and how different kinds of painting affect us differently.[32]

We should note that the criticism of Marion resembles Tsakiridou's critique of Maritain. Both authors are faulted for failing to attend carefully to the givenness or form of artistic objects in their specificity. With respect to Marion, Gschwandtner observes that saturation can come to us in degrees, while different settings can produce phenomenologically different types of experience. Marion has little to say about why some experience such saturation and others do not or about the way in which training or habituation might improve one's capacity for such experiences. Moreover, there is an individualistic bent to Marion's interpretation of these experiences. Community plays little or no role. Again, Marion fails at the task of differentiation. Concerning the purportedly saturated phenomena, Gschwandtner asks:

> If they are truly *phenomena* and hence given to experience in consciousness, are they only *experienced* as saturated or poor and hence the level of saturation is not somehow in the phenomenon itself? The *same* phenomenon can hence appear as saturated to one person but as poor to another, saturated at some time and in some contexts but not at others. And how saturated it appears seems to depend in important ways on the person's (hermeneutic?) preparation for the experience, on the particular (hermeneutic?) context, and on the person's (hermeneutic?) ability to "see."[33]

As a corrective to the deficiencies of Marion's approach, Maritain's metaphysics, especially as articulated in his great work *The Degrees of Knowledge*, can be of assistance. In language reminiscent of Pascal's account of the human condition as a paradoxical mixture of wretchedness and greatness, Maritain speaks of the majesty and poverty of metaphysics. Modern philosophy, on his view, can be seen as a series of oscillations between inordinate claims on behalf of metaphysics and proclamations of intellectual defeat and despair. Descartes is followed by Hume; Hegel, by Nietzsche and Kierkegaard; and Husserl, by Heidegger and Derrida. Maritain's corrective is to see that metaphysics, properly understood, reveals its limits in its highest points of achievement. Metaphysics begins and ends in wonder, in an "avowal of ignorance." Maritain writes, "The very age that is unaware of the majesty of metaphysics, likewise overlooks its poverty. Its majesty? It is wisdom. Its poverty? It is human science."[34] The poverty of metaphysics is most evident in its aspiration: "It awakens the desire for supreme union, for spiritual possession completed in the order of reality itself and not only in the concept. It cannot satisfy that desire."[35]

The metaphysics of Maritain is neither presumptuous nor despairing. It envisions wonder as a characteristic of the middle creature that is the human person. It avoids both anthropocentric idealism, which grounds knowledge and purpose in the subject's spontaneity, and the radical exteriority of the saturated phenomena. It is also a metaphysics open to dialogue with revealed theology.[36] The highest sort of knowledge available to us in this life is a personal communication through love with God, a suffering of divine things rather than a reduction of being to abstract categories. With the help of Maritain's metaphysics, we can discover a basis for distinguishing between the divine and the demonic, goodness and evil, in our experience of the saturated phenomena.

Aware of the gap between aspiration and achievement, some philosophers seek to overcome it with a natural mysticism that would "raise itself dialectically to ecstasy."[37] Maritain is skeptical. He insists that it is only through love, received as a gift, that such an ascent is possible. The paradox here is that a descent, in the form of a gift from above, enables our ascent. There is no natural ascent from the wisdom of philosophy to the wisdom of the saints; indeed, the latter is, to quote Maritain quoting Aquinas, "an experimental knowledge of the deep things of God, or a suffering of divine things, an experience which leads the soul through a series of states and transformations until within the very depths of itself it feels the touch of divinity and 'experiences the life of God.'"[38] As Maritain adds, "Mystical experience ... is a knowledge by connaturality," knowledge by intimate experience rather than by concepts. It is made possible by sanctifying grace, which "lays hold of God as He is really present within us as a Gift, a Friend, an eternal life-companion."[39]

Maritain's notion of connaturality combines intuition with an affective dimension. As Trapani puts it, "Connaturality is a type of knowledge that comes about through a type of immediate and/or spontaneous experience ... through a type of intuition." It is "lived, non-discursive, non-conceptual, and an integrated experience."[40] All conceptual knowledge draws its sustenance from that which is nonconceptual and can never be fully articulated in rational terms, at least by finite, embodied intellects. Reality always exceeds our capacity to articulate it.

Maritain supplies his own version of the saturated phenomena but one that is not as vulnerable to the objections that have been raised against Marion's. For Maritain, the work of art is especially open to indefinite expansion, in part because it does not terminate in an abstract concept. Instead, in its concreteness, it carries with it a host of associations. It always says more than what it is. The work makes present, "together with itself, something else, and still something else, and still something else indefinitely, in the infinite mirrors of analogy."[41] The latent associations may be historical connections to the object, connections of memory, or simply similitudes and correspondences. These are present at the outset of artistic creativity, embedded in the creative intuition of the artist, and in the work of art once it is produced. Such fertile expansion helps account for the natural fecundity of art, the way in which artists are prompted by encounters with beauty to create more and to create what is novel. It also helps to account for the unpredictable character of artistic creation even when art is quite traditional. Because of the infinite mirror of analogy, there is no way to discern in advance the next step in artistic creativity.

Now Maritain also argues that the infinite fecundity of art points in the direction of God as the absolute toward which all experience of beauty tends. As J. W. Hanke points out, it is difficult to discern precisely what Maritain's argument is here. Explicit reference to God, even as a remote source, is not built into the experience of beauty. Let me recur to what I said in the previous chapter about the erotic experience of the beautiful. While it is disinterested in the sense that it does not involve a desire to instrumentalize beauty for some other end, that does not mean that desire or enjoyment is absent. In fact, the experience of beauty, like the apprehension of truth in a particular argument or scientific or philosophical discipline, satisfies only to some extent the desire to know. But just as the desire to know is not sated, and is often in fact incited to greater longing, by the apprehension of this or that truth, so too the experience of the beautiful calls forth a longing for greater beauty. Such a longing points in the direction of an encounter with that which is beautiful in every respect, just as the ultimate end for Aristotle would fully satisfy our longing. Hanke writes, "Beautiful things give joy to the mind: but in their flaws and limitations as they confront our longing for an unalloyed delight, they turn us in the direction of that which can give complete joy, a perfect and unlimited beauty."[42] This is not of course a proof that such an ultimate object or being exists, but it can engender an inquiry, even a quest, to discover the truth of the matter, to encounter a beauty that is the source of all finite beauty.

CREATION AS GIFT:
OUR EVOLUTIONARY HISTORY

Maritain's own version of the saturated phenomenon rests on a specific metaphysics of creation, one that clearly distinguishes divine creation from every other sort of making and that accommodates evolutionary biology and its implicit themes of chance, tragedy, and the sublime. Only in this way can a Catholic aesthetics avoid the pitfalls of the standard genealogy, in its naïveté about nature and its forgetfulness of the motives of modernity. Corresponding to such an account of creation is a sophisticated grammar of being and nothingness, which underscores the complex ways in which we signify "nothing" as well as the ways in which our very ability to signify "nothing" assumes a surplus of being. The allegedly impending darkness presupposes even as it occludes from view what David Walsh calls "the luminosity of existence."

Eager to defend both divine freedom and to avoid arbitrariness in creation, Thomas Aquinas crafts an analogy between creation and art. In a key passage in *LS*, Francis quotes Aquinas on precisely this point: "Nature is nothing other than a certain kind of art, namely God's art, impressed upon things, whereby those things are moved to a determinate end. It is as if a shipbuilder were able to give timbers the wherewithal to move themselves to take the form of a ship" (80). Francis reasons, again with the help of Aquinas, "God's ongoing presence in creation ensures the subsistence and growth of each being" and "continues the work of creation" (80).

Although Francis commends the scientific understanding of nature, he does not hesitate to deploy explicitly theological language. "Nature is usually seen as a system which can be studied, understood and controlled"; creation, by contrast, "can only be understood as a gift from the outstretched hand of the Father of all, and as a reality illuminated by the love which calls us together into universal communion" (76). In his treatment of creation, Thomas quietly highlights these themes as he develops an analogy between creation and art. For the artist, there is some point in making, some desire to communicate, to express beauty and wisdom. Moreover, the design of the artist reaches beyond the overall plan to the intricate details of the artifact. As Thomas puts it, "The causality of God extends to every being, not just to the principles of species, but also to the principles of individuals, not only to things incorruptible, but also to things corruptible."[43] Finally, the artist can continue to work on what is made until the artist judges that it is complete. For Thomas, creation as a work of art thus falls under the plan of divine providence, which orders all things to a cosmic consummation.[44]

Divine creation, as William Desmond brilliantly demonstrates in *God and the Between*, is different from creativity as we normally understand it.

Creativity is a form of making, in which something becomes this or that through a modification of preexisting material. Creation, instead, "makes finite being possible." The distinction between making and creating is palpable; indeed, it is a commonplace of medieval metaphysics. The contingency of finite beings is "not just relative to other finite beings but is inherent in the very being there" of finite beings. Creation is not an event within the whole but rather something that points beyond the whole.[45]

The breakthrough to creation ex nihilo has important implications for metaphysics. God and the whole are not codependent. Creation introduces a radical asymmetry between God and all else that exists. Thus there can be no competition between God and other beings. Finite beings are "seconds," but, in the act of creation, the first is not "cloning itself." Instead, God brings each being into existence out of nothing to stand in its own otherness.

Desmond deploys insights from classical Thomistic metaphysics in a sustained grammatical reflection on being and nothingness. He begins by admitting that nihilism is a perpetual possibility for philosophy and humanity. Modernity, characterized by cycles of presumptive ambition and despairing skepticism, seems particularly vulnerable to the threat of nothingness. But Desmond does not focus exclusively on the Nietzschean theory of nihilism as the "devaluation of the highest values." Desmond wants to slow things down. He offers a cogent, phenomenological analysis of the different senses of nothingness. The word *nothing*—like its apparent opposite, the word *being*—can be said in many ways.

There is, for example, the empty nothing of nihilism; the howling nothing of the damned; the nothing of forgiveness practiced by the merciful; and the kenotic nothing of sacrificial self-emptying. In all this, Desmond insists, there is "no escape from metaphysics." Thoroughgoing nihilism is never possible, even if a variety of trends in modern philosophy, politics, and culture seem inevitably to "return to zero, coming to nothing."[46] Yet Desmond speculates, "Can our return to zero enliven again our taste for the ethos of being and its signs of transcendence?"[47] Instead of simply the nihilism of despair, might we uncover the "nihilating of despair in despair."[48] How is this possible?

> Incomplete nihilism makes the light itself strange. Were nihilism the ultimate truth, we would expect no light, and yet there is light. We see the "truth" of nihilism in a light that nihilism, were it true, would

render impossible. What is that light? Is it something in which we are, in the more primal ethos of being, which we do not bring to be, but rather we are simply what we are as participants in it?[49]

Again, the contrast with Pippin's Kantian accent on spontaneous subjectivity is striking. Sharing the aversion to both philosophical and poetic idealism found in Maritain and Jeffers, Desmond proposes a recovery of wonder. The perplexity is not about evil, or decay, or the lack of clear metaphysical and ethical foundations for thought and life. Rather, it is prompted by the lingering and mysterious presence of being, goodness, and beauty. As Desmond puts it, our experience of the world is "porous to what exceeds finite determination." Even as we protest or lament that it all comes to nothing, we remain ensconced in being. The givenness of being has the character of "surplus generosity." There is no isolated finitude. "In the finiteness of our lives, there is the promise of a generosity beyond finite reckoning. We are given even before we give ourselves to be."[50] We do not seek God merely through negativity but also through the surpluses of finite being.

However we understand the theology of creation, it must, in the tradition of Aquinas, accord with what we know to be true from the natural sciences. Now the neglect of evolution has been mentioned as a weakness in *LS*. Celia Deane-Drummond focuses on the surprisingly scant attention to it.[51] She writes:

> For the sake of brevity, it is worth noting that Pope Francis resists the evolutionary account as adequate to explain human emergence, while recognizing that humans are still evolved beings. What the "direct action of God" might entail in relation to this human evolutionary story is left tantalizingly unclear, except that humans are called forth to a particular task and mission that science can never properly address. What he fails to take into account more broadly is the necessity of situating ecological science in the context of evolutionary accounts, and vice versa.[52]

She adds, "Surprisingly absent is taking proper account of evolutionary aspects of the natural world, including creaturely suffering and death, which would have moved the focus away from any notion of fixed harmony."[53] Where might we find such an account? A supple response to questions concerning evolution and the theological understanding of nature can be found in the writings of Charles De Koninck. He offers a sophisticated rearticulation of traditional anthropology in relation to modern science. One of his most important works is a text on evolution called *The Cosmos*. In this text, De Koninck addresses all sorts of questions: What is the relation between the world as described in mathematical physics and the world of our ordinary experience? Is there chance or indeterminism in nature? Does indeterminism undermine the rationality of science or belief in divine causality? Is the Thomistic conception of the cosmos and human nature friendly or hostile to the notion of evolution?

Contemporary readers are apt to be most surprised by De Koninck's response to the last query, one he was considering some thirty years before Etienne Gilson published *From Aristotle to Darwin and Back Again*. De Koninck's early work shows a philosophical mind, trained in the sciences and in theology, developing a cosmology that accommodates evolution and chance while recognizing order and hierarchy. He develops a capacious theory that accounts for the place of human beings in the cosmos and for the drama of human existence in all its brutality and nobility. He is open to evolution in ways Gilson and others are not.

De Koninck begins *The Cosmos* with a reflection on diametrically opposed tendencies in the universe.[54] The physical order, seen most clearly in the indefinite expansion of the universe, tends to increasing disorder—to entropy—while the biological order tends to "growing concentration." In other words, "Time disperses, life gathers, tending toward structures that are more and more tight." *Tight* here means concentrated or intense rather than enclosed or predetermined; as we ascend in the hierarchy of living things, we encounter beings capable of ever more complex interactions with the world and of greater degrees of self-determination and freedom.[55]

Even more fundamental is the distinction between the living and the nonliving. Going against the modern tendency to begin with the nonliving and then to try to establish the living, De Koninck argues that we know the living better than we know the nonliving and that we define the nonliving by negation of the living. Interiority and self-movement are the marks of the living: "We experience in ourselves that we have a soul and that it is a source of life."[56] The bodily condition of human life signals our animality. The insistence of Aristotle and Thomas on analogies between human activities and those of other animals means that at least one of the assumptions of evolution—the continuity between the animal and the human—does not trouble De Koninck. He detects in much of the resistance to evolution a kind of angelism.[57]

Aristotle's accent on the embodied nature of human rationality arises in part from, and leads him to look for and expect, analogies between the rational behavior of humans and the behavior of other animals. In a sustained examination of these issues, Alasdair MacIntyre defends the notion that nonhuman animals have beliefs and even reasons for action, although they lack the capacity to give reasons for their reasons. They cannot become philosophers or even fully human, deliberative agents. But human children exhibit precisely the sort of prelinguistic skills as do other animals, and these skills in humans are what make possible and underlie linguistic skills. "To acknowledge that there are animal preconditions for human rationality requires us to think of the relationship of human beings to members of other intelligent species in terms of a scale or a spectrum."[58] Of course, the ability to reflect on one's reasons would seem to mark a significant gap between humans and other animals, but for MacIntyre this neither erases the analogies between human and animal reasoning nor eliminates our recognition of the way in which the prelinguistic capacities are conditions for linguistic activity. The prelinguistic capacities do not simply disappear once children become capable of using language. MacIntyre's focus on the embodiment, vulnerability, and dependence of dependent rational animals highlights the analogies and interdependencies between human animals and the natural world.

However much the activities and capacities of other animals might anticipate human intelligence, human persons are distinct. We share with other, higher animals the capacity for memory, but our memory does not merely preserve the past. It also recognizes the past *as* past. Even in the operation of memory, the human animal transcends mere remembering and, in a sense, time. In the human person, we can discern the "triumph of spirit over the dissipation of time." In human persons, the "world is bent in upon itself."[59] In this account of the human, De Koninck comes close to the language of Teilhard de Chardin. As Pat Byrne notes, one of the great strengths in Teilhard's writings is his development of a rich symbolic language for capturing the place of the human in the cosmos. So, the symbolism of return, doubling back, folding in upon itself permeates his writings.[60] Just as for De Koninck, so too for Teilhard, the distinctive feature of human consciousness and thought is "reflection."[61] As Teilhard puts it:

From our experimental point of view, reflection is, as the word indicates, the power acquired by a consciousness to turn in upon itself *as of an object* endowed with its own particular... value: no longer merely to know, but to know oneself; no longer merely to know, but to know that one knows. By this individualization of himself in the depths of himself, the living element, which heretofore had been spread out and divided over a diffuse circle of perceptions and activities, was constituted for the first time as a *centre* in the form of a point at which all the impressions and experiences knit themselves together and fuse into a unity that is conscious of its own organization.[62]

De Koninck draws out the cosmological significance of Aristotle's claim that the human soul is "potentially all things." He makes a nice point—a Socratic point—about the peculiar character of human ignorance. The human intellect's very awareness that it does not comprehend the whole underscores its orientation to that whole, its capacity to make a "tour of being."[63] Whatever cognitive capacities other animals might possess, they do not exhibit tendencies to become philosophers. Human beings are naturally capable of transcendence.

The evolution of the higher from the lower, evident in paleontology, requires for its explanation not ad hoc interventions by some higher power but the intentionality of a universal cause, which acts not so much externally as internally on things. De Koninck has no patience for the sort of occasionalism that passes for creationism. By contrast, the Thomistic tendency, inspired by Augustine, "enriches as much as possible the causality of the creature, not with the goal of eliminating creative intervention, but in order to increase it: For the creative power, envisaged from the side of its effect, is most profoundly at work where created causes are most causes."[64] There is evident here a quite different attitude toward nature and science than that which is characteristic of the most popular modern forms of Christianity.

Of course, matter cannot generate human souls, but the development of the animal body prepares the way for the spiritual soul. De Koninck speculates that in the higher animals, activities enjoyed for their own sake, such as play, might be said to call intelligence into the world. The account of the place of the human species in the cosmos is at once naturalistic and hierarchical. Environmental naturalism and hierarchy need not be incompatible. As Ted Benton puts it:

A non-reductionist naturalism, making use of the ideas of a hierarchy of more or less autonomous levels of organization of matter, each with its own, qualitatively new, "emergent" powers or properties has been one fruitful way of maintaining the insights of a naturalistic approach, without falling foul of what is valid in the anti-naturalistic critique. Such hierarchical, "emergent powers" ontologies enable their advocates to recognize in the various subject matters of the different natural and social sciences more or less discrete and autonomous object-domains.[65]

De Koninck's own argument here goes well beyond what can be established in experimental science, but it is a great merit of his work that he follows the principle of Aristotle and Thomas concerning the irreducible complexity of various modes of human inquiry. For him as much as for Maritain, one must distinguish, in order to unite. Thus, he is careful to distinguish what we know from experimental science, what philosophical reflection on science might contribute, and what further speculation from metaphysics and theology might add to our understanding of the cosmos. One wonders how many contemporary debates about evolution are doomed to futility simply by the failure to make disciplinary distinctions.

Like Desmond, De Koninck is at pains to clarify the very notion of creation, which is different from alteration. The latter entails nothing more than a change introduced into preexisting matter. The failure to distinguish creation from alteration leads some cosmologists to equate the Big Bang with creation without wondering about the origins of the primordial stuff that explodes and expands. Working from metaphysics and theology, De Koninck proceeds to consider God's motive in creating: "If God creates, necessarily he creates in order to manifest his glory outside, not to manifest it to himself, as if by creation he could grow in his own regard." Divine creation is "essentially a communication," but communication involves conscious reception and reciprocal recognition: "His work must be capable of appreciating the gratuitous gift that communication is and that is achieved in the person, that is, in an intellectual creature who can give glory to his principle."[66] De Koninck's account on the motive of divine creation enriches, from a theological perspective, the understanding of the human person as a creature characterized by open-ended wonder. The human soul is, in the words of Aristotle, "in a sense, all things" (*potens omnia*).

The abundant liberality of nature means that we cannot calibrate in detail the way other natural things serve the end of the human species: "The image of the entire cosmos as essentially ordered to man would appear grotesque from the perspective of the astronomy which provides him a poor little planet born of a catastrophe."[67] From the prodigality of nature, together with the presence of chance and randomness, there emerges not only life and biological order but also the most perplexing creature of all, the human being, which has an affinity with the whole. There is a paradox here. The creature most open to contemplating the whole is baffled by that very whole. And yet in the act of knowing, the human creature in some sense transcends the universe. As Pascal put it, "Through space the universe encompasses and swallows me up like a dot; through thought, I grasp it."[68]

In the midst of a vast, cosmic ecosystem, there emerges a creature capable of being its own center. But that capacity to imagine itself at the center breeds dangerous illusions and destructive dispositions. If *The Cosmos* takes us from an ecocentric to an anthropocentric vision, it finally tilts back toward a cosmocentric vision, a vision that urges humility and awe in the face of creation. Johnson associates such a vision with the conclusion of the book of Job, in which God speaks, "out of the whirlwind," to Job and asks, "Were you there when I laid the foundation of the earth?" (38:4).[69] On this view, "we are situated within," and not necessarily "over the magnificent circle of life, whose center and encompassing horizon is the generous God of life."[70]

As the drama of Job indicates, the mystery of the human person reflects another and deeper mystery, concerning the source of the whole. God is a hidden God, whose existence is neither obvious nor provable in such a way as to remove all doubt. Aquinas, known for his proofs for the existence of God, states that without revelation "the human race would be left in the darkest shadows of ignorance" about the most important matters. The few who reach the existence of God through reason will do so only after a long period of inquiry and even then with an admixture of error. They know that God is but not what he is.

The emergent order is compatible with loss, pain, and suffering on an enormous scale. "Tragedy," writes De Koninck, is "essential to cosmic life."[71] The greater the order, the greater the prospect for loss and suffering. As we ascend the scale of being, the passion for living becomes increasingly intense and the desire for preservation more ferocious. Death becomes more "terrible." The God of this universe is a God of paradox and irony. *The Cosmos* offers a corrective to a weakness in *LS*. It provides an account of creation and natural order that contains both what Edwards thinks *LS* contains and what it omits or neglects. It provides both an "acknowledgment of evolution (*LS* 79–81), . . . of God's self-limitation in creating a world that develops with its own proper autonomy (*LS* 80)" and an acknowledgment of "the violence, pain, and death of the natural world."[72]

At one point in *The Cosmos*, De Koninck takes aim at those who construe the "intervention of man in nature as an evil."[73] He confronts here a form of biocentrism. Perhaps the most striking feature of the work is the way it avoids the weaknesses of modern anthropocentrism and biocentrism. Given De Koninck's embrace of evolution, there is no possibility of modern dualism, nor is there any need for the drastic measure of erasing the human to make room for the natural. How woven human nature is into the natural order of things is clear from the way in which he predicates human self-knowledge on an education in metaphysics and cosmology, in history and paleontology. This is a comprehensive ecological education.[74] As Edwards observes, knowledge of and care for nature is "part of coming to ourselves, . . . the discovery of who we are."[75] However restless we might be, our lives as human animals are inexplicable without the entirety of the physical cosmos. De Koninck formulates the point eloquently: "We will only be able to understand ourselves when we understand the universe. Our present is filled with the past."[76]

FOUR

The Ecological Poetics of Robinson Jeffers

One of the most intriguing lines of thought in Nietzsche, which has to do with the project of translating the human back into the natural, touches on the ecological themes broached earlier. Rejecting nearly every extant theory of nature, Nietzsche asks, "When will all these shadows of God cease to darken our minds? When will we complete our de-deification of nature? When may we begin to 'naturalize' humanity in terms of a pure, newly discovered, newly redeemed nature?"[1] Then in a famous passage from *Beyond Good and Evil*, he writes:

> To translate the human back into nature; to become master over the many vain and fanatical interpretations and side-meanings that have so far been scribbled on that eternal ground-text *homo natura*[;] ... to make it that the human being henceforth stands ... before that *other nature* ... deaf to the enticements of all the metaphysical bird-catchers who have been whistling to it for too long: "You are more! You are higher! You are of another origin."[2]

The passage contains themes with which we are now familiar. If Platonism and Christianity depict human nature as dissatisfied with what the merely natural supplies, Nietzsche, we might say, seeks to reverse that. But that's not quite right. A simple reversal, as is evident in Rousseau's account of the state of nature, would be an effete form of Romanticism that thinks that harmony with nature is or at least once was possible. Nietzsche wants us to be at home in a natural sphere that is not pacific, or intelligible, or friendly to human longing. Nature is beyond good and evil.

THE BEAUTY OF NATURE BEYOND GOOD AND EVIL

On the basis of these and other features of Nietzsche's writing, some have gone so far as to see Nietzsche as a "deep ecologist."[3] The thesis here is that Nietzsche "explains change immanently, according to certain homeostasis relations," and "emphasizes the interrelatedness of all things." Such a position—a variant of biocentrism—comes "close to the worldview of modern ecologists, a world in which nature is seen as a living process that is marked by continuous transformation."[4] As Michael Zimmerman has observed, Nietzsche's primary concern is not with environmental devastation but rather with degeneration in the human world.[5] That seems right, but it is also the case that Nietzsche often equates renewal in and of the human world with an alteration in the human relationship to nature. The same point is made quite dramatically in the prologue to *Thus Spake Zarathustra*, where he writes that "the Superman is the meaning of the earth." Zarathustra entreats his listeners to

> remain true to the earth and do not believe those who hold out supernatural hopes for you. They are poisoners, whether they know it or not. They are despisers of life, dying ones and poisoned themselves; the earth is sick of them—let them leave it, then! Once the sin against God was the greatest sin; but God died, and with that these sinners died, too. Now the worst sin is the sin against the earth.[6]

Yet, as we are now quite aware, there are lines of thought in Nietzsche that run in an anthropocentric direction. For this reason, critics of the ecological interpretation of Nietzsche, such as Ralph Acampora, read him as advocating an "aristocratic individualism," deeply at odds with environmental ethics.⁷ Nietzsche's insistence on the distinctive biological and physiological capacities of the human animal cuts against the radical egalitarianism of biocentrism. But then such an egalitarian approach cannot make sense of its own persistent appeal to the peculiar moral sensibility of human beings. The repudiation of hierarchy in the order of intrinsic value engenders what Zimmerman and Esbjorn-Hargens call the "fundamental paradox of environmentalism."⁸ Nietzsche has an abiding awareness of the specific role that the human animal must play in the drama of the cosmos.

One of the distinctive features of Nietzsche's ecological vision is his antiprogressivism. There are liberationist themes in Nietzsche, but they run counter to the dominant Enlightenment motifs of progress. Nietzsche suspects that the notion that history has a telos is a residue of Christianity and an ongoing source of nihilism. On the progressive, historicist vision, the present is deprived of everything except instrumental value. It is a means to something superior. The life we lead is a means to something else. Consequently, where we are is always where we are not supposed to be. As Erazim Kohak, a phenomenologist writing about the environment, puts it:

> The basic reason for questioning the utilitarian justification of the historicist vision is its effect on the only lives that humans actually live, those of the perennial present. The power of the historicist vision is that it seems to endow the present with a time-relative meaning. It does so, however, only at the frightful cost of draining the present of all absolute ... meaning.⁹

Nietzsche's alternative to the progressivist vision of history is eternal recurrence, which allows for the possibility of affirming everything in a kind of perpetual, present moment.¹⁰

Affirmation of the whole is characteristic of the poetic vision of Robinson Jeffers, whose thought embodies a radical version of what Pope Francis calls "biocentrism" but a remarkably sophisticated and self-aware version. According to William Everson, Jeffers is the only twentieth-century American poet to construct a "cosmic vision of man,"¹¹ a vision in which Nietzschean themes are prominent. As a poet and as an essayist, Jeffers is crucial to the development of a post-Romantic environmental aesthetic. Unlike many in the environmental movement who fail to think through the implications of their hostility to the human animal, Jeffers is fully conscious of the implications. He bluntly calls his own philosophy "inhumanism."

Jeffers shares Nietzsche's critique of Christianity, even as he affirms a kind of pantheistic religion.[12] As he once put it in a letter to a correspondent who had inquired about his religious beliefs:

> I believe the universe is one being, all its parts are ... parts of one organic whole. (This is physics, I believe, as well as religion.) The parts change and pass, or die, people and races and rocks and stars, none of them seems to me important in itself, but only the whole. This whole is in all its parts so beautiful, and is felt by me to be so intensely in earnest, that I am compelled to love it, and to think of it as divine. It seems to me that this whole alone is worthy of the deeper sort of love; and that here is peace, freedom, I might say a kind of salvation, in turning one's affection outward toward this one God, rather than inward on oneself, or on humanity, or on human imagination and abstractions — the world of spirits.[13]

The appreciation of vastness does not preclude the commitment to a specific place, namely, Big Sur. Of this location, he writes:

> For the first time in my life I could see people living — amid magnificent unspoiled scenery — essentially as they did in the Idyls or the Sagas, or in Homer's Ithaca. Here was life purged of the ephemeral accretions. Men were riding after cattle, or plowing the headland, hovered by white sea-gulls, as they had done for thousands of years, and will for thousands of years to come. Here was contemporary life that was also permanent life; and not shut from the modern world but conscious of it and related to it; capable of expressing its spirit but unencumbered by the mass of poetically irrelevant details and complexities that make a civilization.[14]

Jeffers's sentiments here call to mind the challenge Nietzsche puts before his readers at the end of *Advantage and Disadvantage*, namely, to cast off sham or artificial needs in order to uncover authentic, natural needs. Jeffers shares much with Nietzsche. He too returns to Greek tragedy. In his writings, he offers a diagnosis of the sickness of the human soul, its antinatural bent, rooted in a certain moral interpretation of existence. Like

Nietzsche, he thinks that the positing of another world, separate from and better than this one, devalues this world. For Jeffers as for Nietzsche, this world is sufficient to satisfy the human need for magnificence and beauty, at least once we have let go of certain transcendental cravings.

This is not to say that there are not tensions between Jeffers and Nietzsche. It seems clear that Jeffers would take issue with the notion of the human being as the esteeming animal, the creator of values. Jeffers's inhumanism attempts to reverse the modern turn to the subject, which makes the human the measure of the real. Instead, the real measures and dwarfs the human. In a sense, Jeffers seeks to make the human person small. Of course, the leveling of the human is what most provokes Nietzsche's scorn, as it gives rise to the last man, whose pusillanimity evacuates human life of every risk and aspiration for greatness. Yet, for Jeffers, the task of measuring the human against the cosmos is no abdication of effort or grandeur. It is an exacting task that requires a disciplined attentiveness to what transcends the human ego. The poet seeks to bestow on human persons a more accurate sense of their place within the whole. The poet thus has a distinct calling, a calling that accentuates the power of art to rectify entrenched misunderstandings of the place of the human in the cosmos. The poet achieves this aim by articulating the beauty of the universe.

Like Nietzsche, Jeffers seeks to translate the human back into the natural, to remove the religious-moralistic interpretation of existence and to substitute for it an aesthetic one. He embraces something like the notion of eternal recurrence: an affirmation of the whole that ignores the morality of good and evil. Such an affirmation would seem to dwarf the particularities of any individual human life, indeed of all human lives together, in both scope and time. It also undermines progressivist impulses, indeed all human desires to control or even adequately interpret the cosmos. It thus shares much with certain forms of biocentrism. Yet the affirmation itself is possible only for the human animal. Jeffers, as we shall see, was acutely aware of this tension.

IDEALISM AND ARTISTIC DECADENCE

In his critique of modern humanism and poetics, Jeffers may unwittingly have recovered elements of premodern conceptions of the human person and nature; indeed, his engagement of modern aesthetic theory shares much in common with the Maritain of *Creative Intuition*. He writes, "The more advanced contemporary poets were ... divorcing poetry from reason and ideas, bringing it nearer to music, finally to astonish the world with what would look like pure nonsense and would be pure poetry."[15] He turns to a direct attack on Mallarmé's Symboliste movement.

> Mallarmé and his followers, renouncing intelligibility in order to concentrate on the music of poetry, had turned off the road into a narrowing lane. Their successors could only make further renunciations; ideas had gone, now meter had gone, imagery would have to go; then recognizable emotions would have to go; perhaps at last even words might have to go or give up their meaning, nothing to be left but musical syllables. Every advance required the elimination of some aspect of reality, and what would it profit me to know the direction of modern poetry if I did not like the direction?[16]

Like Maritain, Jeffers thinks that a kind of idealism has infected modern art, with the consequence that art and human consciousness are, as Maritain put it, "walled in." Jeffers's critique of anthropocentrism resembles that of Maritain and recent papal writing on the environment. Yet his response tends in the direction of a kind of biocentrism; in Nietzschean terms, he seeks to translate the human back into the natural.

Jeffers develops a philosophy that he initially called human naturalism and then later inhumanism. He writes, "Man is a part of nature, but a nearly infinitesimal part; the human race will cease after a while and leave no trace, but the great splendors of nature will go on." He articulates this belief poetically in an early piece, aptly titled "Credo," "a poem that scoffs at ... mind-centered idealism."[17] He eschews the view that "nothing is real except as we make it" and that, in the powers of our mind, we can create an "ocean more real than the ocean, the salt, the actual appalling presence, the power of the waters." Jeffers adopts a "humbler" view, a "harder mysticism." He concludes, "the heartbreaking / beauty / Will remain when there is no heart to break for it."[18]

He counsels a reversal of the notion that human reason is the measure of things. Instead, human reasoning is measured by nature. If we affirm the latter thesis, then philosophy, "which is an endless search for truth, and for contemplation, which is a sort of worship," would find its most "rewarding object" in "the immense beauty of the earth and the outer universe, the divine 'nature of things.'"[19] In "Birds and Fishes," Jeffers describes the ritual arrival of fish, on which the pelicans gorge in "hysterical greed"—an activity that seems a "witches' sabbath of wings." Concerning the slaughter of the fish, he asks, "which one in all this fury of wild-fowl pities the / fish?" No one does, because "Justice and mercy / Are human dreams." What characterizes natural beings is beauty, "not mercy, not mind, not goodness, but the / beauty of God."[20]

Of all the transcendentals, as the scholastics call them, only beauty, for Jeffers, is objective and escapes the world of human dreams. This is a reversal of the standard scholastic assumption that unity, truth, and goodness were obviously transcendentals, while the status of the beautiful remained dubious. Jeffers seems to suppose that standards of truth end up making human persons the measure, while those pertaining to goodness involve our projecting morality onto an indifferent nature. The encounter with beauty, by contrast, involves what Walsh calls "the pull of the real." This conception of beauty and the human will is the antithesis of the model of the human person as esteemer that emerges in some texts of Nietzsche. Marion, as I have already noted, accuses Nietzsche of a kind of self-idolatry. In freeing the image of its connection to an original, he subjects it to the evaluation of the human will. In his own way, Jeffers seeks to devalue the image but in a direction opposite to that of Nietzsche. He wants to bend human understanding and will in the direction of the objective order of the cosmos. The transcendent, encompassing order of nature reduces the image nearly to nonexistence.

Through a careful examination of the texts of thinkers from Kant to Derrida, Walsh argues that modern thought evinces a "remarkably consistent" development, whose terminus is the recognition of the luminosity of existence and the "return of metaphysics in life."[21] The withering critique of propositional, systematic metaphysics has made possible the reemergence of life antecedent to thought. Transcendence reappears as the irreducibly mysterious horizon within which human thought occurs. The consequence, as Walsh provocatively puts it, is that the modern philosophical revolution has succeeded in bringing to light the source of the premodern tradition it opposed. But this is not so much a recovery, much less is it a going backward in time; instead, it is an acknowledgment of what is available to us here and now as implicit in our thinking and living.

In the attempt to transform philosophy from a pursuit of wisdom into a possession of wisdom, Hegel identifies the knowing subject with Spirit. As an ethical whole, Spirit contains rather than being contained. About this, Walsh raises a number of questions. Does the process of self-reflection render further manifestations superfluous? Might there be a role for religion and art beyond the capacity of philosophy to reduce them to thought? Art and religion provide access to "a depth beyond manifestation."[22] Walsh suggests that finite thinking discovers its own possibility within the infinite in which it stands. Such beings as we are cannot grasp the whole except through an existence constituted within that whole.[23] Hence spontaneous subjectivity is secondary to, and parasitic on, receptivity.

One of the problems, according to Walsh, with the tradition of philosophy from Hegel through Derrida, is that it begins from within theory.[24] In contrast, thinkers such as Nietzsche, along with Kierkegaard and Levinas, begin from the question of how we should live. In some measure indebted to the Greeks, these philosophers recover a conception of philosophy as a way of life that seeks, but never achieves, wisdom. The modern philosophical revolution thus reverses the priority of the subject to the real. Luminosity of existence precedes and envelops the subject. These themes are central to the prose and poetry of Jeffers.

The decentering of our thinking and desiring that occurs in the experience of the beautiful is essential to the poetic pedagogy of Jeffers. The problem is that we have relied on a human-centered conception of nature, assuming or wishing that nature accorded more closely with the desires of human persons. The corrective, articulated in "Carmel Point," is clear:

> We must uncenter our minds from ourselves;
> We must unhumanize our views a little, and become confident
> As the rock and ocean that we were made from.[25]

Jeffers takes aim here at the Enlightenment, anthropocentric paradigm of humanity's relationship to the natural world. So twisted and misleading is our assessment of our place in the cosmos that shifting the balance from self to world, from the human to the natural and cosmic, requires a radical reversal of the entire edifice of human self-understanding and activity. A pressing question emerges for Jeffers: How is it that human persons have become so removed from their proper, insignificant place in the universe?

How has arrogant ignorance overshadowed the plain facts of the matter about our status in the cosmos?

JEFFERS'S MYTH OF THE FALL AND THE CONGRUENCE BETWEEN BEAUTY AND SOUL

In *Philosophical Myths of the Fall*, Stephen Mulhall offers an account of the failure of philosophy to liberate itself from theology. Mulhall adopts Stanley Cavell's phrase "truth in foul disguise" to describe Nietzsche's analysis of Christianity. He interrogates the supple dialectical stance toward Christianity adopted by Nietzsche (as well as Heidegger and Wittgenstein). Mulhall's view is that these philosophers "preserve a version of human nature . . . as structurally perverse or errant and yet redeemable from that fallen state."[26] The very notion of redemption is a problem for these thinkers. Still, Mulhall sees these thinkers as countenancing some version of human restoration, an overcoming of our structural perversion. The poetry of Jeffers reinforces the notion that some version of the myth of the fall is nearly indispensable, not just for philosophy, but also for art. Jeffers constructs his own myth of the Fall. Gelpi and Everson go so far as to call Jeffers a poet of original sin. Big Sur, for Jeffers, is like the "garden of Eden before the Fall." It "crystallized his pantheism. It's so extreme in its beauty and titanic scale, in its majesty, that it enabled him to conceive of a humanity-divorcing-symbol, a humanity-reducing-symbol." Jeffers treats humanity "as a mistake, an error in the evolutionary process, a bad turn taken somewhere along the line which produced a species that was cunning and malignant, that was wretched from the start."[27] Jeffers objects to the language of the dignity of the human person because he supposes it countenances human tyranny over nature. Dignity indicates a certain distinctive stature. As Kant put it, only the rational creature has dignity and merits being treated as an end in itself; everything else has a price. While Kant did not draw this conclusion, one might infer from this conception of human dignity that the human person has the freedom to do whatever she wishes with everything that is not human.

For Jeffers, poetry operates as a kind of grace that humiliates the human subject and cures its disorders through self-abnegation. He seeks to foster in readers what Emily Brody calls "an aesthetic-moral relationship between human beings and the natural environment."[28] What Brody describes as a possible result of the failure of the human imagination to comprehend the sublime, namely, that the imagination is expanded and opened out onto the cosmos, is precisely the aim of Jeffers's poetry.[29] Gelpi calls Jeffers the "poet of the sublime without peer in American letters."[30] As noted previously, Romantic aesthetics establishes a contrast between the beautiful and the sublime. If Jeffers is a poet of the sublime, he nonetheless continues to use the language of beauty to describe the goal of his poetry. In fact, he seems to expand the notion of the beautiful to include the sublime.

Because the opening of human consciousness to the external world is not a movement natural to the human soul, there is need for a pedagogy of reproach and humiliation. And yet Jeffers often seeks a kind of mediation between the beautiful and the sublime, an attempt to articulate the place, however small and fleeting, of human persons in a vast cosmos, indifferent to human wishes. His use of the sublime serves to undermine, rather than accentuate, any supposed anthropocentrism. Moreover, he does not push the sublime in the direction of the utter fracturing of experience or language.[31] The focus on the rhetoric of the beautiful and the sublime, on initiating the reader into a certain experience of nature, separates Jeffers from Romanticism and modernism. The goal, we recall, is "to feel / Greatly, and understand greatly, and express greatly, the natural / Beauty."[32] As Gelpi astutely puts it, Jeffers seeks "to stand apart from and yet to be a part of the sublimity of nature."[33] Here Jeffers recapitulates the paradoxes at the heart of Nietzsche's teaching on eternal recurrence. In so doing, Jeffers faces what we have come to call the principal contradiction of environmentalism: the tendency simultaneously to deny any special status to humans and to issue morally infused pleas to humans to change their behavior. But Jeffers's way of managing this paradox is highly instructive. There are times when he seems to find a fitting place for the human person, indeed for human beauty and affection, within the encompassing whole of nature. For example, in the arresting poem "Divinely Superfluous Beauty," he writes:

> Divinely superfluous beauty
> Rules the games, presides over destinies, makes trees grow
> And hills tower, waves fall.[34]

The expression of surplus calls to mind themes of the saturated phenomena and the luminosity of existence. The question is whether pantheism can account for the surplus that exceeds any and all finite determinations. Jeffers strives for a way to transcend nihilism and to overcome negation with affirmation, precisely as Nietzsche hopes great artists will. He even finds a way, despite his inhumanism, to affirm the fittingness of human love in the very midst of nature's indifference. In the lines, "The incredible beauty of joy / Stars with fire the joining of lips, O let our loves too / Be joined," Jeffers finds a place for a naturalized humanism.[35] In so doing, he comes awfully close to undoing the dualism that afflicts so much of modern thought, a dualism repudiated by Nietzsche, among others.[36]

What are we to say of the poet's ability to capture in recollection—and thus to prompt others to experience—such moments of concord between humans and the cosmos? Or of the fitting place of human love in cosmos? Even where the focus is on the negation of the ego, the question arises as to why we find such negation beautiful, even joyful. Is there not great beauty and pleasure in the reading of such poetry? To make sense of the appropriate artistic response to nature, we need to think of these moments as more than simple negations. Instead, these moments are simultaneously self-forgetting, self-transcending, and self-enhancing. In some cases, as in "Divinely Superfluous Beauty," they are self-affirming. In a remarkable passage from one of his letters, he acknowledges the feeling that

> this human and in itself subjective sense of beauty is occasioned by some corresponding quality or temper or arrangement in the object. Why else should a quite neutral thing—a wave or the sea or a hill against the sky—be somehow lovely and loveworthy, and become more so the more it is realized by contemplation? ... The feeling of deep earnestness and nobility in natural objects and in the universe:—these are human qualities, not mineral or vegetable, but it seems to me I would not impute them into the objects unless there is something in not-man that corresponds to these qualities in man. This may be called delusion or it may be called mystical certainty, there is no external proof either way.[37]

Jeffers's artistic honesty is nowhere more evident than in his formulation of this tantalizing wager, which, despite his own protestations, exhibits his own practice of the will to truth.

One is reminded of the paradoxes at the heart of De Koninck's reflections on the strange place in the cosmos of human persons, the natural beings, whose history is a portion of the history of the development of species and who occupy but a "poor little planet born of a catastrophe." The temporal and spatial vastness of the cosmos dwarfs any human presence. In the honest human reckoning with our place in the whole, humiliation and fear compete with wonder and awe. The technocratic regimes that increasingly permeate our politics, economics, and culture encourage a forgetfulness of the whole, even as they foster indifference to persons and natural ecosystems. Jeffers's inhumanism, understood as a moment within a larger pedagogy of reconciliation, is indispensable—a necessary sobering and perhaps humiliation of the human impulse to want to control all of external nature, including the human body. Once purged of its inattentive will to dominate, the human animal encounters in the beauty of the cosmos something more, a call for recognition by beings capable of knowing—beings who seem *intended* to know—nature and to offer thanks and poetic praise in response.

FIVE

The Sacramental Poetics of William Everson

In his mid-twentieth-century essay "Dionysius and the Beat Generation: The Reemergence of the Dionysian Spirit in Contemporary Life," William Everson detects in the rise of the Beat generation a resurgence of the Dionysian spirit. A California Beat poet who spent more than a decade as Brother Antoninus, a monk at St. Albert's Priory, the Dominican house in Oakland, California, Everson sees a rise of the Dionysian in the Beat penchant for jazz and for ecstatic experience. Everson follows Nietzsche in stressing the limits of rationality, which is forgetful of the "darkness."[1] Everson speaks of the need to find a "place" for the "irrational" within "the whole psyche." In its optimism and confidence, the Apollonian refuses to acknowledge its dependence on the Dionysian and "labels ecstasy Satanic."[2] Everson departs radically from Nietzsche, however, in seeing Christianity as an alternative to Apollo rather than one of its chief representatives.

Although not that well known today, at midcentury Everson ranked among the most important of the Beat poets. As I noted in the preface, Albert Gelpi calls him the most significant religious poet of the second half of the twentieth century.³ The great and much better-known poet of the first half, T. S. Eliot, had an impact on Everson. Even more influential was the naturalist poet Robinson Jeffers. Everson thus stands at the intersection of Christian and naturalist poetics. Everson's poetry aims to articulate the relationship of the human person to nature, both to our own embodied, erotic nature and to that of the physical cosmos. As an early commentator, Thomas McDonell, observes, his "quarrel with the world is not that of the whining anti-materialist but of a man who knows something of our human alienation in a world resplendent with beauty and terror."⁴ One of the distinctive features of Everson's poetry is its erotic imagery and themes. His reflection on human desire runs parallel to, and often intersects with, attention to natural processes. For Everson, there is no stable relationship between human persons and the natural world, just as there is no comfortable stasis in the relationship to the divine. As Gelpi puts it, Everson wrestles with "polarities" between the natural and the supernatural, soul and body, sexuality and spirituality.⁵

If Jeffers moves from a biocentric vision to an acknowledgment of the peculiar status of human persons within the natural order, Everson begins within the self and moves outward. It is important to see that this is not an adventitious or forced movement from a clearly demarcated interior to an easily identifiable exterior. The constituting drives, desires, and thoughts of the self bear it ineluctably toward what is other. One useful way to frame Everson's "method," if we can use that word provisionally, is in terms of Charles Taylor's opposition of the buffered and the porous self. An accent on the individual and on the contrast between inner and outer is a distinctive feature of the modern, buffered self.⁶ By contrast, what Taylor calls the porous self, characteristic of premodern conceptions of the human person, is fully embedded in, and vulnerable to, a cosmos, filled with physical, human, and spiritual realities. The buffered self is characteristic of anthropocentrism, which sets up clear boundaries between the self and all else. Everson assumes the contrast between inner and outer and often takes as his starting point the individual self, usually his own self. His goal, however, is to undermine rather than reinforce the assumptions of the buffered self. The self is permeable to all sorts of external influences, even to the unknown elements of its interior life. If he starts, and continuously wrestles with, polarities, he is not committed to any kind of dualism. McDonell amplifies this point: the supernaturalism of Everson "implies neither a divorce from created nature nor a mystical abandonment of our sensuous human nature."[7] Put slightly differently, the experience of the sublime involves an excess that humbles rather than exalts the imagination. Whether in the encounter with hitherto unacknowledged elements of the self or with a God who manifests himself alluringly and whose presence haunts us even as we flee from it, the sublime decenters the self, drawing it into a realm of infinite mystery.

To see what is distinctive about Everson's poetry, I first consider his relationship to two of his great contemporaries, Eliot and Jeffers. Then I turn to Everson's preoccupation with violence, the way it informs his poetic voice and shapes and is shaped by his theological vision.[8]

FROM CHRIST TO DIONYSIUS AND BACK AGAIN

Violence and desire run through the prose and poetry of Everson. In his essay on Dionysius and the Beats, Everson recapitulates Nietzsche's teaching in *The Birth of Tragedy* on two gods, two models of art, and two experiences of the relationship of the individual to the whole of society and nature. For the Greeks, tragedy rests on a symbiotic tension between Dionysius and Apollo, the latter of whom is the source of the precepts "know thyself" and "nothing in excess." Apollo, who individuates and thus makes conscious apprehension and expression possible, is the source of distinctions, including those among objects and between good and evil, and truth and falsity. The pre-Socratic Greeks, particularly the creators of tragedy, realize that the order of Apollo is parasitic on the realm of Dionysius. The "entire existence" of Apollo depends "on a hidden substratum of suffering and knowledge revealed to him by Dionysius," who recalls the Greeks to the primordial source of all things.[9]

In one sense, this is a reversal of a traditional metaphysical view. On that conception, while appearances may be deceptive and replete with evils, the more we probe the depths of being, the more order and truth we discover. For Nietzsche, order, truth, and morality are all epiphenomena. Yet Nietzsche's goal is not to force us to confront the abyss directly. Unmediated access to Dionysius leads to annihilation. Greek tragedy suggests a way of mediating the Dionysian through the Apollonian. It acknowledges the supremacy of Dionysius without denying the indispensable role of Apollo. Tragic culture affirms "wisdom over science," seeks a "comprehensive view," and leads its adherents to encounter "with sympathetic feelings of love, the eternal suffering."[10]

But we moderns have wandered far from the wisdom of the Greeks. In his early work, Nietzsche provides an anticipation of the sort of genealogy he would develop later. With the rise of Socratic philosophy, which equates virtue with truth and happiness and repudiates the insights of tragedy, the dominance of Apollo and the forgetfulness of Dionysius permeate Western civilization. Christianity, modern science, and progressive politics are but variations on a Socratic theme. As is the case in his later works, so too here Nietzsche insists that the Socratic will to truth generates its own demise. Especially in its modern forms, Socratic culture suffers from "the delusion of limitless power," the will to know and control all things.[11] The will to truth finds its denouement in modern science. Nietzsche writes, "Science, spurred by its powerful illusion, speeds irresistibly toward its limits where its optimism, concealed in the essence of logic, suffers shipwreck."[12] The more science claims it knows, the more it is forced into the realization that its knowledge is a mere construct, a set of theories imposed on reality. In this way, logic "bites its own tail" and gives rise to a "tragic insight." The "limits of theory" engender a "turn to art." Nietzsche provides his own genealogy of the way in which Romanticism can arise from Enlightenment rationalism.

Nietzsche seems to side with the Romantics here against the rationalists. He does indeed detect in tragic art an approach to human life that serves rather than thwarts health and that nourishes rather than eviscerates the conditions of human greatness. Yet he is also quite critical of certain features of Romanticism. As Peter Berkowitz notes, Nietzsche's account removes self-consciousness and autonomy from the artistic process.[13] As a communicator of the Dionysian primordial unity, the artist "becomes a work of art."[14] Nietzsche goes so far as to say that the "individual with egoistic ends" is the "antagonist of art." He also rejects the Romantic—and in some cases, environmental—ideal of an innocent nature to which human persons might return: "This harmony[,] . . . this oneness of man with nature . . . is by no means a simple condition that comes into being naturally. . . . It is not a condition that, like a terrestrial paradise, must necessarily be found at the gate of every culture. Only a romantic age could believe this."[15] This is one passage, among many, that makes clear Nietzsche's repudiation of the notion that a return to some sort of pure nature is possible for human beings. He seeks a way around the mutually exclusive alternatives of anthropocentrism and biocentrism.

Like Nietzsche, Everson speaks of a tragic wisdom that mediates between the Apollonian and the Dionysian. He traces the Catholic understanding of *sacramentum* to its origins in the military oath, a ritual involving the sacrifice of the blood of animals and the offering of one's own life in a potentially bloody battle. The pagan world contains disordered anticipations of the Christian understanding of violence. Everson writes, for example, "in some places the cult of Dionysius took the form of Zagreus, meaning 'torn-to-pieces,' the god whose dismembered body rose each spring to redeem the people from the ravages of winter."[16]

There are two crucial differences between the preeminent accounts of nature in the Christian and the pagan world. The first is that the latter is always tempted to see evil as inherent in the natural order, inextricably woven into the very fabric of being. By contrast, the Christian understanding sees evil as an unnatural intervention in an otherwise good cosmos. Creation itself is good. In Genesis, God repeatedly affirms the goodness of the created order. But disorder has emerged within order. In contrast to the Nietzsche of the *Birth of Tragedy*, Everson insists that the "natural resolving synthesis" of the two gods is "not possible." The Beat generation is just the latest failed attempt to achieve such a synthesis. By setting out for ecstasy at any price, it "roves restlessly from the delirium of sensational licentiousness to compulsive flights at the infinite through drugs or dythrambic aestheticism."[17]

This second difference, which is related to the first, has to do with the question of whether what escapes reason must always be seen as sub- or antirational. Relevant to this point, Nietzsche offers an intriguing proposal in the *Birth of Tragedy* that we embrace the Socrates who practices music. Throughout much of that work, Nietzsche excoriates Socrates for equating virtue with knowledge and for striving to eliminate tragedy from human life. But he also finds in the late Socrates, the Socrates of the *Crito*, who is facing death and now composing poetry, a model for thinking about the relationship of reason and nonreason. Nietzsche detects in the final Socrates an openness to nonrational inspiration. But the source of the inspiration and how it stands in relation to reason are precisely what Socrates (not to mention Maritain and Everson) would want to interrogate.[18]

The question is whether the inspiration is from above or from below. Maritain and Everson are critical of conceptions of inspiration that unleash the Übermensch, the celebration of arbitrary and irrational self-expression. Platonic *mousikè* is, by contrast, a madness from above reason. Maritain calls it "a kind of divination," an "intercommunication between the inner being of things and the inner being of the human Self."[19] In his correspondence with the artist Jean Cocteau, Maritain elaborates at length this sort of inspiration:

> Poetry is from on high—not like grace, which is essentially supernatural, and which makes us participants in what belongs to God only, but like the highest natural resemblance to God's activity. . . . [I]n the natural order . . . there is special inspiration which, too, is above the deliberations of reason, and which proceeds, as Aristotle observes, from God present in us. Such is the inspiration of the poet.[20]

This *mania* is not to be confused with Dionysian chaos and violence, even if both conceptions of madness curb the illusions of human autonomy and undermine the anthropocentric paradigm.[21] Because it has a transcendent source, it is not to be confused with biocentrism.

REWRITING T. S. ELIOT

For all his willingness to embrace the mystical and the erotic, Everson nonetheless insists that the "way of perfection is hard, rigorous, and disenchanting, as the great religions have ever taught."[22] Everson might well have lifted the notion of discipline from T. S. Eliot, with whom he shares a great deal. Both seek to engage modern art and poetics from an orthodox Christian perspective. Both admire Dante, John Donne, and Baudelaire. While Eliot keeps, or tries to keep, Romanticism at a distance, Everson aims to bring together strains of Romanticism with the concrete intellectualism of the metaphysical poets. Gelpi compares Everson and Eliot in these terms: "Where Eliot's Christianity was ascetic, conservative, and apollonian—'masculine,' . . . Everson is radically feminine, incarnational, and Dionysian."[23]

There are numerous points of contact between Eliot and Everson, but the easiest way to compare them is to consider Everson's first postconversion poem, "Triptych for the Living," a poem about the birth of Christ and the Epiphany. The poem reworks material from Eliot's "Journey of the Magi," which reconstructs the scriptural narrative mediated through a consciousness typical of dislocated modernity. The narrator is caught between an old and a new dispensation, uncomfortable in the old world because of the unsettling experience of Christianity but lacking the framework to make sense of the new. The opening lines issue a series of complaints about the conditions of the journey. It ends with the lines, "With the voices singing in our ears, saying / That this was all folly."[24] The scriptural allusion is lost on the narrator, as it would be on many modern secular readers no longer conversant with scripture. The narrator fails to recognize the folly of the Christian faith as a blessing. The second stanza begins on a more promising note, as the travelers reach a "temperate valley, smelling of vegetation." Yet the temperate climate and the promise of nature renewed do not yield a rebirth of spirit. As was true in *The Waste Land*, so too here ambiguity and uncertainty concerning the prospect of renewal haunt this poem. The scriptural allusions proliferate in the second stanza: "vine-leaves," "pieces of silver," and "wine-skins." But they are merely fragments of some larger vision that escapes the narrator. He ends by saying that "the place," their destination, "was (you might say) satisfactory." The final stanza encapsulates the confusion and bewilderment of the narrator, who does not know whether they were led all that way for "Birth or Death." This particular birth feels like death. They experience an event that thwarts their working assumptions. They see contradictions that baffle them; they are unable to apprehend the paradox at the heart of the Christian story. To put it more precisely, they experience an event but not a revelation. The result is yet again a kind of paralyzed despair, a willed nihilism: "I should be glad of another death." The narrator is surrounded by the signs, both verbal and natural, of the gospel but is unable to orient his life in accord with them. The Magi are dislocated, resigned, void of hope, and exhausted; they embody modern ennui.

Everson's triptych echoes Eliot's "Journey" in a number of respects. It too begins with a journey situated in the natural environment, but Everson is much more expansive in his description of inclement weather. Moreover, the triptych does not begin with the Magi. Instead, it begins with a section titled "The Uncouth," about the shepherds who witness the virgin birth. The poem's opening lines describe the harsh conditions, not of a single journey, but of an entire way of life. The shepherds endure the world's disdain. They, who had "only the crude capacity to survive" and on whose brow hope "never had recourse," were "fated" to receive the "transforming grace," about which the rest of the world "dreamed blindly."[25] Everson here undercuts Eliot's focus on the literate and wealthy Magi. Instead, he begins with those whose lives are barely human, almost bestial.

The second poem in the series, "The Coming," also begins with imagery of nature, in this case, a specific patch of the earth on which livestock have given birth and on which another birth is about to occur. In language resembling that of Eliot, Everson assimilates birth and death: "birth, / Like death, ravenous—." Now, on the same patch of bloodstained earth, the "Bull-trodden earth, where the cow / Had bled of the womb-blind calf," we have a human birth. Yet this time there is a difference. An intervention breaks the linear cycle of the "device of the flesh, the need of the flesh."[26] In contrast to Eliot's rather abstract talk about a "birth," Everson narrows in on the flesh, the physical realities of birth. Filthy animals provide the setting for such a strange birth, a birth in which God enters the universe through the most unlikely of avenues, the womb of a woman living at the margins of the civilized world. In entering and taking on flesh, the Word of God takes on the entire physical universe. John Paul II puts this well:

> The Incarnation of God the Son signifies the taking up into unity with God not only of human nature, but in this human nature, in a sense, of everything that is "flesh": the whole of humanity, the entire visible and material world. The Incarnation, then, also has a cosmic significance, a cosmic dimension. The "first-born of all creation," becoming incarnate in the individual humanity of Christ, unites himself in some way with the entire reality of man, which is also "flesh" and in this reality with all "flesh," with the whole of creation.[27]

Everson articulates in poetic language the truth of the cosmic significance of the Incarnation. But this is no mere naturalistic event. He goes on: "the flame sprang through, . . . / Hued with the flush of Godhead, / Set round with the tongues of angels."[28]

Everson here conflates the Nativity and Pentecost, the birth of Christ and the birth of the church through the descent of the Holy Spirit in the form of tongues of fire. The breaking of the natural, linear cycle by the insertion of a vertical dimension, a dimension that marks the intersection of time and eternity, marks a common pattern in Everson's poetry. The result, as he puts it, is that "birth, like death" is "transcended." Everson's poem overcomes the cyclical alternation, and sterile confusion, of death and birth that permeates Eliot's "Journey of the Magi." The occasion of the intervention is some sort of physical violence or rupture, a wound that allows the victim to be entered and for life to flow out. This night, this particular moment in time, cannot contain this birth: temple, kings, and Empire will be affected and toppled by the "bare power, which is love." As the unknowing oxen "crunch their corn," the response of man, "seized in that vortex / Breaks on his knees / And prays!"[29] Everson here speaks the language of prayer and praise: *laudato si*'!

In the final poem in the sequence, "The Wise," Everson at last comes to the subject matter proper to Eliot's poem. Both poems begin with a description of the journey as an exhausting quest. If Eliot underscores the lingering gap between the two kingdoms, Everson stresses the ceding of one to the other. But it is not precisely the fulfillment of the one by the other, since the wise have wasted their time "reading the wrong texts, / Charting the doubtful calculations." After the fact, or, as Everson puts it, "under the Sign," they no longer regard the preceding work as "search but as preparation." They learn not just the truth but something equally important about the revelation of truth: "When sought and at last seen, / Is never found. It is given."[30]

Revelation arrives as a gift disproportionate to any antecedent effort expended to achieve it. In this case alone, the disproportion is infinite, as it marks the entrance of the eternal God into time to reconcile all things to himself. This is indeed the singular event, not just for those, such as the shepherds and the Magi, who happen to be present in time and place, but also for the entire human race: "Once, as it may, in the life of a man; / Once, as it was, in the life of mankind, / All is corrected."[31] The triptych ends where it began, on the filthy bloodstained earth. The wise worship in tears on the same plot of earth inhabited by the uncouth.

Where Eliot is hesitant, uncertain, and negative, Everson is enthusiastic, confident, and affirmative. Nature permeates Eliot's poetry. Yet Eliot writes *about* nature, observing it from a certain distance. Everson's writing immerses the reader in the concrete realities of the physical world, as *The Triptych* amply illustrates. Another difference between Eliot and Everson has to do with the explicitly scriptural framework of Everson's triptych.

"Journey" is replete with allusions to scripture, but these are fragments rather than parts of a coherent narrative of the birth of the savior. Everson establishes the setting for each poem in the sequence with a direct quotation from the Gospel according to Luke.

The rewriting of Eliot's "Journey" is at once an acknowledgment of debt to the greatest religious poet of Everson's time and a signal that his own poetic vocation would take a different course. Indeed, the objective third-person narration of the triptych would prove to be atypical for Everson, whose sense of his own calling as a Christian poet was rooted in a deeply personal experience of the God who beckons alluringly. Everson's poetry is personal, erotic, and ecstatic. Everson affirms the irreducibly complex reality of the human person, who is both body and soul, emotion and reason, sense and intellect. He seeks not so much to find a restful balance as to keep these elements in a kind of creative tension.

THE POROUS SELF, PIERCED BY THE DIVINE

The key event in Everson's life preceding the composition of the triptych is his attendance at Christmas Mass in 1948. Feeling a bit of Nietzschean superiority (recall Nietzsche's quip that we should avoid church if we wish to breathe clean air) to the credulous, inferior souls around him, Everson is suddenly moved by the smell of fir trees. The operative sense, the bodily vehicle of grace, is not vision, touch, or taste but smell. The result is an experience not of a naturalist, pantheist divinity but of a transcendent person communicating directly to him in time and space. He discovers "for the first time that synthesis of spirit and sense that I had needed and never found." As a result, he enters "into the family and fellowship of Christ—made my assent, such as it was—one more poor wretch, who had nothing to bring but his iniquities."[32] Here we find the first instance of an abiding theme in Everson's work and life: the attempt to articulate, to re-create in language, the experience of the immanent presence of a transcendent, hidden God, an instance of the wrestling with "polarities" that Gelpi has rightly identified as constitutive of Everson's poetic vision.

Two years later, while working at a Catholic Worker House in Oakland, he had another profound experience during Mass: "I was seized by a feeling so intense as to exceed anything I had previously experienced, a feeling of extreme anguish and joy, of transcendent spirituality and of a great, thrilling physical character." He writes about this experience in "The Encounter": "My Lord came to me in the deep of night." His shame surfaces: "I was a thing of flesh for His despise; / I was a nakedness before His sight."[33]

Shrinking from God in shame, he cannot escape God's pursuit of him. God "broke beyond the burning and the blame, / And burned the blame to make that pain of praise." The divine presence terrifies; it provokes a piercing awareness of nakedness and shame. The burning is at once a burning from shame, the difficulty of enduring exposure, and a burning for Christ: "all my body burned to bear his name."[34] Wanting to escape but not being able to, the soul is paralyzed. The soul would remain immobile except for the fact that God purges the blame itself to make "that pain of praise." Poetry as praise is rooted in purgatorial fire.

The key source in the Christian tradition for Everson's erotic spirituality is the Song of Solomon. As Paul Griffiths writes in his reflection on that text, "Singing is a complex speech-act of confession that may include praise, gratitude, and lament and that establishes a relation of peculiar and profound intimacy between singer and hearer, reconfiguring the being and understanding and aspiration of the singer by conforming her more closely to the Lord to whom she sings."[35] Such singing is the vocation of the Christian poet. In Everson's case, the poet speaks in first-person language, attentive to his instability, his precarious location between nothingness and infinity, in imagery that is often violent and almost always erotic. The ecstasy that results from erotic love propels the self beyond itself toward the object of its desire. The response is praise, gratitude, and awe.

With the departure of the divine, the poet is struck by the realization that he "could not be." A tellingly ambiguous phrase, it indicates how tenuous and uncertain his existence is (he might not be) and how, in God's absence, he simply cannot be. He falls, "forever through Time's windless flight / To meet the waters of eternity."[36] Again Griffiths: "To become as nothing before love's delights is the only way to become something: it is to respond to the Lord's gift by accepting it.... There is no other substance than that given and taken in love's economy."[37] Everson recasts the oblivion and dissolution of the self through immersion in the Dionysian, to the relationship with a personal God, who awakens human creatures to their own nothingness in order to restore them to themselves.

Everson and Griffiths call to mind Desmond. Nothingness signifies in many ways. In Everson's poetry, the sense that our very existence comes from and rests on nothingness undoes the human assumption of a stable, sufficient self. That is an illusion, punctured by the very presence of God whose infinite and radiant beauty inspires in the self a sense of its own nothingness. A philosophy that "comes to nothing," in which "our reasoning reduces to zero," can be seen "as an end that is also a beginning." The recognition of one's own nothingness, a willingness to be as nothing, allows for a "new interface with creation" and the creator.[38]

In flight from metaphysics, contemporary philosophers of religion often speak of God as without or beyond being. Desmond prefers to speak of God as "beyond the whole," existing in a mode that cannot be located on the same plane as other beings.[39] If philosophers wonder about the order, beauty, and goodness of being, they are invited to ask about the source of the whole, a source that escapes delimitation by the categories we deploy to understand beings within the whole.

The seemingly natural, commonsense certainty of our own existence, the assumption that we stand on solid ground, is put into question in the poetry of Everson. The poet finds himself perched precariously between God and nonbeing; what sustains and supports him is his grace-given attention to the one who gazes at him. Here we find a reversal of idolatrous viewing. As Marion puts it, "The idol remains ... proportionate to the expectation of desire; thus, it fulfills ... expectation. The icon definitively exceeds the scope of expectation, terrifying the desire, annulling the anticipation."[40] In place of our control over the object, the "icon inverts it while substituting its own—its aim toward us—in place of ours toward it."[41] Everson here begins from the subject and stresses throughout the difficulty of finding a resting place, the elusiveness of a natural home. But this is coupled with a deeply antimodern insight, namely, that any attempt at control is based on the mistaken suppositions about our fixed place in nature and our capacity to master the natural world. The poet discovers that nature itself, indeed all of created being, is porous, dependent for its very existence on the gratuitous action of a transcendent God.

Throughout Everson's poetry, there is a close connection between poetic and mystical experience, both of which are, according to Maritain, "born near the center of the soul, in the living springs of preconscious or supraconscious vitality of the spirit."[42] The very notion of creative intuition for

Maritain signals the key role of the preconscious in the work of the artist. The artist is affected by the external world; emotions are moved in a certain way. What the poet apprehends in "creative intuition," a phrase Everson himself uses, is not an essence, as is the case with philosophical knowledge of the world. Instead, the apprehension is directed to "concrete existence," to an experience of the world in a "soul pierced by a given emotion."[43]

The framework for creative emotion in Everson is the place and afflictions of human persons in the natural cosmos. Everson's focus on nature and the earth predates his Christian conversion; it is part of his own rootedness in the land of Northern California. Regionalism is crucial to the ecological poetry of both Jeffers and Everson. In the introduction to the second volume of his trilogy of collected poems, Everson writes, "In retrospect my life emerges as a kind of Californian odyssey—an odyssey in the sense that every life is a mythic journey through time; and Californian in the sense that the scale of the American west casts its presence over the scenario of the quest, determining the broader ethos within which the ideological progression is enacted."[44] As Gary Snyder puts it, "Bioregional awareness teaches us in specific ways.... Our relation to the natural world takes place in a place."[45] Regional language is a sign of a particular "place—an indication that the speaker has a place, feels part of a place."[46]

The sense of place or home is compatible with a lingering sense of homelessness. Prior to his conversion, Everson had an instinctive affinity for pantheism. He then believed that the main task was "recovering a bond with nature," from which we had been separated by "cities and machines."[47] As we have seen, these are pervasive themes in the poetry of Jeffers. There is a cosmic accent to his sense of beleaguered humanity, lost in the universe. Everson reflects on the "nameless galaxies" whose indifference embodies a kind of "vast, universal enmity against the human heart" and its longings.[48] On top of the natural disparity between human persons and the vast cosmos, human beings have established technologies that further alienate them from nature.

In his autobiography, he writes of his experience, before his conversion, of the dread of an infinite and hostile universe. In Pascalian language, he speaks of human persons "dissevered from God, adrift on the raft of earth in a universe of night, a universe of fog, of galactic dust, and no port to make." He adds, "We in our enlightenment know that the old gods are dead, the stars no more than titanic blobs of fire, unthinkably vast, and going nowhere."[49] Despite its proud accomplishments in the areas of science and technology, modern humanity is bereft, adrift in a world whose cold indifference makes all the more necessary, even as it makes ultimately pointless, the task of reshaping it in accord with human wishes. Everson affirms a version of Jeffers's notion that God has withdrawn (or been cast out) from the "sterility of modern consciousness" and now reposes in nature.[50]

However religious it may be, sublime pantheism is not to be equated with the mystical encounter with a personal God, who at once transcends time and enters it to engage human persons. The difference that the latter conception of God makes is evident in an early Everson poem, "The South Coast." With its regional flavor, the poem features intricate descriptions of creeks and the sea, herons and mud hens, winds and mountains, salt grass and cypress—all in constant motion in an ever-changing scene of grandiose proportion. Early in the poem, the poet wonders, "Whose mind conceives?" His meandering description continues until the abrupt and compressed proclamation: "God *makes*." Here is the finale, reminiscent of Hopkins in the intensity of its phrasing and its revelatory tone:

> God makes
> On earth, in us, most instantly
> On the very now,
> His own means conceives.
> How many strengths break out unchoked
> Where He, Whom all declares,
> Delights to make be![51]

The piling of short phrases on top of one another heightens the dramatic intensity of the poem. The strategy of composition reflects the activity of God in creation: manifold, constantly active, at work in ways we cannot begin to fathom. The active causality of the Being who exceeds all his effects is manifest in the surge of beings, in a surplus of actuality permeating the universe. Here the saturation of the phenomena invites meditation on the benevolence of the creator who "delights to make be." What provokes wonder is the irrepressible fertility and incomprehensible diversity of created things. In a twist on the sentiment I have already borrowed from Johnson, Everson detects in biodiversity, not just a "manifestation of the goodness of God" that "goes beyond the imagination," but a plethora of created beings that at once entice and overwhelm the imagination.[52]

We are brought closer to God, not by abstracting from the created order or receding to an order of thought, but by immersing ourselves in the multiform beauty of the sensible order itself, an order whose sheer exuberance calls to mind a cause present everywhere and nowhere, the presence, as Pascal puts it, of a hidden God.

God creates in order to let other things exist in their otherness. The motive for creation is agapeic: "The good of being is for nothing, nothing but goodness itself."[53] The "nothing" is important for our understanding not only of creation but also of redemption and forgiveness. In the face of the "absolute nothing," we encounter the question of ultimate trust. "In . . . ultimate forsakenness," trust is "the opposite extreme" of "self-willing absoluteness."[54] Such a logic of nothing and being informs Everson's poetry in his religious period.

Recapitulating, even as he transforms, Jeffers's teaching on the primacy of beauty, Everson asserts, in distinctively theological language, "Beauty is the blood of God." It both "sustains and moves the cosmos." He expands:

> Beauty pulls back fragmentation from diffusion into coherence, restructures the rudimentary basis of things upon a higher principle of synthesis. The gash of violation is accommodated into the unity of its dismembered wholeness. . . . As the blood of God, beauty intoxicates as well as refreshes, maddens as well as invigorates. The excesses of God are the feminine allure of divinity, forever calling forms out of their equipoise to immolate themselves on impossible ideals that transcend their capacities.[55]

This is the divine madness of Socrates or, as Everson noted in his essay on Beat poetry, of the disciples at Pentecost. Everson's incarnational or sacramental poetry highlights the concrete and the specific. Lines from the late poem "The Blood of the Poet" bear repeating here: "His vivid signature, dazzlingly / Calligraphed on trees, rivers, rocks, buttes, and benchlands."

VIOLENCE, SEX, AND THE SACRED

The "gash of violation" permeates the religious poetry of Everson. Christ's passion, reflected in nature, is prominent in the short poem "Passion Week," in which a simple cut in a cedar tree is a sign of the violence and blood in salvation history. With the intensity of its short lines, the poem creates, through a concatenation of allusions and references, an intensity of feeling and perception. By the end of the poem, the cedar's bleeding pours out, "as Christ, / Those pearls of pain, / Bequeathed." It is the "The earth's / Old ache." Everson joins the cedar cut with the "lance wound under the narrow rib" of Christ on the cross, with the post-Edenic pain in childbirth ("Eve's orifice"), and with the violence of fratricide ("the agony of Avel"). In the middle of the poem, there occurs a violent disruption of the atmosphere in the descent of the Holy Spirit at Pentecost:

> The Holy Ghost
> Gusted out of the sky
> Aghast
> Our guest.[56]

There is marvelous, compressed alliteration here, but there is also a momentary rest in the shortest stanza in the poem: "Our guest." Violence arises from the unexpected intervention of the divine, but it does not call forth an endless chain of violent reactions. Instead, it reverses or decisively interrupts that chain and is an occasion for reconciliation and peace.

In his focus on expiatory self-sacrifice as the key to violence, Everson anticipates the work of René Girard, whose account of the connection between mimetic desire and violence offers a religious sociology of the roots of violence. Desire for Girard is intimately connected with mimesis or imitation. We want what others want. Shared wants create competition for the objects of desire. "Rivalistic desire" generates "reciprocal escalation."[57] Such violence can swell out of control and threaten the very foundations of society. By turning attention from the war of all against all to the war of all against one, the scapegoat "protects the entire community from its own violence."[58] Although the identification of the allegedly guilty scapegoat is arbitrary, this truth must remain hidden. As Girard puts it, the "sacrificial process requires misunderstanding."[59] Because the scapegoat mechanism unites and diffuses the violence, the guilt of the scapegoat is confirmed. Something like the scapegoat mechanism is operative in the tearing of the god to pieces in the orgiastic rites of Dionysius. Everson notes, "There will always be a victim."[60] A consequence of Girard's view is that the gospel frees believers from the envy and the perpetration of violence that otherwise pervade human community. As Everson makes clear, it does not free us from the experience of natural or human violence, or from the responsibility to reckon with a cosmos that is wracked by violence.[61] The Christian narrative and its liturgical language inform Everson's poetic exploration of violence.

To see more clearly what is at stake in Everson's approach to violence and the sacred, we might compare it with the great Romantic mythmaking on the same topic, particularly in the work of Richard Wagner, who was perhaps the most influential advocate of the Romantic hope that art could replace religion in modern culture. Toward the end of Wagner's *Tristan and Isolde*, Tristan tears a bandage from his body, allowing the life to flow out of himself. For Wagner, the act represents Tristan's free embrace of a sacrificial death, the decisive testimony of his love for Isolde and his desire for a union so absolute that it can be realized only in death. In Wagner's depiction of erotic love as a kind of sickness unto death, Roger Scruton finds a remedy for what ails the modern world, a "morbidly unheroic world," dominated by "cost-benefit calculation," which tempts us to regard our own existence as nothing more than a "cosmic mistake."[62]

In contrast to the sacramental, marital bond, which bends erotic desire to the task of reproduction and succors rather than subverts the social order, Wagner isolates the sacred moment of erotic consummation, "to show us that it is indeed sacred, and to reawaken in us a knowledge that the erotic is . . . an aspect of our freedom and an avenue of redemption." Against the abstract, bloodless, and calculative reason of modernity, Wagner sought to revive through art a distinctively premodern and originally religious conception of the world, wherein "rituals, oaths, acts of heroic sacrifice" are woven into the very fabric of communal life.[63] Despite Scruton's eloquent plea, the rehabilitation of modern humanity through the self-conscious construction of myth is problematic. Wagner's peculiar way of framing our path to redemption raises the questions: How are we to understand the intimate connection between erotic desire and death? How are we to avoid the possibility of a macabre celebration of the self-destructive pursuit of whatever is forbidden? This is a version of the problem of violence that surfaces in Nietzsche's *Birth of Tragedy*; that issue, as we saw at the outset of this chapter, preoccupied Everson, who offers quite a different diagnosis of the problem of violence.

Another difficulty is this. Wagner and Scruton's return to a premodern experience of the sacred is decidedly incomplete, since the premodern experience would have been wedded to a belief in the actual existence of heroic love and fidelity, not predicated on a belief in the value of living "as if" such devotion were possible.[64] Scruton's Kantian defense of the salutary nature of myth reposes on a conception of the sacred as entirely manmade. This raises the question, voiced in other contexts by the late British philosopher Bernard Williams, whether a conception like this is not unstable under reflection.[65] Can we give our sacred honor, indeed our very selves, to a conception of redemption that we know to be a human construct? Before and after Nietzsche, Wagner and Scruton succumb to the same dilemmas that contemporary philosophers have identified as fatal to Nietzsche's project of overcoming nihilism through human artifice.

For Everson, poetry as a form of making is a participation in the ongoing order of divine creation. Because he discerns the restoring and reordering action of providence in and through the violence of the natural and human orders, Everson finds beauty in it. Everson himself cites the Thomistic notion that the experience of the beautiful is a kind of "participated beatitude," or better, "participated theonomy."[66] To Maritain's pairing of the aesthetic and the poetic, Everson adds the erotic. Maritain writes of the "alert receptivity" of the artist. He sees an analogy between the mystic's suffering of the divine and the poet's "suffering of the things of the world."[67] Everson focuses on the ecstasy involved in the erotic as mediating between the things of this world and the divine.

Whatever mysticism there is in Everson is a fully embodied mysticism. He detects telling correspondences among the human, the natural, and the divine. In the poem "In All These Acts," Everson discerns in the violence suffered by animals an intimation of redemptive suffering. "Dawn cried out: the brutal voice of a bird." Animals hear the "big wind / Boom back on the cliff, crunch timber . . . the staggering gyrations of splintered kindling." If the birds escape, not all other animals are so fortunate: a "great elk, caught midway between two scissoring logs, / Arched belly-up and died." Everson's description of the violence of this death is detailed and blunt. He writes of the "snapped spine / Half torn out of his peeled back" and then shifts his attention to "far down below" where the results of the "mountain torrent," the "avalanchial wrack . . . spun down its thread."[68] Violence permeates nature. But Everson invites us to to detect in the violence the passion of Christ. The final stanza begins:

> In all these acts
> Christ crouches and seethes pitched forward
> On the crucifying stroke.

There is an overlap here between Everson's vision and that of classical tragedy. Violence permeates nature; in its acceptance, there is a kind of tragic glory. Yet there is something new in Everson. He detects in natural agony the patterns of redemption displayed by the God who takes on the matter of the cosmos and the flesh of the human animal in order to take violence into himself: "These are the modes of His forth-showing, His serene agonization."[69]

Everson develops a poetic expression of eros that is reducible neither to Freudian nor to Wagnerian erotics, although it has points of contact with each. In "The Mate-Flight of Eagles," a poem with the subtitle "The Savagery of Love," composed on the Feast of Mary Magdalen, Everson magnificently pairs natural and human, secular and sacred, violence and redemption. He imagines a scene in ancient Palestine, which begins from an observation of the coupling of eagles in flight and then turns to Mary Magdalen at the foot of the cross, the "grief-tree, tree of the desolation." Her love is "savage as sin." The sexual imagery of penetration and union runs parallel to the wounding of body and soul in love, the archetype of which is the passion of Christ, specifically in this case, the lance that pierced his side. Here eros, which desires union with the beloved, generates passion, understood in its etymological sense as a suffering or receiving. Elsewhere, Everson writes about his own study of Thomas Aquinas, which led him to the realization of the important role of the passions in the human discovery of truth and in the virtuous life.[70] The anthropology derived from Thomas Aquinas takes seriously the fact that human beings are animals, whose embodiment is not a punishment or a cosmic accident. In a pertinent passage, Thomas writes, "The lover in some sense passes over into the beloved. For this reason, love is called a piercing. Piercing reaches the interior of something by separating or dividing. Similarly, the beloved penetrates internally. Thus love is said to wound, in that it transfigures the passions."[71] In its openness to wounding, eros mirrors the condition of art. The parallel is the source of the laments of artists about their own suffering as a result of their peculiar calling. Maritain speaks of art itself as having a kind of "imperfection through which the infinite wounds the finite."[72] Everson continues: "What plenitude of power in passion loosed, / When the Christ-love and the Christ-death / Find the Love-death of the cross."[73]

We should note Everson's use of the phrase "Love-death," a term made famous in Wagner's *Tristan*. For Everson, the modern obsession with death as a consummation devoutly to be wished is a residue of, a secularized replacement for, the Crucifixion, in which God embraces death in order to bring rebirth. Violence, itself unnatural, is paradoxically necessary for our redemption because the soul is in an unnatural, disordered state. Once again, we see Everson's conjoining of the mystical and the poetic. Ecstasy can move us beneath or above reason.

Everson's emphasis on the erotic-ecstatic and his rhetorical focus on moving his audience have implications for his style. In the *Naked Heart*, he describes the chief stylistic difference between his poetry and that of Jeffers, a contrast that has to do with the "increase in density at the syllabic level." He explains:

> My rhythmic unities are much more closely moulded than his. He can tolerate a more relaxed line because he's dealing with more phenomena. Going back and down to the drama of the Self, I build up rhythmic intensity in order to get the emotive urgency across, the travail of experience, to register the ordeal. And so the line becomes shorter, a lot more enjambment[,] . . . a cumulative and intensifying factor that you see in Hopkins or Donne.[74]

The stylistic arena is the one in which Everson departs most dramatically from his mentor. His erotic, personal, and ecstatic style is closer to that of John Donne than it is to Jeffers. As was true of Donne, so too in Everson there is an avoidance of any dissociation of sensibility: thought and feeling, intellectual insight and transforming emotion are not severed but integrated.

The telescoping of images, their almost violent repetition, is characteristic of Donne and Everson. The latter's use of "rhythmic intensity" and "enjambment" reflects the brokenness of human life in a fallen world. It is meant to address human persons where they are, blind to their own blindness, often overcome by their disordered desires, and fearful of unsettling interventions from outside their own settled sphere of desire and perception. His poetry is accusatory and decentering even as it invites a self-knowledge that allows for ecstatic healing.

"Suffice it to say," Everson writes in *Birth of a Poet*, "that when I left the monastery for academe the method that I brought with me was meditative rather than discursive. For I had learned how concepts seemingly exhausted by endless repetition could suddenly, under the probe of intuition, blossom into life."[75] Another convergence between the Beat poets and the Dominican order, the order of preachers, has to do with the preference for the oral over the written, for the living speech of the word rather than its printed record. Everson was famous throughout the United States and Europe for his live performances of his poetry. As a preacher-poet, he came to see these encounters as "vehicles for making contact between God and other souls."[76]

THE PASSION FOR ELSENESS

The union of souls, as well as bodies, is an abiding theme in Everson's poetry. As is true for Donne, so too in Everson there is a range of erotic desire. Whereas Donne devotes a great deal of attention to the poetry of seduction, Everson attends especially to the imaging of God in the erotic and procreative love of man and woman. There is ample theological precedent for this approach. The theme runs from the opening of Genesis through the Song of Songs to Saint Paul's reflection on the way in which the love between husband and wife mirrors the love between Christ and his church.[77]

Everson's poetry of consummation seeks to revive premodern motifs. In contrast to his sacramental conception of sex, contemporary views of sex tend to strip it of its ecstatic, erotic, and procreative dimensions. Sex is thus reduced to the mechanical interaction of cells, a matter of chemistry. The viewer or reader of explicit depictions of sex is led to attend to surface, bodily interactions. In our increasingly pornographic culture, fantasy takes the place of imagination with dreadful consequences. As Wendell Berry writes:

> Fantasy is of the solitary self, and it cannot lead us away from ourselves. It is by imagination that we cross over the differences between ourselves and other beings and thus learn compassion, forbearance, mercy, forgiveness, sympathy, and love. . . . In sex, as in other things, we have liberated fantasy but killed imagination, and so have sealed ourselves in selfishness and loneliness.[78]

So great is our addiction to fantasy that its correction requires a kind of violent reordering of our passions and perceptions. As Scruton puts it in his study of beauty, eros "singles out . . . not an assemblage of parts but an embodied person." The singling indicates the irreducible individuality of the other person, a "free being revealed in the flesh" and encountered in love. Such love is "sacred" in the sense that it is "removed," "set apart"; it simultaneously draws us to it and warns us that we must be willing to sacrifice or do without it rather than "despoil" it.[79]

One of his longer poems, "River-Root: A Syzygy," is an extended reflection on sexual congress between a man and a woman, who experience the "incarnational join: body to body, twain in one flesh."[80] Married with children, the couple has grown distant. Awakening to one another's embrace in the middle of the night, they have sex and conceive another child. The poem, which contains explicit descriptions of the sexual act, includes a parallel narrative of the flowing of a river. From the "merest wet," the least element of moisture, the water gathers to a cascading flow that pushes forward until it reaches the sea. The paired opposites, stressed in the word *syzygy*—a connection or conjunction of two distinct, often opposed, things—include not just male and female but also human persons and nature.

The poem begins with drops of water whose accumulation will create the river, the incessant motion of which indicates that a "passion for elseness lurks in his root."[81] The river is "life-bestowing," the "father of waters."[82] Everson supplies the history of the river and charts its purposive course. Along its path, the river travels by the "somnolent night-lying cities of men."[83] Here we encounter another history, that of man and woman, who have grown apart, even somewhat hostile. They wake, and their touch prompts an acknowledgment of the need for forgiveness and reunion. Passionate, whispered apologies give way to physical caresses and then further intimacy.

The act of unitive love is also procreative. The sacramental element is prominent. The conceiving of children is, in "River-Root," the "prototypical act of creation." The couple's union is also a union with God: "For God grows in them. /In the sacramental oneness."[84] Everson here revives in quite contemporary language an ancient Christian account of eros. As David O'Connor notes in his study of ancient conceptions of love, the scriptural account of the source of the union of male and female is distinctive. It underscores the "radical incompleteness" of human persons; neediness is natural and intended by God for the good of human persons. In influential pagan accounts, by contrast, the sexual coupling of humans is often the result of a punishment.[85] Moreover, on the Christian view, the chief way of mirroring God is to be fruitful through the procreation of children.⁸⁶ As Everson puts it, "Seed must be sown that a soul might be made."⁸⁷ There is a striking overlap here between De Koninck's account of how matter reaches upward toward spirit and Everson's biological depiction of the conception of human life.

Meanwhile, "out in the night the River runs." Everson moves back and forth between the act of human sexual intimacy and the river, which always "runs by the house." What follows is a lengthy, florid depiction of the act of lovemaking, its "pounding concentration, a stunning rhythm, a terror of pace, and an enveloping thunder." The scene encompasses not just man and woman, not just human persons and the local environment, but the entire cosmos. He expands beyond the river to the continent, the earth, and the sun. Finally, "beyond the sun," he depicts "all the orgiastic fire of the stars, / Seething and seeding down the web of space."⁸⁸

Here Everson approaches Dante's vision of the indissoluble connection between individual and cosmic love. The particular desire of each and every person is a participation in the "love that moves the sun and all the other stars." The shifting back and forth between an anthropocentric and a bio- or ecocentric perspective gives way to a cosmocentric perspective. Everson couples the sense of human participation in a cosmic whole with a reflection on the integrated levels of communion between husband and wife, physical, human, and divine: "They have touched transcendence, a syzygy / Greater than wonder ever could know."⁸⁹ Syzygy is operative on a number of levels: male and female; human and natural; the couple and the cosmos; the physical and the spiritual; the flux of time and the intervention of the eternal in time.

"River-Root" merits consideration alongside another poem, "Kingfisher Flat," a compressed rewriting of the classical myth of the Fisher King. Prompted by an experience of the absence of love and the paralysis of desire, the narrator traces drought in the human and natural orders. The poem begins:

> A rustle of whispering wind over leaves,
> Then the stillness closes: no creek music,
> No slurred water-sound.⁹⁰

The scene expresses the lack of what "River-Root" exuberantly portrays: the flowing of life-giving fluid. In "Kingfisher Flat," by contrast, there is only the "starved stream." But drought is not an attribute reserved for surrounding nature. As in "River-Root," so too here the natural and the human mirror one another. While in the former poem Everson develops leisurely analogies, here he moves with much greater immediacy to tie the natural and the human orders tightly together: "dry turning of leaves, cessation of desire."[91]

Perhaps because he finds only mutually confirming negation in the human and the natural order, he reaches out to the past and to the realm of myth for illumination. The poet's insights call to mind an ancient myth: "I think of the Fisher King, / All his domain parched in sterile fixation of purpose, / Clenched on the core of the burning question / Gone unasked."[92] It is never clear in the context of this poem what the unasked question is. The collusion of natural and human and the allusion to the ancient myth raise other questions: Is there a causal connection and not just a parallel or a coincidence between human impotence and the drought of the land? If so, what is its source? Is its cause some recent violation of nature or the result of an ancient curse?

Having invoked large mythic questions, the poet returns to the personal drama of husband and wife. He observes that the "masks of drought deceive us."[93] The poet's gift for concrete detail draws his and our attention back to the local plot of land and the sleeping woman next to him. Like the earth, she "aches for rain."[94] Procreation is not mentioned here. Age may be a factor. Still, the same parallel between life-giving, life-renewing water and human sex is present.

"Kingfisher Flat" by negation and "Syzygy" by affirmation indicate the need for reciprocity of response between the two lovers, and on numerous levels: physical consent and desire, natural human affection and union, and spiritual awareness. Everson typically begins with the human order, with an individual human person and his or her desires. But the human self is encompassed by and immersed in a biosphere, a physical cosmos, shot through with moral and spiritual significance. Sometimes he deploys a natural image as a kind of symbol of the human order or a sign of the divine. At other times he traces out the human and the natural in parallel lines of exploration. The two orders mutually illumine one another, intersect, and become inseparably entangled. What results is a highly discursive treatment of the complex relations between inner and outer, human and cosmos, cosmos and God. Violence, inflicted or at least undergone, cannot be eliminated. Can there be a natural resting place for a self whose dynamic structure is ecstatic, whose telos is to stand outside itself, whose soul is structured by what Everson calls the "passion for elseness"?[95]

The autonomous self is as much an illusion as is the picture of nature as raw material at our disposal; nature cannot be so easily understood or subdued. It is suffused with contingency and violence. It is also open to intervention from the God who fashions it from nothing and sustains it in being. Moreover, the self, despite its illusions of autonomy, is porous not only to external things and persons, but even to the unknown depths within itself. In these ways, Everson's poetry takes up and develops themes present in *LS* even as it overcomes the limitations of that document. Yet the goal is similar: to craft practices of cosmic praise.

SIX

Georges Rouault

Artist of Alienation and Transfiguration

The sociologist James Davison Hunter describes nihilism as the loss of contact between the word and the real. He borrows from George Steiner the notion that nihilism has to do with the decline of the "civilization of the word" and the loss of the "instauration of truth between word and world."[1] The "covenant between signified and signifier is broken."[2] Great poets, such as Jeffers and Everson, are acutely aware of the break between word and world; their poetics attempt to restore the covenant. More than Jeffers, Everson deploys an erotic-ecstatic discourse that befits the strange creature that feels homeless in its home. The crisis of modernity, however, might be said to begin with what Jean-Luc Marion called the "crisis of the visible." The problem of the image, doubts about whether it refers to anything beyond other images, is coterminous with modernity.

The painter Georges Rouault had a sense of the crisis of the visible and its connection to the threat of nihilism in modern civilization. In his early period, he is captivated by the degradation of modern society and its impact on the bodies and souls of members of every echelon of society.

Pierre Courthion, a friend of Rouault and author of the magisterial *Rouault*, writes, "The [great] war confirmed Rouault in his skepticism about progress."[3] Rouault finds the hell of the imagination in the real-world degradation of prostitutes, the sorrow of clowns, and the hypocrisy of judges. Despite the many interpretive theories concerning what Rouault was up to in this early period, his intentions remain opaque, as they may well have been to Rouault himself. What is clear is that Rouault had a dark view of modern civilization: "A new world is dawning. Tragic is the light I see on the horizon. . . . Material appetites have gone beyond all bounds. The entire universe is out of joint, spiritual values are being destroyed ever more rapidly. There is scarcely any time left for leisure or higher things. . . . [M]an is a wolf to man—*homo homini lupus*—under the guise of civilization."[4] His reaction against optimist progressivist views of modernity took the form of an obsession with shame, misery, and disgrace. Lionello Venturi describes Rouault's early career as his "voyage into hell."[5] Along with many of his contemporaries, Rouault recognized that the linear progress promised in modernity was a deception. The pursuit of progress had led to regress; the desire for absolute knowledge, to ignorance and unreason; and the quest for untrammeled freedom, to novel and barbaric forms of enslavement.

Rouault does not treat these matters as academic abstractions or philosophical exercises. Instead, he focuses on depictions of the degradation of the natural and moral worlds that we inhabit. He detects the sources of nihilism in ordinary human life, in the experience of grief, sadness, and loss without recourse to mercy, and of injustice that debases both victim and perpetrator. He depicts the human person as a "vagabond of misfortune," whose wandering indicates a dislocation from nature and community. Yet he does not rest in despair or nihilism. Instead, he provides a "language of hope in exile."[6] Rouault's vision, particularly as it emerges over time, is what Maritain has called "transfigurative" realism, a realism that neither discounts the pervasive sense of alienation nor succumbs to temptations to despair.

Rouault mixes medieval with modern, a Dantesque sense of judgment and of the sacramental character of the natural world, with some of the most innovative stylistic techniques of any twentieth-century artist. One of the key influences on Rouault is Baudelaire, whose art seeks to "disrupt the senses" and to startle readers into an experience of recognition.[7] By the strategy known as "dedoublement," Baudelaire constructs an "aesthetics of shock" whose goal is to enable readers to see themselves from an external point of view and thus to come to a painful self-knowledge. A similar approach runs through much of Rouault's work, especially the *Miserere*, which combines images of ordinary persons with those from the life of Christ, particularly from his passion.

In my examination of Rouault, I begin with the *Miserere* and then turn to his early works featuring prostitutes, clowns, and judges. Finally, I consider his late religious landscapes. Although Rouault focuses on the human drama of degradation and redemption, his art also attends to the natural environment. Critics see his late landscapes as among the most remarkable works of art in the twentieth century. These arresting works suggest a visual alternative to the dichotomy of anthropocentrism and biocentrism. In a distinctive way, he underscores the inseparability of natural and human ecology as he seeks to display the "cosmic affinity between man and his natural surroundings."[8]

THE CRISIS OF THE VISIBLE

The anthropocentric turn in early modern thought is in part a response to an epistemological problem of the early modern period that has to do with whether images or ideas have any purchase on the real world. The early modern period in philosophy is dominated by what has been called since the time of Thomas Reid the way or "theory of ideas."[9] The assumption that we start from within ideas and then try to make our way back to real has no cure. Once we believe that what we primarily know is ideas, there is no way back to the real order. Every attempt to break from the circle of consciousness must be by means of another image. Hence we have an infinite regress from the real order. The logical result of this early modern turn to the idea or image as the object of knowledge is the idealist teaching of Berkeley, "to be is to be perceived," the very claim that Marion takes to be definitive of a Nietzschean anthropology and of the contemporary crisis of the visible, wherein the image becomes indistinguishable from the idol.

One might instructively contrast contemporary reflections on our enslavement to images with the account of images in Plato's famous allegory of the cave. The contemporary dilemma is less optimistic. For all its negative assessment of the condition of most human beings, Plato's allegory presents a remedy, in terms of an ascent from image to reality. The contemporary difficulty is the supposition that images reflect only other images. In this way, the insight into the distinction between image and reality, rooted in the realization that what we have taken to be real is but an image, becomes a self-canceling one.

In *Crossing of the Visible*, Marion frames his analysis of modern painting in terms of the crisis of the visible itself. Central to Marion's analysis is the difference between the icon and the idol, the latter of which is "proportionate to the expectation of desire." Rather than transform or educate our desire, the idol simply satisfies the preexisting desire of the spectator. Reducing all value to that of the viewer, the implicit assumption of the idol is that "to be is to be perceived."[10] The idol feeds the lust to behold (*libido videndi*) all things without being seen. The idol produces only mirror images of the gaze of the viewer. The resulting conception of the human being is the Nietzschean conception of the human person as esteemer; the only values are those constructed by the choosing subject. In this respect, Marion's analysis accords with Hunter's thesis that the roots of nihilism are found in unfettered autonomy, in the elevation of choice as an end in itself.

Although Marion is inconsistent in his use of the terms "idol" and "icon," it seems clear that painting, or at least what Marion refers to as authentic painting, functions in the manner of the icon, as described in the previous paragraph.[11] Rejecting the notion that painting is the imitation of nature, Marion argues that painting brings the "unseen to light."[12] It captivates by its depiction of what has hitherto been unencountered. In a nihilistic context more than any other, "the painting becomes for us one of the rare but powerful challenges to mastery."[13] In the context of the idol, which Marion sees as increasingly pervasive in modern society, eros becomes debased and the beautiful becomes degraded into an object of consumerist preference.

THE *MISERERE* AND THE QUEST FOR THE TRUE ICON

For Marion, true painting, in bringing the unseen or the unexpected to light, annuls our antecedent desire in order to give rise to a new one. It thus subverts the visible by the invisible and overturns the relationship of the spectator and the spectacle. Marion takes his point of departure from

Saint Paul's usage of *icon* in Colossians 1:15: "Christ is the image (icon) of the invisible God." Attempting to see, we discover ourselves being seen; the viewer is exposed and revealed, by an "other-than-itself." What does this have to do with Rouault?

In his masterpiece, the *Miserere*, Rouault recovers an iconic understanding of art.[14] Universally acknowledged as Rouault's supreme achievement, the *Miserere*, begun in the 1920s but not published until after World War II, is a series of fifty-eight black-and-white prints. The title comes from Psalm 51, a penitential psalm recited every Friday morning, the day of the passion of Christ, in the Catholic liturgy, as a reminder of the need for repentance.[15] Central to the *Miserere* series is the veil of Veronica, whose name means "true image or icon." By interspersing images of Veronica's veil and images of Christ's passion within a series of prints of contemporary scenes and character types, Rouault offers viewers the opportunity to come to see ordinary lives, indeed their own lives, in relation to that of Christ. The aim is to recover an appreciation of Christ as at once the image of God and the image of the human condition. By embracing the disorders and evils afflicting modern society, Rouault responds to a particularly vexing problem for contemporary Christianity, what Hunter calls the "weakened plausibility structures" of the Christian faith in the modern world.[16] The assumption that God exists and is active in the world cannot be easily sustained because the most important symbols of social, economic, political, and aesthetic life no longer point to him.[17] Rouault starts fresh; he puts the secular and the sacred in conversation by juxtaposing images from each.

The complex artistic pedagogy of the *Miserere* serves a further purpose. Much of contemporary art is divided between facile transcendence, superficially affirmative stories, and debased Gothic narratives, depicting a world of unrelenting evil. Rouault follows a third path, one that embraces the suffering, doubt, and evils of our age, yet offers a vision of hope. Only in this way can nihilism be engaged and overcome. The kenotic emptying of Christ in his passion and death provides the corrective to the nihilism that threatens to engulf the modern world.

Before viewers begin to grapple with the complex iconography of the series, they are mesmerized by the look of the images. The stark contrast between dark and light in the prints has been hailed as Rouault's revival of chiaroscuro. But this is misleading. As John McCoy shows, in "Technique and Space in the *Miserere*," in comparison to the standard mechanisms of chiaroscuro, Rouault's prints have no light source, and the contrast between dark and light does not produce the effect of volume or depth. Instead, he "imbues the static statuesque compositions with vibrant energy."[18] In place of the illusion of space, his work exhibits a "depth of texture and tone." McCoy also qualifies somewhat the common notion that Rouault's own art mirrors closely the techniques and effects of stained glass in which Rouault was trained early in his career. Whereas stained glass is "regular, rigid, and geometrical," Rouault's prints are "calligraphic, intuitive, and expressive."[19] Rouault also opts for heavy, thick outlines, in contrast to the distinct, discrete lines of stained glass. Rouault exhibits a penchant, characteristic of modernism, for flattened surfaces and for an acknowledgment of the materials used by the artist.[20]

The opening sequence of four images in the *Miserere* is striking. The first, a title piece for the first half of the book, locates Christ beneath a semicircle in the lower half of the image, above which is a depiction of an angelic figure. Christ appears in the mutable, sublunary world with his head bowed—a posture that recurs. The next image, also of Christ with head bowed, has the text, "Jesus despised." Following that is another image of Christ, accompanied by the words, "always flagellated." From these opening images of the passion of Christ, we turn to an ordinary man with a child. The man's posture mirrors that of Christ from the previous image, even as he reaches out in a gentle gesture toward the child. He is a fugitive, a wanderer. The inscription reads, "Take refuge in your heart, you vagabond of misfortune." The mutual reflection of Christ and ordinary human beings repeats itself throughout the *Miserere*. We are apt to think of human beings as made in the image and likeness of God; here Christ imitates human suffering.

Throughout, Rouault depicts Christ as the suffering servant. Rouault acknowledges the problem of evil; at times he seems obsessed with its reality. As William Desmond puts it:

> Why the ultimate allowance of evil? . . . Is not the forbearance of the good God horrifying? Creation is saturated with the cries of horror, and the sky smiles serenely. One looks up at the battered face of the crucified man. Is the crushing weight of limp death taken into the heart of the divine? Must the agapeic God taste evil, not taste but become subjected to death—death the outcome in nothing of the free

refusal let be by the first agape? Free being has been given, but finite free being gives itself to itself and comes to be lord of death not life. The horror of the inversion cannot be turned around, or turned over by that free finite being, for now its freedom is unfree, for there seems to be no release of agapeic being intimate to it any longer.[21]

This is a remarkably fitting articulation of Rouault's vision. Alas, the knowledge of our own evil as well as its cure is something we resist.

The triptych of images in *Miserere* 6–8 begins with the question, "Are we not all convicts?" The next text is, "Supposing ourselves kings." The final text is again a query: "Who does not wear a mask?" The first is a tragic figure; the second, a leering, vain, almost insane pretender to royalty; and the third, a sad clown. The universal practice of self-aggrandizing deception precludes the possibility of real self-knowledge. As Pascal puts it, we hide and disguise ourselves from ourselves. One of the chief reasons that images are not transparent has to do with our own manipulation of images, something we do consciously and unconsciously, as we are moved by our passions. Given our resistance to self-knowledge, the images in the *Miserere* are designed to shock us with the immediacy of death, degradation, and vanity. Thus Rouault fashions his own aesthetics of shock. If we wish to see ourselves in the images of the *Miserere*, we will have to allow ourselves to be accused. We will have to allow the text to read us as we read it. We will have to be seen even as we see. We will have to admit that we are convicts, operating under the self-delusion that we are kings, adept at presenting false faces to those we encounter.

The initial alternation of images of Christ and of ordinary human beings gives way to the depiction of bourgeois female characters (14–17), whose affluence and prestige generate high self-regard. Following images of a condemned man and a lawyer and a set of images of Christ, interspersed with images of desolation, there is a print (28) of a morgue with piles of skulls surrounding a crucifix. What seems morbid is in fact a hopeful scene, indicated both by the central location of the cross, surrounded by light, and by the accompanying scriptural text: "Whoever believes in me, though he die, will have life" (John 11:25). Immediately after the statement of resurrection, we have a scene of rebirth (29), as the text urges viewers, "Sing Matins, the Day is Renewed." The image is that of an open landscape flooded with light from a bright sun.

The next two scenes (Christ's baptism and an image of the crucifixion beneath which is the text, "Love one another") reach fruition in the subsequent plate (32), an image of an individual person turned toward Christ speaking the words, "Lord, it is you, I recognize you" (figure 6.1). This plate brings together what had previously remained separate, the depiction of human persons and of Christ. It also contains the key moment of recognition, knowing Christ for who he is. As Stephen Schloesser shows, Rouault brings together here two post-resurrection passages from scripture: the journey to Emmaus, in which the disciples come to recognize Jesus in the breaking of the bread; and the confession scene of the doubting Thomas.[22] Immediately after the scene of recognition, in the last plate of the first half of the *Miserere*, Veronica's veil appears (33) (figure 6.2). Thus the first half ends with the presentation of the true icon of the invisible God, the proper recognition of which the preceding series of plates has prepared the viewer to receive.

The second half, "Guerre," begins with an image that calls to mind the first plate: a frame neatly divided into upper and lower parts, with the lower containing a figure in an oval or semicircle. Instead of Christ with a bowed head in the lower, sublunary world, there is a corpse-like figure. Christ here appears in the upper portion, in resplendent glory, framed by the shape of the veil (34). The plate supplies a glimpse, however fleeting, of beatitude. Veronica's veil, in one of its numerous occurrences in the *Miserere*, here functions as the hinge linking the two parts of the series. As Schloesser notes, the image expresses Rouault's central conviction: "The visible world is the outward expression of unchanging invisible realities—the ongoing passion of Christ and the ongoing compassion of Veronica."[23] The veil makes other appearances in the second half. In *De Profundis* (47), a plate that marks the midpoint of the "Guerre" section, a fallen soldier lies supine, with his face illumined by the light flowing from the image of the veil on the wall.[24]

The last three images of the entire series are of Mary, of Christ crucified, and, finally, of Veronica's veil, at once the most brutal and most hopeful of all: a depiction of the crown of thorns with the accompanying text, "by his wounds we are healed." In the culminating image of the *Miserere*, we find the innocent, incarnate God, tortured and mocked. Rouault's text for that plate comes from the book of Isaiah, a passage that begins with the query, "Who would believe what we have heard?" It continues:

Figure 6.1. Seigneur, c'est vous, je vous reconnais. Lord it is You, I recognize You. Plate 32 of *Miserere*. Portfolio EX.88. Rouault, Georges (1871–1958). Photo: Georges Meguerditchian. CNAC/MNAM, Dist. RMN-Grand Palais / Art Resource, NY.

Figure 6.2. Et Véronique au tendre lin, passe encore sur le chemin. And Veronica with her tender linen, still passes along the way. Plate 33 from *Miserere*. Rouault, Georges (1871–1958). Photo: Philippe Migeat. CNAC/MNAM, Dist. RMN-Grand Palais / Art Resource, NY.

He was spurned and avoided by men,
a man of suffering, knowing pain,
Like one from whom you turn your face,
spurned, and we held him in no esteem.

Yet it was our pain that he bore,
our sufferings he endured.

> We thought of him as stricken,
> struck down by God, and afflicted,
> But he was pierced for our sins,
> crushed for our iniquity.
> He bore the punishment that makes us whole,
> by his wounds we were healed.

How ironic of God to appear in a way utterly unanticipated by the philosophers and in a guise that is offensive to civilized canons of taste. Christ comes into the very cosmos that he fashioned and he enters through a woman's womb. He lives in a particular place and time, on the outskirts of the world of politics and power. His culminating act is one from which human beings are inclined to turn their gaze in horror and scorn. He embraces the images of humanity that we hold in "no esteem." A sublime image indeed.

Here the dedoublement of Baudelaire is inscribed with the very pedagogy of the divine. The veil is the means by which Rouault addresses the crisis of the visible. Veronica's veil is itself an image of Christ, who, as Colossians teaches, is the image of the invisible God. Rouault sometimes simply portrays the veil; at other times, he presents the veil as an image within an image. In the latter instance, we have an image within an image of an image of the image of the invisible God. Rouault seems here to invite, almost to demand, an indefinite extension of images. He gives us a print, which is itself an image, which contains an image (the veil), which is in turn an image of Veronica's veil, which is the original image of Christ, who is himself the image of the invisible God. And yet the multiplication results not in the dissolution of meaning by proliferation, an endless regress of traces, but in a compression and reordering of meaning. The multiplication of references is a decidedly postmodern mechanism that Rouault embraces with astonishing enthusiasm. Even more remarkable is the effect, an unraveling of the postmodern undoing of signification and significance. Rouault's dedoublement of postmodernism supplies a profound response to the crisis of the visible.

Whether or not they are aware of it, contemporary artists operate in the context of the threat of modern nihilism, which obscures not only the divine but also the human presence. The artist is dependent on external matter and on the surrounding culture and cannot abstract the work of art from time and place, from the conditions of human life in the here and now. If modernity means any one thing, it means or involves a break from antecedent traditions and a fracturing of the sources of communal and artistic life. As we shall see more clearly below, that has interesting consequences for the artist's relationship to any ongoing tradition.

Just as Christ meets Veronica along the way, so we can encounter Veronica along any path and at any time. Rouault has crafted in the *Miserere* a modern series of icons, which "always show a gaze belonging to a human face." The exchange of gazes crosses the visible and opens up a "face-to-face relation," in which "two invisible gazes" cross themselves "through the visible witness of their bodies."[25] The true image of God and the human person provides self-knowledge, a proper ordering of our passions, and a liturgical reintegration of the individual wanderer into the body of Christ. The *Miserere* may accurately be termed a "prayer book of hope," but whatever theological aims it achieves, it does so through a lengthy and circuitous interplay of secular and sacred images.[26]

ROUAULT'S PASCALIAN PARADOXES

Rouault was a remarkably productive artist over many decades. While there is much stylistic variation, there is a remarkably consistent focus on certain social types. As Kang convincingly argues, Rouault concentrates on a "limited number of social types [prostitutes, judges, and clowns] whom he constantly depicted throughout his life." In her book, *Rouault in Perspective*, she insists that Rouault's "iconography" requires "an interpretive effort on the part of the viewer," who is invited to trace the types as they appear in different contexts.[27] After an initial period in which Rouault painted traditional religious scenes in the style of Rembrandt, he immerses himself in the contemporary world. The pictorial result is violent and jarring.

Rouault's prostitutes are usually completely nude; but there is little that is erotic about them. They are large, bulky women, with disheveled hair and worn faces. In their composition, one can detect the influence of the sculpture-like forms of Cézanne. Rouault underscores the sheer physicality of the prostitutes; their suffering is manifest in and through their bodies. Their gaze is not in the direction of the viewer, much less is it enticing. They look absently toward the horizon or vacantly into a mirror.

The penchant for distorted and apparently debased figures led some to see in his painting an obsession with human degradation. A fellow Catholic and an influential novelist, Léon Bloy, faulted Rouault for imagining "the most atrocious and avenging caricatures" and for being "attracted exclusively by the ugly."[28] What are we to make of these accusations?

These paintings have been the subject of a great debate. Maritain defends Rouault against Bloy's charge; evil, he urges, must be depicted as ugly. Rouault's prostitutes bear in their bodies the effects of original sin. At times, Rouault seems to point his viewers in this very direction; for example, when he titles one of his paintings of a prostitute, *Fallen Eve*. For the most part, however, he refrains from such commentary. As he describes his own condition at the time of the composition of these works, he seems to have been overcome by an obsession with the disorder in the world immediately around him in Paris. He began to paint with a kind of fury, creating on canvas the images that had entered his soul and taken possession of his imagination.

Discounting Maritain's interpretation, Mary Roberts rejects the notion that the distortion and ugliness of Rouault's prostitutes constitute moral judgments of sin. She cites Rouault's claim that "art is infinitely above morality."[29] For her, Rouault is not judging the prostitutes but depicting the spiritual damage, the erosion of self-esteem, inflicted by the moral judgment of society. Maritain anticipates Roberts's point when he calls Rouault's prostitutes "sacrificial victims," the "ransom of a bourgeois society."[30] Both agree that Rouault's prostitutes have little in common with the ironic self-presentation of Manet's *Olympia*. As if to underscore the contrast, Rouault painted an "Olympia" of his own, whose self-presentation and physical appearance is much closer to Manet's famous image than it is to the rest of his own paintings of prostitutes. The latter are melancholy and never display themselves alluringly to the viewer. Rouault's physically malformed and spiritually desolate street prostitutes lack the individuality of the figures of Manet or Toulouse-Lautrec. There is a certain inconsistency in Roberts's account; she seems not to realize that her interpretation simply substitutes one kind of moral interpretation for another. On that score, Roberts is right to see in Rouault's prostitutes a critique of the culture of commodification, the culture of seeing and being seen.[31]

Courthion suggests that the distortions and deformities in Rouault's works are akin to those in medieval cathedrals. But this is not quite right.

In these early paintings, the deformities are not part of some larger aesthetic whole, as is the case with the gargoyles on the cathedrals. The same is true of Rouault's depiction of clowns and judges. They stand alone as riveting individualized portraits of character types. If the types are not included within a larger cycle of images, they nonetheless provide insight into the human condition. The clowns with their distorted features, rueful countenances, and stark contrasting color do not entertain, much less prompt laughter. They haunt the viewer. Meanwhile, the judges, portrayed in formal legal settings with garments and chambers that reflect their claims to dignity and authority, often have bloated physiques, sneering expressions, and supercilious attitudes. Infinite sadness and the gap between the surface presentation of the self and its inner truth are prominent themes in Rouault's early subjects.

We would be wrong to adopt a stance of disengaged judgment of these characters. Rouault sees himself, indeed all humans, in the clowns' barely concealed sorrow. Even in his most degraded characters, Rouault seeks the soul, not merely the body. In his *Souvenirs intimes*, he writes, "We are fallen, it is true, but my clowns are really only dispossessed kings; their laugh is familiar to me; it reaches the realm of a million stifled sobs."[32] "Dispossessed kings" is precisely the language Pascal deploys to describe the paradoxical combination of wretchedness and greatness characteristic of the human condition. Wretchedness is proof of greatness, since it arises from a realization of a lack, an absence, a disorder, that is not proper to us. The horror of the prostitutes and the sorrow of the clowns are tinged with mournful regret. Judgment gives way to pity. In an astute commentary, Jean Grenier writes, "His judges however monstrous make us think of real justice. His prostitutes in their disgrace recall both degraded and real love, while his sad, bewildered clowns evoke by contrast innocent children at play."[33] This is a quintessentially Pascalian approach to the human condition. Rouault's allusion to Pascal's paradoxical account of the human condition counts against the notion that he was wallowing in degradation or asserting that human beings are but calculating beasts.[34] Rouault accentuates the wretchedness of the human condition, but, as Pascal argues, the very judgment that something or someone is wretched presupposes a sense of the greatness or dignity that has been lost.

The abiding sense that something has gone awry is a leitmotif of the poetry and prose of Baudelaire, whose influence on both Maritain and Rouault is profound. Schloesser goes so far as to say that Maritain reads Aquinas through the lens of Baudelaire. In *Creative Intuition*, Maritain states that it is to Baudelaire that "modern art owes its having become aware of the theological quality and tyrannical spirituality of beauty." He then quotes at length a passage from Poe that Baudelaire himself had quoted. "By and through" the arts, "the soul divines what splendors shine behind the tomb." When beauty incites tears, "such tears are not the sign of an excess of joy, they are rather a witness to an irritated melancholy, an exigency of nerves, a nature exiled in the imperfect which would possess immediately, on this very earth, a paradise revealed."[35] Toward the end of the book, in a section devoted to Dante, Maritain notes that Baudelaire perceived "what kind of hell is our modern universe." He may not have been able to show forth a path toward transcendence, but to identify something as hell is to recognize disorder and implicitly at least to glimpse the possibility of order.[36]

To make depravity the whole picture is to grasp only one part of our duality, to exaggerate our wretchedness and to neglect entirely our greatness. Without a residue of greatness, we could not recognize our condition as wretched. Pascal makes this point explicitly: "All these examples of wretchedness prove his greatness. It is the wretchedness of a dispossessed king" (#116). It might seem that Rouault focuses almost exclusively on the wretchedness and ignores human greatness. But this would be to misunderstand both Pascal and Rouault. For Pascal, greatness arises from a recognition of loss, of disorder, and of deprivation. Greatness is thus elusive; we cannot by our own efforts restore it. Yet it is the very reason we call something wretched. As Pascal observes, no one objects to having two eyes rather than three, but those who lose one can be inconsolable. Thus the sorrow and horror that we experience in the face of Rouault's paintings is precisely a recognition of a vanished greatness or lost dignity that is characteristic of the human condition. As Pascal writes, "Man must not be allowed to believe that he is equal either to animals or to angels, nor to be unaware of either, but he must know both" (#121).

Contemplation of the human condition inspires, not dispassionate calm, but distress and confusion. Pascal writes: "What sort of freak then is man! How novel, how monstrous, how chaotic, how paradoxical, how prodigious! Judge of all things, feeble earthworm, repository of truth, sink of doubt and error, glory and refuse of the universe!" (#131). Rouault's penchant for the grotesque and the tragic rests on Pascalian insights about human nature. What accounts, not just for our failure to achieve happiness, but for our self-destructive pursuit of it? What explains the strange and horrifying way in which nature can turn against itself and its own good? Our ignorance is dual. We are often enough ignorant of the good, but a more profound ignorance is evident in our ignorance of our own ignorance. Our lack of self-knowledge supplies the motivation for the poetic strategy of Baudelaire, the dedoublement, the aim of which is to decenter and astonish the audience. In a world permeated by visual idolatry, Rouault's whores, judges, and clowns are modern Baudelairian icons, taunting self-images that turn back upon the viewer.

In a much-discussed plate from the *Miserere*, Rouault turns to the line from Virgil's *Aeneid* where Aeneas, in the underground, encounters images of the fall of Troy. He sadly exclaims, "Sunt lacrimae rerum et mentem mortalia tangunt" (There are tears of things and mortal matters touch the mind and heart). What unites Aeneas with the marginalized characters populating Rouault's works is the experience of devastating loss. The plate also implicates the viewer. Aeneas sees in the painting before him images of his own history and thus grieves at the loss. So too should viewers of the *Miserere* see the history of their time and thus be led to mourn the vanishing of an array of goods. Rouault never makes obvious the connections between our lives and the lives of others; nor does he force conclusions on viewers.

Because the *Miserere* has as its centerpiece the desecrated image of the invisible God in the passion of Christ, Rouault does not leave his viewers to wrestle hopelessly with their guilt and despair. As Desmond puts it in words that describe quite accurately Rouault's portrayal of the suffering servant:

> This abandon is the redeemed release of agapeic being at the furthest limit of the evil. God is given over to desecration: not an insulted warlord requiring blood ransom; an agapeic servant revealing God as there in the instance of death itself, and not outside, but within this instance with the most intimate immanence. This intimate immanence is nothing other than generosity transcending for the other as other, for its good as the gift of life itself. Creative coming to be recreates the promise of becoming.[37]

This is the logic of the "agapeic servant who consents to the good by being willing to be as nothing."[38]

NATURE, PERSON, AND *SACRAMENTUM MUNDI*

Maritain argues that the first and chief victim of modern art's commitment to recasting the visible fabric of things is the human figure, the natural sacrament.[39] One of the distinguishing features of the art of Rouault (as of the other leading religious artist of the twentieth century, Chagall) has to do with an ongoing focus on the human figure. Rouault was aware that his attention to the human face distinguished him among contemporary artists.[40] Throughout his entire career, the human figure remains an object of study. But, as discussed above, Rouault's portrayal of the human form is not from the genre of classical portraiture. Especially early on, his focus is on the degradation of the human form—through maltreatment by others and particularly through the self-inflicted ugliness of the vices of pride, greed, and vanity. Human beings are wolves not just to one another but also to themselves.

From the early description of human degradation, Rouault moves on to focus on the face of Christ, especially Christ as bearing the image of sinful man in his passion and crucifixion. In the final period, the human face reappears, full of holiness and splendid pity for fallen mankind. As I have noted, Rouault portrays human figures without distinctive features; at times the human form itself is barely recognizable. Yet he is certainly not portraying abstract types. Avoiding modern art's oblivion of the human figure does not entail a bland, photographic naturalism.

In his defense of certain strains of modern art against its traditionalist detractors, Maritain devotes a great deal of attention to the question of imitation, which is central to the classical understanding of art. As scholars have noted, Maritain's rejection of the mimetic theory of art has to do with the thoroughgoing materialism of modern accounts of mimesis.[41] Maritain appeals to the scholastic dictum that art imitates nature "in its operation," not in reproducing its surface appearances. Moreover, in the *Poetics*, the very work in which Aristotle advances the notion that tragedy is an imitation, Aristotle himself argues that what distinguishes poetry from history is that the former is about possibility, not about a simple reiteration of what has happened. The possible of course is something latent within the world as given to us, but the gift and discipline of the artist is to bring it to light: "What is required is not that the representation exactly conform to a given reality, but that through the material elements of the beauty of the work there truly pass, sovereign and whole, the radiance of a form."[42] The delight that human beings take in imitation is not a delight in the material reproduction of what is already given in immediate experience. Poets have what Aristotle calls a mastery of metaphor; they apprehend the likenesses between unlike things. The gift is not a capacity for mere reproduction. Instead, the artist grasps what others do not, indeed what is not immediately given. Still, what the artist apprehends is something intelligible and communicable. The "formal element of imitation" is "the expression or manifestation, in a work suitably proportioned, of some secret principle of intelligibility which shines forth."[43] Maritain points to an artist such as El Greco, who, in his distortion of the natural look of the human figure, grasps "something more human than human appearances."[44]

Rouault's presentation of the human form, particularly the face, aspires to this deeper realism, as do his late landscape paintings. One strain of Rouault's mature art focuses on the presentation of the human form with lavish attention to the details of the human face, particularly faces that embody holiness and joy, as in the late painting of Veronica (figure 6.3). Another strain occurs in his landscapes, in which the distinctive features of the human body merge with the shapes in the immediate pictorial environment. Put slightly differently, in the latter case, the human body takes on the shapes and contours of the natural objects in its vicinity. Courthion astutely observes that in the late landscapes the "spiritual tension communicated to the paint itself is no longer derived from the story, or from the action of the characters, but from the interrelationships of proportions, planes and colors." In accord with this new style of Rouault, the human figure is inscribed within a pattern of proportions, planes, and colors. This is perhaps the most artistically innovative way in which Rouault captures the "cosmic affinity between man and his natural surroundings," the inseparability of natural and human ecology.[45]

So prominent are the landscapes in his later career that, as Kang notes, they come to displace the human figure as the primary medium through which Rouault expresses his artistic vision.[46] His color palette during this time most nearly resembles Fauvism, as "gloomy scenes" give way to settings of "vibrant light."[47] As impressive as the late landscapes are, it is important to note that landscapes are common throughout Rouault's entire painting career. We have already noted their presence in his great work, the *Miserere*.[48] Other landscapes appear as minimalist drawings,

Figure 6.3. Véronique. Veronica. 1945. Rouault, Georges (1871–1958). CNAC/MNAM, Dist. RMN-Grand Palais / Art Resource, NY.

with barren lands and trees that provide a strong, narrow vertical focus to the canvas. Attention to vertical shapes is present in the Cezanne-influenced "Bathers" (1910). There are other, more lush and colorful early landscapes such as the winter scene in *Christmas Landscape* (1920).

Later in his career, Rouault seems to have heeded the counsel of his friend Andre Suares, who urged him to pursue more vigorously the painting of religious landscapes: "you can achieve something not done for a long time since Rembrandt: religious landscape ... the mystic landscape."[49] The result is something quite distinctive in the history of painting. The integration of persons and buildings into nature—with shapes mirroring one another, edges bleeding into one another, and colors complementing one another—underscores the unified whole that is created nature. Rouault supplies a visual counter to anthropocentrism and biocentrism, even as he overcomes the Romantic dilemma of the problematic status of human persons in the cosmos. He recovers nature, of which the human person is a part, as a creative manifestation of divine splendor.

In the late paintings, beauty overwhelms the senses and invites the imagination into the "infinite openness of the riches of being."[50] Although we have need of honest depictions of the spiritual and physical hazards of modern life, the soul cannot feed only on images of desolation. The strain of modern art that dismisses the beautiful itself as always implicated in structures of deception and manipulation is "dangerous." Maritain calls this an "unholy mortification." The human person, he writes, cannot live without delight in beauty.[51] Rouault's late landscapes are remarkably serene even as they entice the viewer into a beauty that envelops perception and desire. He achieves varied kinds of harmony in these works: harmony of human persons with nature and of the artistic object with the perception of the viewer. But he does so while also communicating a transcendent or supernatural source of the beauty—the world as sacrament (*sacramentum mundi*).

We should cite in particular *Stella Vespertina*'s first image, *De Profundis*, which features two individuals draped in black and purple, mourning and comforting one another in front of a grave. Courthion rightly praises the "powerful structural lines—verticals and horizontals crossed by diagonals" that "create a curiously impressive, timeless atmosphere."[52] The sun shines brightly over the scene of apparent grief. The note of death and mourning underscores that, even for the late Rouault, serenity is not achieved by circumventing tragedy.

Another print from *Stella Vespertina*, *Crepuscule*, is a marvelous image of twilight, dominated by dark greens and blues with sharp colorations of red, orange, and yellow. Three figures stand together in the foreground. Behind them are multiple paths leading to a home and off into the horizon. The mood is warm and calm; nature seems at once dark and light, as if sunset were the time of day when the richness of natural hues is most evident. The setting sun is still distinct and clear; if the sky is dark, it is nonetheless translucent and richly colored. In these late works, the paint is a kind of "congealed lava," in which "luminous tones . . . crackle among dark, rugged impastos. . . . The light does not come from without, does not fall upon the forms, but emerges from the canvas itself."[53]

A similar if more subdued version of this strategy is at work already in the *Miserere*, particularly in the role of landscapes in that series. While Rouault focuses mainly on the human image in *Miserere*, landscapes are not entirely absent. They appear in at least a dozen of the prints. In plates 9 and 10 ("at times the road is beautiful" and "in the old district of longsuffering"), the dearth of natural vitality in the background contrasts with the scenes of human warmth in the foreground, while in the third ("tomorrow will be beautiful said the shipwrecked man") the violent disorder in nature underscores the futility of human hope in the accompanying text. In others, for example, in plates 24 ("winter, leper of the earth") and 26 ("in the land of thirst and fear"), the landscape features dark, oppressive clouds. In plates 37 ("*homo homini lupus*") and 54 ("arise, you dead"), the foreground features upright skeletal human figures. In the former the landscape is littered with human skulls, while in the latter skeletal figures look to be arising, imitating and following the one fully erect figure. There are also images of crosses, perhaps denoting graves, dotting the horizon. Both of these make reference to war. In fact, the saying, "Arise, you dead," was a chilling phrase used to encourage men to enter the front lines of battle. In one of the most striking landscapes (plate 44, "my sweet country, where are you?"), barely perceptible human figures lay supine in the foreground. A few buildings stand on a hillside void of vegetation. There is more light in this image than in most of the *Miserere* prints, but here it serves to highlight the smoke, whose source is unclear, that pollutes the entire environment.

As noted above, the series has a Christocentric structure. Approximately one-fourth of the plates in the *Miserere* series contain images of Christ; in these, the background landscapes are typically distant and minute.

Yet two landscapes promise transformation. In the third to the last print (56), just before the final images of Christ as suffering servant, there is an image of Mary holding the Christ child. The text for this image is, "In these dark times of vainglory and unbelief, our Lady of the Ends of the Earth remains vigilant." Vigilance here is a matter of loving devotion, not of strenuous, anxious effort. The image comes perhaps the closest of any in the series to the look of a traditional religious icon. Mary occupies the center of the scene, with her head slightly tilted toward the infant Christ, whose own body, cradled in Mary's arms, makes a circular image with Mary's head. Emanating from that central circle, light illuminates the sky and the horizon. Mary's vigilance enlightens and blesses the human and natural world.

The most important landscape occurs in the middle of the series, plate 29, "Sing Matins, a New Day Is Born." Indeed, this is the only true landscape in the sense that it contains no buildings or human figures. The contrasting use of dark and light, which permeates the *Miserere* series, is more pronounced and more moving here than in any of the other images. A radiant, clear sun shines in the darkness and begins to illuminate the sky and the earth. Because there are 58 plates, no one plate can be called the center. Instead, plates 29 and 30 jointly occupy that spot. Plate 30 ("We who were baptized into Jesus Christ, were baptized into his death") depicts the baptism of the Lord with the Spirit in the form of a dove descending above Christ's head. The transformation wrought in baptism, an immersion in the waters of death and rebirth, is anticipated in the previous print (29), which marks the liturgical celebration of the new dawn, the joyous reaffirmation of creation through the descending grace of Christ.

In the later landscapes, the sacramental vision is often eucharistic. The sun often occupies a central and illuminating position, with its shape resembling the physical form of the monstrance containing the Sacred Host in the Catholic practice of eucharistic adoration.[54] One need not have liturgical forms in mind to appreciate these landscapes. As Bernard Dorival notes, the "openness of the sky" and the activity of illumination from above give both a sense of transcendence and an emphasis on the participation of human figures in an enveloping reality.[55]

Rouault avoids pantheism by displaying nature as a glorious revelation of the hidden God. In fact, it would be more accurate to say that he

Figure 6.4. Autumn (Nazareth). 1948. Rouault, Georges (1871–1958). Scala / Art Resource, NY.

resolves the place of persons in nature not simply by reinserting them into nature, but by a construal of nature itself as sacramental sign. The resolution deepens the sense of mystery. Of the many examples of these late landscapes, *Autumn* or *Nazareth*, from 1948, stands out (figure 6.4).

The sense of a restoration of harmony among human persons, the environment (both natural and built), and the divine permeates *Autumn* or *Nazareth*, one of the first twentieth-century works to be accepted by the Vatican Museum, where it remains on display. The color scheme—deep blues, strong vertical browns, soft yellows, and fiery orange—is stunning. As is often the case, the sun acts as a source of light and warmth. The barren trees divide up the canvas but in a way that brings unity and concord rather than separation or opposition. Buildings, scaled to fit the human and natural environment, populate the horizon. Smaller human figures, which occupy the center, lack detailed definition. In this they reflect the natural objects that surround them. Indeed, the human figures are enveloped by and seem to take on the posture of the trees. The human figures are shadowy, "hardly distinguishable from" their "surroundings."[56] Near the very center of the painting is a figure in white, with a slight halo, not a white halo but a yellow halo that mirrors in hue the sun. That figure appears to be Christ. He occupies the center not in a commanding but in a humble way. The human figures, including Christ, are at the center, but their size and the way their posture mirrors that of nature indicates that they are also a part of the natural whole, as are the buildings, the results of human techne. Here is truly a common home, a home transfigured by the grace of beauty and the suggestion of a transcendent presence, manifest in the radiance of the entire image.

Related strategies are on display in the remarkable series of works in the *Stella Vespertina* (1947). In the preface to that work, Rouault writes, "He who has once apprehended the absolute can see its evidences throughout the relative, and of all things can make a sign."[57] In *Ransoming the Time*, Maritain writes, "The birth of the idea and hence of the intellectual life in us seems to be bound up with the discovery and the value of the meaning of the sign."[58] The humble task of Veronica informs Rouault's artistic mission to recover the meaning of the sign and to restore the covenant between sign and signified. This is especially true of the human face, the image nearly banished from twentieth-century art. Rouault transforms the quest for meaning into a search "to discern the divine presence in humanity."[59] He sets his art against the dominant, technocratic tendencies of the age: "In this mechanical age would not art seem to be a miracle? at times well-nigh a miracle.... True beauty remains hidden; it has always been thus."[60] By setting lowly human beings against the background of a "brilliant biblical landscape," Rouault shows that outcasts experience the "glorious fruit of spiritual reality ... while they endure the hardships of daily life."[61]

As Courtion notes, although Rouault was never a member of the Fauves, the scenes in *Stella Vespertina* come the closest to adopting their stylistic tendencies.[62] The prints "exhibit an intensity and a resonance with respect to color pushed to their extremes, without ever seeming strained."[63] The Thomistic notion of splendor (*claritas*) is an apt description of the beauty of many of Rouault's sacred landscapes. Thomas Aquinas speaks of beauty's radiance, an influx or overflow of beauty, especially in light and color, in which the experiencing subject finds herself immersed. If many of the late paintings dwarf and humble persons, they also elevate and satisfy our longings. Rouault's art brings something new into being and helps us see what we otherwise would not.

EXPRESSIVISM AND THE PROBLEM OF TRADITION

Rouault manages to incorporate the past in ways that allow him to speak to the present moment. He thus solves in his work the problem of generativity, to which Nietzsche devotes much attention in his early work *On the Advantage and Disadvantage of History for Life*, a work composed "against the age," in the hope of having an impact on the age.[64] In Nietzsche's time, he worried that his age had become weighted down by history (for our own time, we might substitute information), held back from creative renewal, and deprived of living fully in the present. Modern culture is no real culture but only "knowledge of culture."[65] Hyperconsciousness of the past can paralyze creative instincts in the present.[66] The modern aspiration to total transparency and complete awareness ignores the fact that some of our knowledge is always tacit, unarticulated. At any moment, we can be aware of only a part of our experience.

The remedy is to balance the historical with the unhistorical, remembering with forgetting.[67] Historical knowledge ought to inform and nourish life rather than substitute for it. The more of the past one aspires to take in, the deeper one's roots must be. Nietzsche deploys, in addition to the image of soil, the image of a horizon, a more or less definitive context in which generativity can flourish. The attempt to think and live within an "infinite horizon" engenders a retreat to the self, to the isolated ego, where cleverness or jaded irony is the highest virtue.

Nietzsche lays out three types of history: monumental, antiquarian, and critical. Monumental history encourages those in the present to believe great deeds are possible because they have occurred at least once in the past. But the danger here is that we become so taken with comparisons between present and past greatness that we develop misleading analogies and distort large portions of the past. Antiquarian history conserves what is of value in the past, but too great a commitment to preservation "mummifies the present."[68] The weakness of both these modes of historical knowing underscores the importance of the third type of history, critical history, which supplies the strength to "shatter" the past. But critical history for its own sake and in isolation from the other types of history cannot be generative.

Nietzsche's own text would seem to involve all three types of history. It is most obviously a kind of critical metahistory that seeks to liberate contemporaries from the stultifying excesses of encyclopedic knowledge. It shares much with the Enlightenment genre of critique, but it is a critique on behalf of life. It seeks not so much liberation from the past as a proper relationship to it and thus circumvents both radical progressive liberation and Romantic nostalgia. In his return to the Greeks and in his ambition for some sort of grand renewal of civilization, Nietzsche is also engaging in forms of monumental and antiquarian history.

Nietzsche insists that we need all three modes of history, with the virtues of each correcting the vices of the others. But historical consciousness alone is insufficient. In what might seem an unusual claim for Nietzsche, he argues that a flourishing culture needs a quite different sense, that of the "superhistorical," an orientation to what is "eternal and stable." Transcending the mere flow of time, the superhistorical is the realm of art and religion rather than historical science.[69] It involves "unconditional love" and "faith in something perfect and righteous."[70] Every type of faith operates within a horizon, a veil, which protects and demands reverence.[71]

As I noted in my discussion of another early work of Nietzsche, *The Birth of Tragedy*, Nietzsche avoids both progressivism and Romanticism. One of the dilemmas inherited from the contest between the two has to do with tradition. On the one hand, in its reaction against the progressive rationalism of the Enlightenment, Romanticism often appeals to tradition, to premodern societies characterized by a greater sense of organic unity. On the other hand, Romantics exalt individual creativity or authenticity in a way that encourages flight from, or dismissal of, the past. Post-Enlightenment, post-Romantic art has thus an inescapably complicated relationship to tradition. Connection to antecedent traditions is broken; reestablishing it is not a matter of simply asserting fidelity to it. Rouault's earliest works illustrate his devotion to the old masters, especially Rembrandt. As an apprentice to Moreau, his painting continues to be deeply traditional. Yet, in the wake of the death of his mentor, Rouault undergoes a spiritual crisis that was ultimately purifying: "I was only thirty when Moreau died. Then there was a desert to cross and painting: an oasis or a mirage? Well, knowing that I knew nothing—having certainly learned quite a bit ... but considering that I perhaps did not know the essential thing, which is to strip oneself, is the grace accorded us after having learned so much."[72] One might say that Rouault engages in a kind of critical engagement of history, both the history of painting and history in the form of autobiography, the history of his own artistic and spiritual development. He "shatters" his inheritance and enters into a more direct encounter with his own age, with the ambient cultural conditions and the new techniques of painting. Yet he eventually would bring together the old and the new in a remarkably personal synthesis.

Rouault was acutely aware that we cannot settle for monumental, antiquarian, or critical history. He observes in *Stella Vespertina*, "One does not enter into tradition the way one climbs aboard a city bus. More hidden affinities are necessary."[73] As T. S. Eliot puts it in his influential essay "Tradition and the Individual Talent," the artist must have a sense not only of the "pastness of the past but also of its presence."[74] Atrophied repetition is not to be confused with a living tradition. Instead, it is mere nostalgia, a vague aspiration to return to what once was, or at least to an image we now have of what was. Such banal sentimentality is a powerful advertising tool.[75] With the lines of tradition broken and with the legitimate, although always potentially excessive, emphasis on novelty in art, tradition becomes a very complicated affair. As Cocteau puts it, "Tradition appears at every epoch under a different disguise, but the public does not recognize it easily and never discovers it underneath its masks."[76]

Without resolving them, Rouault embodies the existing tensions regarding tradition in late modernity. Anticipating in certain respects a thesis of T. S. Eliot, Rouault urges that the artist "should disappear behind his work." He sometimes claims that he would prefer to leave his works unsigned and admits his kinship with the anonymous craftsmen of the medieval cathedrals. And yet he concedes that it is impossible to "re-create" the art of the cathedral or even of the conditions that made such anonymous craftsmanship the norm.[77] In ways similar to Nietzsche, he worries about an inordinate devotion to the past; "just as we don't wear the same clothes as our ancestors," so too it would be absurd for us slavishly to imitate their artistic styles. Rouault seems well aware of the advantages and disadvantages of artistic history for the life of contemporary art. Antiquarian history exalts preservation of the past to such a degree that it "mummifies the present."[78] A critical approach to inherited traditions can, if taken to an extreme, deprive the artist of the freedom to build in the present.

But building is not always possible or at least not always equally possible. Maritain reflects on the conditions of art that are beyond the control of the artist in a section of *Creative Intuition* devoted to Dante. He cites

T. S. Eliot's remark that "many people who enjoy Dante enjoy Baudelaire."[79] Maritain proceeds to offer a comparison of the two that stresses the influence of the preexisting and enveloping culture on the artist. He refers to Dante's good fortune:

> Dante's luck was to have all the *presences*, the existential certitudes which are the natural soil of poetry, integrated with absolute firmness in a consistent universe of thought rooted in reason and faith — and radiant to his emotion in the blissful innocence of the intellect. Never has creative innocence enjoyed so favorable a climate and such exceptional assistance. A whole cosmos could pass through the creative night of his poetic intuition.[80]

By contrast, Baudelaire (and one might add, Rouault) was not so fortunate. Of Baudelaire, Maritain writes, "He was wounded and destroyed by his time, as Dante was served by his. He waged within himself a hopeless spiritual war against his time, as Dante assumed his in exultation. He revealed the eternal and supernatural in man in man's perversity as Dante revealed it in God's justice and mercy." Without any of Dante's ensconcing certitudes, he maintains a "sense of the reality of sin and of the transcendent destiny of the soul." Maritain disputes the claim that "in the adjustment of the natural to the spiritual, ... Baudelaire is a bungler compared with Dante."[81] He counters that Baudelaire, "in the place where he was, and from which he looked at things, was precisely required by poetry not to perceive the adjustment, but to feel the split and derangement."[82]

Like Baudelaire, Rouault continues to listen to the "unquiet" matters that secularizing modernity wants to silence. Although his art never achieves the sovereign grandeur of Dante's, he comes closer than Baudelaire to healing the rift in the modern soul, at least part of which has to do with our vain anthropocentrism. Accusing his viewers, Rouault castigates pride and vanity — a strategy particularly prominent in the *Miserere*. The human face eventually emerges not as an object of scorn but as an icon, an object of beauty. Finally in the late landscapes, Rouault's painting might be said to "refuse any final rivalry between humanity and creation, between anthropocentrism and ecocentrism."[83] But that is to put things far too negatively and woefully to underestimate the achievement of these works; for they offer a cosmos, in which the human, the natural, and the constructed are "resplendently transfigured" through the grace of art, reflecting in its humble way the grace of God.

Standing outside the mainstream, Rouault reappropriates traditions neglected, in some cases disdained, by the dominant trends in art. The reappropriation and extension of tradition allow for a recovery of what has been lost and for envisioning something new in the tradition, for the realization of unanticipated possibilities latent within it. Of course, one of the goals of the builders of the cathedrals, whom Rouault admired, was to build works of art that would stand the test of time. Remaining in contact with vital traditions of art can help restore art to its lofty aspirations. In such a context, the artist can aspire, as Eliot writes in "Ash Wednesday," to "redeem the time, redeem the unread vision in the higher dream."[84]

SEVEN

Culture Care, Generativity, and the Calling of the Artist

The aspiration to read the unread vision in the higher dream is rare in contemporary art; indeed, the very ambition is often held in contempt. In one of his occasional essays, Makoto Fujimura describes his experience of viewing the art of Fra Angelico at an exhibition at the Metropolitan Museum in New York. Contemplating beauty that "was too much to behold," he staggered, "almost feeling ashamed to be in the presence of such greatness."[1] Retreating from the exhibition to gain perspective, he posed for himself the "500-year question," the question why in contemporary culture we no longer aspire to create art that will last for centuries. The question moves in a diametrically opposed direction to that sense of time and art encapsulated in Warhol's proclamations of the democratization of fame, lasting fifteen minutes. Fujimura laments that contemporary art lacks roots in the past and ambitions for shaping the future.

He embraces Maritain's account of creative intuition. Like many artists, he finds that Maritain's description of the creative process resonates with his own experience as an artist. Like Maritain, Fujimura is attentive to the way in which cultural conditions shape the possibilities of art in a given time and place. He goes further than Maritain, however, in underscoring the role of art and the artist in cultivating cultural renewal. His accent on culture care and generativity links his concerns directly with those central to the project of *LS*. In Fra Angelico's art, he detects a hope that is "not only the hope of an individual genius, but also of patronage, of society and the church." The challenges that Fra Angelico's art puts forward to artists today are, "Would we see another Renaissance in the days to come? Would we have another chance to steward our culture, without losing our identity and faith in the process?"[2] Fujimura highlights the role of the ambient culture in fostering art, nurturing grand aspirations for artists, and providing public occasions for the creation and appreciation of art. While he certainly upholds a notion of artistic freedom compatible with that of Maritain, he repudiates dichotomies between the fine arts and other activities of making and generating.

In this final chapter, I focus on the art of Makoto Fujimura. His vision of culture care is of interest not only because it echoes *LS* but also because it is informed by the work of Jacques Maritain and Georges Rouault. Moreover, his painting directly addresses the crisis of twentieth-century art, especially in its abstractionist mode. His work can guide us in reflecting on questions about abstraction. What are we to make of so-called abstract art? Is this merely an attempt to escape from the human and natural world? Is it a dead end for art? Can it foster ecological virtues? Can it tap into neglected elements in traditional art to revive, in a contemporary key, the grand ambitions of art? I begin with a consideration of the way in which Fujimura's notion of culture care broadens the implications of art and making beyond that of the fine arts to the entirety of human making. Such a broadening is necessary if something like the ecological vision of *LS* is to be realized. Then I turn to Fujimura's art. Since there is a special affinity between his work and that of Mark Rothko, I briefly consider Rothko's art as a prelude to that of Fujimura.

CONSERVATION AND GENERATIVITY

Fujimura defends a version of the account of human making that we have found in numerous Catholic thinkers, not least in the writings of the current pope. It is a mark of human dignity, an essential part of our human vocation, that we should cultivate the earth and make it fruitful. Maritain quotes John of St. Thomas: "To be fertile, to manifest that which one possess within oneself, is a great perfection." The artist "continues God's creative act."[3] Labor, Francis writes, is meant to be fruitful (124). We are not merely recipients of the results of God's creative activity; we are active participants in God's creative action (131). I have already noted Francis's claim that it is a mark of the "nobility of the human vocation" that persons can "participate in God's creative action" (131).

To articulate the full Catholic ecological vision involves overcoming a host of dichotomies: between person and nature; reason and passion; the beautiful and the sublime; the natural world and the human, built environment; and tradition and innovation. As already noted, Fujimura's art intends to undo settled oppositions. He writes, "I encourage people not to segment art into an 'extra' sphere of life and decorations. Why? Because art is everywhere and has already taken root in our lives." The question is not whether we should have art but which kind of art: "This choice is a responsibility of cultural stewardship. Just as we have responsibility for natural resources, so do we have to take stewardship care of our culture."[4] The connection between art and a broader project of culture care involves an implicit questioning of any deep divide between fine arts and useful arts. I have already raised this question with respect to the development of Maritain's own views of the fine arts. What Fujimura invites us to see is that any unbridgeable gulf between the two is antithetical to the renewal of culture. Locating the fulfillment of art in the utterly free acts of the fine arts, as Maritain is sometimes wont to do, risks exposing the rest of culture to thoroughgoing instrumentalization, wherein the motives of profit and narrow utility predominate.

Such an instrumental culture is easily co-opted by technocracy. It feigns moral neutrality, which Fujimura identifies as an enemy of culture care: "If we do not teach our children, and ourselves, that what we imagine, and how we design the world, can make a difference, the culture of cynicism will do that for us."[5] Cynicism generates hopelessness and callous detachment; its highest artistic expression is jaded, purportedly all-knowing irony. Such a culture leaves youth to their own devices, as it has nothing substantive to offer by way of an alternative to the consumer model of preferential choice, which has infiltrated the dominant ideologies of our time.

ROTHKO'S COLOR FIELD PAINTINGS AS NIETZSCHEAN DRAMAS

The sense of civilization in decline has haunted many twentieth-century artists and philosophers. Among the many analyses of, and remedies for, cultural decline, Nietzsche's *Birth of Tragedy* has had a notable impact on the self-understanding of many twentieth-century artists. For Mark Rothko, *Birth* supplies a rich vision of the conditions and ambitions of art. By channeling the chaotic substratum of reality through an Apollonian veneer of order, art makes reality palatable. Like the early Nietzsche, he supposes that the experience of awe in the presence of great art could supply something of what religion once offered. He was famous for the saying that a painting must be a miracle.

There are numerous reasons to consider the work of Rothko, not least is that he seeks to embody a Nietzschean vision in his art. Rothko and Fujimura stand in relationship to one another in a manner similar to that of the stance of Everson to Jeffers. Jeffers and Rothko were both influenced by Nietzsche, while Everson and Fujimura adopt conceptions of art and beauty informed by Christian sources.

Like many artists, Rothko is simultaneously diffident about discussing the nature and significance of his own art and in search of a language that would help him articulate his own artistic process and the products of his work. Like Nietzsche, Rothko believes that traditional religions were myths enabling fragile human psyches to live in a world fundamentally indifferent to human desire and morality. As James Breslin shows in his book on Rothko, tragic art, understood in Nietzschean terms, is for Rothko the only honest art. These are not mere academic matters for Rothko, of whom his first wife observed that he had a "tremendous emotional capacity for despair."[6] He once commented that the "only serious thing is death."[7] In a stark vision of the human condition, he speaks of "the boundless aspirations and terrors, the welter of restlessness, the senselessness, the alterations of hope and despair out of context and out of reason, on which is constructed the shaky security of our ordered life." The contrast between Dionysius and Apollo, already familiar to us from previous chapters, captures Rothko's sense that reality is ultimately unintelligible, grounded in a violence that ordinary human consciousness could not fathom. "Eternal symbols" help individuals grapple with "primitive fears" that arise from the "brutality of the natural world and the insecurity of life."[8] As Rothko puts it, Dionysius possesses the "secret of direct access to the wild terror and suffering and the blind drives and aspirations which lay at the bottom of human existence and which relentlessly assault our ordered lives never thoroughly allayed or initiated by our catalogues and categories."[9] Although he thinks tragic art remains possible, he does not suggest that the modern artist can achieve the reconciliation that the Greeks realized in their own work or that art can revivify culture in the way it once did.

Rothko finds much of modern culture, even in its artistic forms, bankrupt. Language and images are no longer capable of feeding our souls in the way they once did. Here his views echo those of a number of authors whom we have already encountered who see the crisis of modernity as one of dislocation of persons from one another, from nature, and from God. The dislocation manifests itself most pointedly in the severing of the natural link between images and reality or between language and meaning. The decline or absence of creative myths in modern culture is at the root of the dislocation of humanity. In such a situation, one must, as Nietzsche urged, destroy in order to create. The desire to destroy is often attributed to strains of twentieth-century art. So-called abstract art can be seen as the natural termination point of a series of destructions, negations, or subtractions. The human figure and natural objects are deconstructed and then rejected or ignored entirely: the notions of depth and perspective are eliminated; what remains is abstract shapes. In its rebellion against decadence and against external control, it adopts an entirely negative way: freedom from politics, freedom from having to represent the world, and "freedom from . . . the collective ethos of style."[10] As we have seen in the analysis of Maritain, the danger of the autonomous thrust in art is that negation becomes an end in itself. Art ultimately has nothing to say or communicate; it is "walled in."

If we understand abstraction in these terms, we are likely to conceive of abstract art in mainly negative terms, as the reduction of a rich artistic perceptual field to its barest elements. But that would be a misinterpretation, at least of the work of Rothko. Before painting the works in the 1950s for which he is most famous, he experimented with an approach often called multiform. How did he make the move from multiform to what is called abstract or, more accurately, color field paintings?

The turn was decisively influenced and informed by a single work of art, Matisse's *Red Studio*. Soon after it was installed at the Museum of

Modern Art, Rothko spent many hours in front of it. The painting is large, one of those in which Matisse violates nearly every rule of perspective. The eye, led in one direction by an apparent base of a wall, follows that line. Expecting to reach a corner, the eye is brought up short by the sudden dissolution of depth. Objects that from one angle seem attached to a wall, from another angle seem to float freely. The color red dominates the frame and overwhelms the viewer. Rothko observes, "When you looked at that painting, you became that color, you became totally saturated with it."[11] So many of Rothko's own methods and goals in his large color field paintings can be traced to the inspiration of this single Matisse painting. There is another feature of the *Red Studio* that carries over into Rothko's paintings in the immediately ensuing period. The violation of the principles of perspective creates a dynamic and lively interplay between the objects.

The active interaction between fields or objects is important for two reasons. First, it underscores the way in which the transition to color field paintings is not simply a subtraction or negation, but rather a way of presenting objects such that they come to life. In a helpful exposition of an early color field painting, *Number 10, 1950*, Breslin describes its "pictorial space" as having "properties — its colors, shapes, weights, spatial relationships" that "keep shifting, keep *moving.*"[12] In striking contrast to the abstract art of, say, Piet Mondrian, who divides up the canvas, Rothko puts things on it. Second, the interaction is seen by Rothko as dramatic, and thus as a way of fulfilling Nietzsche's mythic prescriptions for tragic art. On this last point, Breslin's comments are astute: Rothko combines freedom with constraint. His paintings create "dramas"; with the shapes as "performers," they stage a *struggle* to be free.[13] The Nietzschean sense of art as re-presenting a struggle or contest between opposed forces is present here in the very manner of juxtaposing color fields. The Nietzschean result is palpable. These paintings "transform the hollowness and despair into transcendent and nurturing beauty. These empty canvases are full."[14]

Given his aims and achievements, Rothko's work is not, I think, vulnerable to the critique leveled by Maritain at surrealism, as the abandonment of reason and form for the sake of nihilistic unreason. Rothko's art is more authentically Nietzschean. First, Rothko's work is not simply about Dionysian chaos; it is about the communication of the Dionysian through the Apollonian. Second, it aims at transformation and splendor, not negation. It empties in order to fill. The aim is a kind of transcendence. Rothko insisted that his interest was "only in expressing basic human emotions—tragedy, ecstasy, doom, and so on." These are fundamentally religious emotions. Rothko observes, "The fact that a lot of people break down and cry when confronted with my pictures shows that I can communicate those basic human emotions.... The people who weep before my pictures are having the same religious experience I had when I painted them. And if you, as you say, are moved only by their color relationship, then you miss the point."[15]

For Jean-Luc Marion, the paintings of Mark Rothko are exemplary. At times, Marion depicts the painter in religious terms, as having special access to resources of a divine origin. The painter is "the porter who filters the unseen's access to the visible" and "grants visibility to the unseen, delivering the unseen from its anterior invisibility, its shapelessness."[16] The painter brings the "unseen to light."[17] In Rothko's work, Marion detects the realization of the completion of the art of painting as supplying access to the "pure seen, reduced phenomenologically to its visibility, without remainder."[18] For Marion, Rothko's paintings are paradigmatic instances of phenomenon, occasions for the examination of pure appearance. He describes Rothko's *No. 7* as establishing a

> fragile peace where the frontiers are sketched less by a common accord than by a miraculous and simultaneous exhaustion of their rival tides, present[ing] a miraculous equilibrium, so supple that it seems at the same time almost indestructible. The canvas distends itself and breathes from the free commerce ... of colored stripes, which remain docile enough to go on their own, without nevertheless being separated.... The canvas no longer rests on a material foundation, but is detached from it.[19]

If Rothko's works do indeed pulverize the world of everyday experience, there is another sense in which these works call out to that world, at least to that part of it capable of vision. The movement and interplay of the various fields remain dormant without an embodied viewer. The paintings invite viewing, as if they need completion by being seen. Rothko expresses the relationship between the work of art and the viewer in eloquent terms, even if his assessment of viewers contains a dose of Nietzschean scorn for the uncouth:

A picture lives by companionship, expanding and quickening in the eyes of the sensitive observer. It dies by the same token. It is therefore a risky and unfeeling act to send it out into the world. How often it must be permanently impaired by the eyes of the vulgar and the cruelty of the impotent who would extend the affliction universally.[20]

LEARNING TO SEE, FEEL, AND SPEAK

For all the talk about companionship in Rothko, there remains a high level of suspicion of the audience, as is evident from the final sentence in the preceding quotation. Some critics see the Nietzschean heritage operating in Rothko's art in simply nihilistic terms. In "Nothingness Made Visible: The Case of Rothko's Paintings," Matali Kosoi suggests that Rothko's paintings re-create a primal experience of anxiety, prompted by the realization of the emptiness of human existence: "In anxiety the entities in the world recede from us and we cannot get hold of them, leaving us with only our own being, which is being-toward death."[21] Even if we have seen reasons to doubt the nihilistic interpretation, Rothko himself remains dubious as to how much art can provide by way of overcoming nihilism. By contrast, Fujimura crafts paintings that are more welcoming, one might say more hospitable, to viewers but not by a return to naive realism or by ignoring the complex modern relationships between artist, art, and audience. The differences stand out amid many similarities. The active interaction among the color fields in Rothko's paintings means that what he presents is not an inert flatness. In the juxtaposition of the fields and in the gaps or edges, rough or smooth, there can emerge a sense of depth. Moreover, the situation of the viewer in relation to the painting involves an experience of depth. Rothko once commented that he preferred large to small paintings because the former encompass the viewer and invite active participation in the drama depicted.

Similarly, Fujimura prefers large-scale compositions, which provide an immersive experience. In a series of paintings that he composed in response to some works of George Rouault, Fujimura creates large-scale paintings, with vibrant color schemes and layers of depth that provide an experience of the luminosity of existence. In the painting titled *Genesis*, for example, the surface is dominated by blues of varying shades, accompanied by segments of black and some small sections of white and faint yellow. Some sections appear to be swirling, while others are more stable. More than in Rothko's paintings, Fujimura's work puts the viewer in a conversation between the artwork and the capacious whole of our natural environment. *Genesis* calls to mind, at one moment, the colors and depths of the ocean and, at another, the deep blue of the sky; and, at yet another, a storm that merges sea and sky. The title might lead one to think of the book of Genesis, particularly the lines, "in the beginning, God created the heavens and the earth" and "the spirit hovered over the abyss." Or one could be led to ponder generativity, the creative process, and the ways form gradually emerges from what Maritain calls creative intuition.

The more one contemplates the painting, the more one feels enveloped by the whole. *Genesis* invites the viewer into an experience of shifting depth, as layers appear on the surface at one moment and then seem to recede in the next. There is no sharp, clearly delineated front and back, yet there is depth and mystery. The color schemes are as vibrant as anything in Rothko's color field paintings but with greater fluidity and richness. In a perceptive essay on Fujimura's work, David Gelernter situates it in relationship to twentieth-century abstraction. He writes:

> Depth of field is a rare quality in abstract art. Abstraction emerged, after all, when the rear plane of the picture-space (like the back wall of a giant aquarium), having moved steadily forward over half-a-century, finally collided with the front plane—leaving a flat field to be decorated rather than a volume to be filled. This gradual squashing of the picture-space was evident in Manet and urged forward by the startling, nose-pressed-to-the-glass immediacy of van Gogh and Cézanne. The cubists were left with staved-in, flattened figures inhabiting the narrowest of gaps, and the conclusion was inevitable. Most abstract paintings are accordingly flat—but Fujimura gives us a surface with a vast space opening behind it.[22]

In another painting in this series, titled *Passion*, there are strong contrasts between rich reds and deep blacks. In some sections, the red is draped over the background with a thick brush, while in others it appears to have been splattered. Of course, red can connote the heat of passion, physical love, and the burning of desire. It can also call to mind purgatorial passion, the blood of sacrifice, and perhaps even the specific passion of Christ, shedding of blood in his torture and crucifixion — a sacrifice that takes violence into itself and thus undoes the chain of reprisal and victimization of the scapegoat mechanism. Viewers can encounter and be moved by Fujimura's art without having any religious views whatsoever. Of course, viewers might ponder whether the deeper mysteries of things indicate an infinite source of beauty. I say "might." Art is not apologetics; it is not argument. Its method is surprise, suggestion, and splendor.

For Fujimura, as for Everson, there is an alternative to the Dionysius/Apollo contrast, with its supposition that at the foundation of being is irrational violence. The mystery of being is deeper and more comprehensive than the simple contrast between Dionysius and Apollo allows. The experience of Fujimura's paintings definitely does not call to mind the word *tragic*, the term Rothko thought was the most apt description of his art. Instead, the experience is much closer to that of joy, which is in fact a title of one of Fujimura's paintings.

In *Joy*, Fujimura makes ample use of a common material in his paintings, gold leaf in small square shapes. The gold stands out magnificently against a black background. On one side of the painting, there is a consistent and well-ordered pattern of gold squares. That the pattern of squares breaks off and that gold squares show up elsewhere on the surface at odd angles might lead one to think that this is an unfinished project. Even in the segment of the painting in which the gold leaf is organized into a clear arrangement, the gold is more or less transparent. In some parts, other colors bleed through. In other parts, the gold squares are less evenly placed, with some of them overlapping one another or juxtaposed at unpredictable angles. Some simply dangle alone. There are also areas of green and blue, perhaps signifying fertility and renewal. There is a sense of movement, almost a dancing of the images in relation to one another. But this is hardly a tragic interplay of irreconcilable opposites. The experience is one, not of death and despair, but rather of the infinite richness of being, of sublime beauty, and joy — dispositions of the soul conducive to the practice of ecological virtues.

It is interesting to compare Fujimura and Rothko in their fashioning of titles and in their sense of the resources afforded by language. Thinking that language had become bankrupt, Rothko, particularly in the period I am discussing, wants to free his art from titles. So he numbers them.

But Fujimura offers titles that can suggest ways of interpreting the paintings. Sometimes he goes further, as in the painting *Matthew 6*, a reference to the chapter in the Gospel of Matthew containing Christ's Sermon on the Mount. As one contemplates the image created by Fujimura, one can see finely embedded in the colors words from that sermon pertaining to the lilies of the field. As I have already mentioned, Fujimura's use of titles and themes from religious traditions does not seek to offer peremptory hermeneutic guidance. For those who are religious, interpretation might lead in the direction of scriptural narratives. But even here there is an invitation to recover a new capacity to see, to feel, and to articulate the beauty of creation. Put slightly differently, Fujimura's art has elements of the icon. It does not leave viewers with their antecedent desires but engages them in a way that invites transcendence and transformation.

If Fujimura gives us more in the way of verbal cues and hints, he does not force interpretations on us. The words certainly can enrich the images. Conversely and more important, the imagery can enrich the language. If it is right to say with Rothko and others that the twentieth century witnessed a debasement of language, particularly regarding terms expressive of goodness and beauty, then an encounter with arresting imagery might well provide a path back to a more supple and more resonant use of language. This is yet another way in which art is wiser than philosophy. It can help restore the bond between sign and signified, between self and world.

NEGLECTED TRADITIONS

Among the most important influences on the thought and art of Fujimura is Georges Rouault. Many of the themes and characteristics of Rouault's art find a place in Fujimura's artistic vision. Both refuse to settle for the allegedly exclusive alternatives of despair or facile transcendence. As Fujimura says of Rouault, he "probed deeply into both the malaise and despair ... and at the same time held to a deep abiding reality of greater hope." In contrast to the taunting, proud, and despairing statements of "No Exit" that so many artists post in front of their art, Rouault provides a "window that looks out into a vision of wholeness."[23] Despite their radically contemporary artistic methods, Rouault's "paintings are a portal that peaks into the ages past, and then, magically, invites us into a journey toward our future."

Fujimura adds, "They transport us to a past beyond the fragmentation of Modernism into the enchantment and mysteries of medieval aesthetics. Before rationality was segregated from passion, and our hearts divorced from faith."[24] Fujimura, like Rouault, deploys quite contemporary techniques to ends that are congruent with premodern conceptions of art.[25]

If Fujimura's interpretation of Rouault sounds strikingly similar to that of Jacques Maritain, that is no mere coincidence. Fujimura is, as noted above, influenced by Maritain's conception of creative intuition. Fujimura's work is at least equally influenced by Eastern models and methods. Indeed, his work is an attempt at bridging divides of many kinds. The renewal of the virtues of human making overcomes the divisions between the natural and the artificial, the constructed and the human, and the secular and the sacred. Beyond the dichotomies sacred and secular, contemporary and medieval, natural and artificial, there is an additional opposition that Fujimura's art seeks to bridge: the divide between East and West.

Fujimura studied under a Nihonga master, and his work betrays the influence of the Japanese decorative screen tradition called Rimpa. For his work, the materials are not merely instrumental. Gold and silver are "the most mysterious of all the materials."[26] Pure gold affixed to glass, Fujimura observes, is transparent and opens the viewer to the transcendent. He adds, "In such a Reality, materiality has direct connection with the sacred, and gives conviction to an artist . . . to see the spiritual, heavenly presence and to manifest itself in the reality of earth." There is an important contrast here with Rothko, who had a fear, even at times a revulsion, of bodily reality. Breslin observes, "Life in the flesh left Rothko uneasy, restless."[27] He saw his task as an artist as in part to "keep from being smothered."[28] By contrast, Fujimura embraces the reality, goodness, and beauty of the physical. Or rather he depicts the way in which human seeing, thinking, and living are embraced by a comprehensive physical order. There is a biocentric dimension to Fujimura's art, a dimension that underscores a perhaps surprising kinship between Fujimura and Jeffers.

In the very materials he elects to use, finely distilled elements of gold and silver, as well as elements that change over time, Fujimura highlights the temporality of finite, material existence. But the emphasis is not on nothingness so much as it is on the goodness and mystery of temporal, material things—on the miraculous fact of their sheer existence. In a brilliant integration of Eastern and Western, Fujimura brings the resources of

Japanese screen painting to bear on the central teaching and mystery of the Christian religion, the Incarnation of God, the audacious claim that the Word of God has entered time and taken on human flesh, thus dignifying both time and flesh.

ART AT THE STILL POINT

The dialogue between East and West mirrors to some extent an underappreciated dialogue of the same kind in perhaps the greatest poet of the twentieth century, T. S. Eliot, who himself sought to revive neglected traditions in fresh language. Reviving marginalized traditions is a way of enlivening art in the present. The echo of Eliot is instructive, since among the most striking of Fujimura's projects is a brilliant set of four paintings inspired by T. S. Eliot's *Four Quartets*, a series of poems that Eliot wrote in the most mature phase of his career and at a time when he had fully incorporated the insights of his conversion to the Christian faith into his own poetic calling and vision. Eliot, whose influence on the poetry of Everson I have already addressed, is among the artists who strive to offer a hopeful vision. Yet no poet dwells in greater detail on the nihilism of the twentieth century. His art does not discount or occlude from view the confrontation with the disorders and violence in nature or in the human world. Eliot makes the "hell of the imagination" the starting point of art. Because we lack self-knowledge, indeed because our blindness often extends to a willful and giddy blindness to our own blindness, the direct engagement of readers is difficult. Thus artists have recourse to the dedoublement of Baudelaire, whom Eliot invokes at a pivotal point in *The Waste Land*.

Eliot is heavily influenced by Eastern philosophy and religious practice. There is a kind of reconciliation of the two in his *Four Quartets*, even if the understanding of time and timelessness leans in the end in the direction of a Christian understanding of incarnation.[29] Eliot's contrast between empty and full time, between flux and permanence, and between the nothingness of ennui and the nothingness of sacrificial self-abasement in the face of infinite goodness: all of these themes are familiar from previous chapters. Stillness can indicate vacuity or concentrated fullness. So too silence can signify inarticulacy, expectation (anxious or hopeful), or communion beyond words.

In conversation with Eliot, Fujimura constructs four large paintings, whose color schemes and use of layering resemble the paintings I have already discussed.[30] Three of the titles—all derived from lines in Eliot's poems—pick up on precisely these themes. *Between Two Waves of the Sea*, *The Still Point*, and *Zero Summer* underscore stillness, silence, and absence. Only the fourth painting, *Fire and Rose Are One*, accentuates natural imagery and transformation. Or at least that's what one might gather from the titles. The paintings themselves are all richly layered, with multiple colors, including the characteristic gold leaf. They are hardly vacant. Brimming with color, the paintings invigorate rather than short-circuit the imagination. *Zero Summer* shimmers with a nearly blinding gold leaf. *Fire and the Rose Are One* highlights bursting sections of red with tinges of orange or yellow. The red intersperses with black and deep blue—producing an elevating and transforming experience of sublime beauty.

The visual experience of the paintings enables viewers to grasp the deeper meaning of stillness and apparent absence that Eliot himself aims to communicate. Of the still point, Eliot in "Burnt Norton" writes in paradoxical terms, denying that it is pure stillness or motion, bodily or nonbodily. It gathers all of time and is the center of all other motion.[31] Fujimura's large, multilayered canvases are visual realizations of Eliot's poetic exhortation that we need to be "still and still moving." They provoke feelings of being at once overwhelmed and invited, motionless and yet moving into deeper levels of meaning.

Here we find an expansive use by Fujimura of the pairing word and painting, text and image. Even as the allusions enrich the experience of the paintings, so too do the paintings point us back to Eliot's great poem, with fresh insights and new questions. The difference in the media allows for the painting to work on its audience through its peculiar mode of communication. What Eliot says of a poem, namely, that it can communicate before it is understood, is perhaps even more true of a painting, which has the further advantage of being able to be taken in as a whole at one glance in a way that a poem cannot.

What I have already said about the need for attention, for purgation and emptiness as conditions of the experience of the beautiful, is a common theme in Fujimura and Eliot. Both supply arts that foster in readers and viewers habits of attention. In many and subtle ways, then, Fujimura's art offers what *LS* calls an "aesthetic education" (215). Such an education fosters what Iris Murdoch calls attention, the great enemy of which is fantasy. To learn to love is to learn to see others in their irreducible particularity.[32] Opposed to fantasy is the cultivation of imagination, which enables us to "reach out toward what is real."[33] For this task, we need the arts. Pure reason is insufficient.[34] In the encounter with beauty, we are arrested, seized, held; we experience nature, human artifacts, and human persons in a noninstrumentalist, nonutilitarian way. At its peak, such experiences are ecstatic, enabling us to transcend ourselves and even time, if only momentarily. We are thus decentered. The cultivation of the habits of the beautiful nourishes intellect, will, and heart and thus counters the "internal deserts" that threaten our souls.[35] The vices attending to the technocratic paradigm are countered by dispositions and virtues arising from our experience of beauty: awe, wonder, and gratitude (111–12).

Aesthetic education involves habits of self-emptying and attention. Art here is on the cusp of the religious. Many artists, including Rothko, have gone further and suggested that aesthetic experience is itself a form of religious experience. I spoke earlier of myths of the Fall and of the way they recur even in purportedly secular contexts. We might here speak of myths of the beautiful or the sublime. Even in secular environmentalism, the language of the sacredness of nature surfaces with some regularity. Such language is also prevalent in Romanticism. The question is whether such discourse can be meaningfully maintained without some sort of theological underpinning.

In Nietzschean fashion, Rothko relies on classical myth. Yet he does not suppose that his own art can function in the way classical art did in its own time and place. Is there reason to think that art can perform its vivifying role apart from a religious context in which the transcendent is grounded, not in self-constructed myths, but in an affirmation of the reality of the divine? As I noted in the opening chapter, one of the strategies of *LS* is precisely to raise the question of whether modern, secular environmentalism can supply human persons with a self-understanding and motivation sufficient to implement a robust ecological vision. The question is whether human persons can find strong enough reasons to care about the natural or human orders without some sort of overarching affirmation of the goodness of both. As Rémi Brague notes, it is hard to see why humans should care for the cosmos or themselves without such divine affirmation of the goodness of creation and of the human creature.

He writes:

> The question is not to know if man can know on his own how he ought to live and live well. It is rather to know if he can *will to survive* without a superior instance to affirm him, without someone who has not only granted him his humanity—by breathing into him a soul or, more prosaically, by ensuring the conditions for an evolutionary emergence of superior mental functions ("mind")—but also granted him *legitimacy*. On his own, man cannot pronounce on his own value; he cannot be party and judge.[36]

The problem of legitimacy is a legacy of radical anthropocentrism. It is not solved by variants of biocentrism. Perhaps the question of the solution of our environmental crisis, which is itself a symptom of much deeper disorders, concerns not so much genealogy as eschatology, not so much the past as the future, not so much how we got here as where we are going and how we can envision a hopeful future, for us and our common home. What are the resources for shared hope, grounded in a "shared experience of awe" and responsibility and in a shared anticipation that all creatures, "resplendently transfigured," will find their "rightful place," in the cosmos (243)?

NOTES

PREFACE

1. It would be interesting to compare Malick's opening with the stages of cosmic development (physical, chemical, biological, and cognitive) outlined in Marcelo Gleiser's essay, "From Cosmos to Intelligent Life," *International Journal of Astrobiology* 11, no. 4 (2012): 345–50.

2. In an essay, "Meaning in a Silent Universe," *New Atlantis* 47 (2015): 76–86; and a book, *The Islands of Knowledge: The Limits of Science and the Search for Meaning* (New York: Basic Books, 2014), Marcelo Gleiser cites Pascal and argues that we need to come to terms with both our cosmic loneliness and our cosmic significance, what Pascal might call our wretchedness and greatness.

3. All quotations are from the official English-language version of *Laudato Si': On Care for Our Common Home* (Vatican City: Libreria Editrice Vaticana, 2015); hereafter *LS*. I have included paragraph references parenthetically in the text.

4. Jacques Maritain, *Education at the Crossroads* (New Haven, CT: Yale University Press, [1943] 1960).

5. Makoto Fujimura, *Culture Care: Reconnecting with Beauty for Our Common Life* (Westmont, IL: IVP Books, 2017).

6. Ibid., 22.

7. Albert Gelpi, Introduction to William Everson, *Dark God of Eros: A William Everson Reader*, ed. Albert Gelpi (Berkeley, CA: Santa Clara University and Heyday Books, 2003), xxxv. Also see the appreciation by the poet and former chair of the National Endowment for the Arts Dana Gioia, "In Memoriam: William Everson," *Robinson Jeffers Newsletter*, nos. 93–94 (Winter–Spring 1995).

8. Pierre Manent, *Seeing Things Politically: Interviews with Benedict Delorme-Montini*, trans. Ralph Hancock (South Bend, IN: Saint Augustine's Press, 2015), 92.

ONE. Laudato Si', Technocracy, and the Renewal of Human Making

1. See Dennis Edwards, "'Sublime Communion': The Theology of the Natural World in *Laudato Si'*," in *The Natural World and God: Theological Explorations* (Adelaide, South Australia: ATF Press, 2017), 101–2. The essay first appeared in *Theological Studies* 77, no. 2 (2016): 377–91. Also of note in the same issue is Celia Deane-Drummond, "*Laudato Si'* and the Natural Sciences: An Assessment of Possibilities and Limits," 392–415.

2. A theme of Francis's encyclical *Lumen Fidei* is that faith encourages science by infusing in the human soul a spirit of wonder and a supposition that nature is always greater than whatever thus far has been understood.

3. On this issue more broadly, see the chapter "Environmental Virtues: Charity, Nature, and Divine Friendship in Thomas," in Willis Jenkins, *Ecologies of Grace: Environmental Ethics and Christian Theology* (Oxford: Oxford University Press, 2008), 132–51. Among other discussions of ecological virtue, see Celia Deane-Drummond, *The Ethics of Nature* (Hoboken, NJ: Wiley-Blackwell, 2004), with a particular emphasis on wisdom (9–28); Elizabeth Johnson, *Ask the Beasts: Darwin and the God of Love* (London: Bloomsbury, 2014), with special attention to humility and joy (272–73); and for an analysis focused on Aquinas, James Schaefer, "The Virtuous Cooperator," *Worldviews: Environment, Culture, Religion* 7 (2003): 171–95.

4. Naomi Oreskes, Introduction to the encyclical *Laudato Si'* (London: Melville House, 2016), vii–xxiv.

5. The raising of moral concerns is commonplace in the standard environmental science textbooks. See, e.g., G. Tyler Miller and Scott Spoolman, *Living in the Environment: Principles, Connections, and Solutions*, 18th ed. (Boston, MA: Cengage Learning, 2014), 491.

6. Ralph Ellison, *Invisible Man* (New York: Vintage Books, 1995), 6.

7. Michael Hanby, "The Gospel of Creation and the Technocratic Paradigm: Reflections on a Central Teaching of *Laudato Si'*," *Communio* 42 (2015): 724–47.

8. See Ryszard Sadowski, "Inspirations of Pope Francis' Concept of Integral Ecology," *SEMINARE* 37 (2016): 69–82. The best study of the shape of the document and its complex set of sources is Kevin Irwin's *A Commentary on "Laudato Si'": Examining the Background, Contributions, Implementation, and Future of Pope Francis's Encyclical* (Mahwah, NJ: Paulist Press, 2016).

9. Walker Percy, *Lost in the Cosmos: The Last Self-Help Book* (New York: Washington Square Press, 1984).

10. Francis is quoting from Aquinas, *Summa Theologiae*, I. 47, art. 1–3.

11. G. K. Chesterton, *Chesterton's Biographies: Saint Thomas Aquinas and Saint Francis of Assisi* (North Yorkshire: House of Stratus, 2008), 5.

12. Johnson, *Ask the Beasts*, 149.
13. Ibid.
14. See the discussion in Jenkins, *Ecologies of Grace*, 135–51.
15. Jenkins, *Ecologies of Grace*, 138.
16. Chesterton, *Saint Thomas Aquinas and Saint Francis of Assisi*, 13.
17. Ibid., 10.
18. Ibid., 40.
19. Ibid., 147.
20. Edwards, *The Natural World and God*, 102–5.
21. Gerald Manley Hopkins, "Pied Beauty," in *Selected Poetry* (Oxford: Oxford University Press, 1996), 118.
22. Chesterson, *Saint Thomas Aquinas and Saint Francis of Assisi*, 147.
23. Ibid., 188.
24. Fujimura, *Culture Care*.
25. Ibid., 40.
26. Ibid., 29.
27. Ibid., 22.
28. Ibid., 24.
29. Ibid., 25.
30. Ibid., 34.
31. Ibid., 47.
32. Makoto Fujimura, *Refractions: A Journey of Faith, Art, Culture* (Colorado Springs, CO: NavPress, 2009), 125.
33. Manent, *Seeing Things Politically*, 92.
34. Thomas Hobbes, *Leviathan*, ed. Edwin Curley (Indianapolis, IN: Hackett, 1994), 25.
35. Edwards, *The Natural World and God*, 116.
36. Ibid.
37. Augustine, *Confessions*, trans. F. J. Sheed (Indianapolis, IN: Hackett, 2006), 3.
38. This is a prominent theme in the writings of Peter Augustine Lawler, who traces the roots of this view of the human condition to Augustine, Pascal, and—in our time—Walker Percy. See, e.g., his *Homeless and at Home in America: Evidence for the Dignity of the Human Soul in Our Time and Place* (South Bend, IN: Saint Augustine's Press, 2007).
39. Jacques Maritain, *Art and Scholasticism with Other Essays* (Minneapolis, MN: Filiquarian Publishing, 2007), 28.
40. Mathew Croasmun and Miroslav Volf, *The Hunger for Home: Food and Meals in the Gospel of Luke* (Waco, TX: Baylor University Press, 2022), 1.
41. A bizarre mixture of these two modern tendencies can be found in a form of utilitarian pragmatism that seeks to transform human nature in such a

way that human persons would no longer be capable of experiencing themselves as unsettled in what is apparently their natural habitat. In its application of medicinal and therapeutic cures, in its eschewal of longings for transcendence as relics of superstition, and in its politics of egalitarian uniformity, a certain strain of modernity aims to domesticate the wildest animal of all, the only animal that is a problem to and for itself. "An alien extermination program," that's the pithy way Peter Lawler describes the project of modernity; see *Aliens in America: The Strange Truth about Our Souls* (Wilmington, DE: Intercollegiate Studies Institute, 2002), x.

42. Jenkins, *Ecologies of Grace*, 147.

43. Ibid., 148.

44. Jacques Maritain, *An Essay on Christian Philosophy*, trans. Edward H. Flannery (New York: Philosophical Library, 1955), 23.

45. See Lynn White, "The Historical Roots of Our Ecological Crisis," http://www.uvm.edu/~gflomenh/ENV-NGO-PA395/articles/Lynn-White.pdf; originally published in *Science* 155 (1967).

46. Ibid., 150.

47. Johnson, *Ask the Beasts*, ix.

48. Rémi Brague, *The Kingdom of Man: Genesis and Failure of the Modern Project* (Notre Dame, IN: University of Notre Dame Press, 2018), 97.

49. It suffices by way of contrast on this matter simply to note that Aquinas has a very different notion of property from that of Locke, a view that distinguishes between the nature of external things, which are subject only to God's power, and their use, which is granted to us by God. But even that use is governed by virtue and by the obligation to share what is common with all. See *Summa Theologiae*, II-II.66. For a good treatment of Aquinas on property, see the following works by Mary Hirschfeld: *Aquinas and the Market: Toward a Humane Economy* (Cambridge, MA: Harvard University Press, 2018); "Rethinking Economic Inequality: A Theological Perspective," *Journal of Religious Ethics* 42, no. 2 (June 2019): 259–82; and "Neither Left nor Right: Toward a Catholic View of the Economy," *Horizons* 42, no. 1 (June 2015): 140–49.

50. For a feminist critique, see Carolyn Merchant, *The Death of Nature: Women, Ecology, and the Scientific Revolution* (San Francisco: HarperOne, 1990).

51. See Anthony Mills, "Is Pope Francis Anti-Modern?," *New Atlantis* 47 (2015): 45–55.

52. William Cronon, *Uncommon Ground: Rethinking the Human Place in Nature* (New York: Norton, 1995), 69–90. In response to the all too common lament in the environmental movement, encapsulated in Bill McKibben's *The End of Nature* (New York: Random House, 2006), that human persons have killed nature, Cronon states that that could only be possible if we conceive of nature as pristine. The same dualism, according to Cronon, underlies the program of the Earth First movement.

53. In *Green Writing: Romanticism and Ecology* (London: Palgrave Macmillan, 2000), James McKusick argues that the nineteenth-century British Romantic poets were more than protoecologists. They were in fact well-developed forerunners of the twentieth-century environmental movement. McKusick also objects to Cronon's thesis that these poets conceived of nature, particularly the landscape, as pristine.

54. Cronan cites Wendell Berry as offering an alternative to the dualistic account. One might go further and note the indispensability of developing an ecology of cities. See, e.g., the work of the Thriving Cities Project at the Institute for Advanced Studies in Culture, University of Virginia: http://iasc-culture.org/THR/channels/Common_Place/tag/thriving-cities/. Also see the discussion in Jenkins of Aquinas's thought as providing a basis for a "land management ethos instead of romanticizing nature" (*Ecologies of Grace*, 150).

55. Jacques Maritain, *The Degrees of Knowledge* (New York: Charles Scribner's Sons, 1959), 233.

56. Ibid., 234.

57. Ibid., 236.

58. A lengthy study could be written on the various strains in the Romantic influence on Catholic thinkers. Among the authors who would have to be included are J. R. R. Tolkien, who in both his fiction and his letters engages the Romantic conception of nature; Jacques Maritain, whose writings on aesthetics feature an encounter with Romanticism; Gerard Manley Hopkins, whose poetry is heavily influenced by the Romantic poetic tradition; Karl Schmidt and his Romantic politics; Thomas Merton, who wrote a thesis on Blake and for whom Romantic themes endure in his writings, particularly in the attention to landscapes in his poetry and early monastic writings; Hans Urs von Balthasar, whose theological aesthetics takes as its departure an engagement with Romanticism; and Charles Taylor, who has written on the sources of modern aesthetics and on authenticity.

59. Cronon, *Uncommon Ground*, 69–90.

60. The literature on Romanticism is vast and far too complex for detailed examination here. I shall, however, have occasion throughout this book to attend to some of the central and most informative debates in that literature. Here is a list of some of the works that have been consulted. For the connection between Romanticism and environmentalism, see Cronon, *Uncommon Ground*; McKusick, *Green Writing*; and Timothy Morton, *Ecology without Nature* (Cambridge, MA: Harvard University Press, 2009). For general studies, see Isaiah Berlin, *The Roots of Romanticism*, ed. H. Hardy (Princeton, NJ: Princeton University Press, 1999); Dalia Nassar, *The Romantic Absolute* (Chicago: University of Chicago Press, 2014); Andrew Bowie, *Aesthetics and Subjectivity: From Kant to Nietzsche* (Manchester: Manchester University Press, 2003); Peter Thorslev, "German Romantic Idealism," in *The Cambridge Companion to British Romanticism*, 2nd ed., 82–102; Marshall Brown,

"Enlightenment and Romanticism," in *The Cambridge Companion to British Romanticism*, 34–55; Jean-Marie Schaeffer, *Art of the Modern Age: Philosophy of Art from Kant to Heidegger* (Princeton, NJ: Princeton University Press, 2000); and Colin Jager, *Unquiet Things: Secularism in the Romantic Age* (Philadelphia: University of Pennsylvania Press, 2014). For studies more specifically focused on Romanticism and the arts, see Emily Brady, *The Sublime in Modern Philosophy: Aesthetics, Ethics, and Nature* (Cambridge: Cambridge University Press, 2013); Roger Scruton, *The Death-Devoted Heart: Sex and the Sacred in Wagner's Tristan and Isolde* (Oxford: Oxford University Press, 2004); Edward Lobb, *T. S. Eliot and the Romantic Critical Tradition* (London: Routledge, 2015); Northrup Frye, *A Study of English Romanticism* (New York: Random House, 1968); Albert Gelpi, "Introduction: The Janus-Face of Romanticism and Modernism," in *A Coherent Splendor: The American Poetic Renaissance, 1910–1950* (Cambridge: Cambridge University Press, 1990); Albert Gelpi, "Robinson Jeffers and the Sublime," in *The Wild God of the World: An Anthology of Robinson Jeffers*, ed. Albert Gelpi (Stanford, CA: Stanford University Press, 2003).

61. David Jeffrey, "Romantic Religion and the Sublime," in *In the Beauty of Holiness: Art and the Bible in Western Culture* (Grand Rapids, MI: Eerdmans, 2017), 219–52. The emphasis on subjective feeling and the role of the imagination is of course at work already and quite decisively in Kant. As Robert Pippin points out, "The Kantian sublime should also be distinguished from modern, religious views of the sublime, as in nature's void or infinity in Calvin and Pascal, and that will make clear the heretical character of Kant's position. Rather than provoke a humbling awe, the experience of the sublime is a *two*-step process in Kant and finally confirms a sense of man's absolute supremacy over all of nature by virtue of his moral vocation and its independence from any natural condition or power." See Pippin, "What Was Abstract Art? From the Point of View of Hegel," *Critical Inquiry* 29, no. 1 (Autumn 2002): 1–24. Julianne Dolan provides an extensive treatment of Maritain and Romanticism in "Being Laden with Love: A Theological Development of Jacques Maritain's Creative Intuition" (PhD diss., University of Notre Dame, 2020), 136–210.

62. Similarly, distorted conceptions of rationality have given rise to reactionary and equally warped conceptions of religion, in various forms of fundamentalism and mythologies of quite varied types. On this, see the essay by Stephane Symons, "Same City, Another Universe: On Jacques Maritain and Walter Benjamin," in *The Maritain Factor: Taking Religion into Interwar Modernism*, ed. Rajesh Heynickx and Jan de Maeyer (Leuven: Leuven University Press, 2010), 128–37.

63. Jager, *Unquiet Things*, 7.

64. Ibid., 23.

65. David Walsh, *The Modern Philosophical Revolution: The Luminosity of Existence* (New York: Cambridge University Press, 2008), 128.

66. Frajam Taylor, "The Rebellious Will of Gerard Manley Hopkins," *Poetry* 59, no. 9 (1942): 270–79, at 276. The most extensive treatment of Jeffers's relation to Nietzsche can be found in Arthur Coffin, *Robinson Jeffers: Poet of Inhumanism* (Madison: University of Wisconsin Press, 1971). The book, which focuses on the longer-form poetry of Jeffers, is marred by an overly allegorical reading of characters in Jeffers's works as representatives of themes in Nietzsche's philosophy.

67. Gelpi, *The Wild God*, 175.

68. William Everson, *Prodigious Thrust* (Los Angeles, CA: Black Sparrow Press, 1996), 197.

69. Edwards, "Sublime Communion," 379. While De Koninck's *Cosmos* takes seriously the cosmic conditions of tragedy, suffering, and violent death, it does not go in the direction of claiming that sin is inevitable, with the implication that God would be responsible for evil. De Koninck is not attempting to resolve the problem of evil in this text. As we will see, his account of the cosmos takes seriously the varied contributions of distinct and relatively autonomous sciences. His theoretical account is underdetermined. Although there are many similarities between his work and that of the famous Jesuit cosmologist Teilhard de Chardin, he avoids the traps that Chardin could not.

70. As quoted in Pierre Courthion, *Rouault* (New York: Henry Abrams, 1962), 240.

71. Ibid., 244.

72. Ibid., 240.

73. Ibid., 238.

74. Such a position is perhaps better described as off-modern rather than antimodern. On this, see Stephen Schloesser, *Jazz Age Catholicism: Mystic Modernism in Postwar Paris 1919–1933* (Toronto: University of Toronto Press, 2005).

TWO. Jacques Maritain and the Twilight of Civilization

1. The famous Thomistic Study Circles, hosted at the Maritains' home, were hardly purely academic affairs; indeed, as Yves Simon, perhaps Maritain's most gifted philosophical pupil, observes about these gatherings: "The living room was generally crowded, less by teachers or students than by writers, poets, painters, musicians, persons interested in mysticism, missionaries and friends of the missions. Most of the artists were of the vanguard description." See John Howard Griffin and Yves Simon, *Jacques Maritain: Homage in Words and Pictures* (Albany, NY: Magi Press, 1974), 5. See also the chapter "Major Formative Influences: Artists and Saints" in John G. Trapani Jr., *Poetry, Beauty, and Contemplation: The Complete Aesthetics of Jacques Maritain* (Washington, DC: Catholic University of

American Press, 2011), 18–26. Among the artists present were Gide, Mauriac, Cocteau, Picasso, Chagall, Stravinsky, and Satie (25).

2. Griffin and Simon, *Jacques Maritain*, 5.

3. Maritain's correspondence with Cocteau became a remarkable little book, *Art and Faith*. See Jacques Maritain and Jean Cocteau, *Art and Faith* (New York: Philosophical Library, 1947). See R. Mathias, "Exploring the New Classicism: Reflections on Stravinsky and Maritain c. 1920–1940," *Maritain Studies* 17 (2001): 79–86; and Robert Fallon, "Composing Subjectivity: Maritain's Poetic Knowledge in Stravinsky and Messiaen," in *Jacques Maritain and the Many Ways of Knowing*, ed. Douglas A. Ollivant (Washington, DC: Catholic University of America Press, 2002), 284–302. On Maritain's relationship with Cocteau, see Daniel B. Gallagher, "Sympathy or Sell-Out? Maritain's Relationship with Cocteau and the Avant-Garde," in *A Piercing Light: Beauty, Faith and Human Transcendence*, ed. James M. Jacobs (Washington, DC: Catholic University of America Press, 2015), 3–24. Also see the chapters on Maritain's many friendships with artists in the section "Grandes Amities" in Heynickx and de Maeyer, *The Maritain Factor*.

4. Maritain's aesthetic thought remains understudied. The two most important book-length studies are Trapani, *Poetry, Beauty, and Contemplation*; and J. W. Hanke, *Maritain's Ontology of the Work of Art* (The Hague: Martinus Nijhoff, 1973). For other works on Aquinas, see Umberto Eco, *The Aesthetics of Thomas Aquinas* (Cambridge, MA: Harvard University Press, 1988); Armand Maurer, *About Beauty* (Houston, TX: Center for Thomistic Studies, 1983); and Mark Jordan, "The Evidence of the Transcendentals and the Place of Beauty in Thomas Aquinas," *International Philosophical Quarterly* 29 (1989): 393–406.

5. Raïssa Maritain, *We Have Been Friends Together*, trans. Julie Kernan (New York: Longmans, Green, and Co., 1945), 194.

6. Ralph McInerny, *The Very Rich Hours of Jacques Maritain: A Spiritual Life* (Notre Dame, IN: University of Notre Dame Press, 2011), 92, 94.

7. Aidan Nichols, "The English Uses of Maritain's Aesthetics," in *Redeeming Beauty: Soundings in Sacral Aesthetics* (Farnham: Ashgate, 2007), 125–42.

8. Thomas Merton, *Seven Storey Mountain* (New York: Harcourt, Brace, 1948), 217–30.

9. Flannery O'Connor, *The Habit of Being*, ed. Sally Fitzgerald (New York: Farrar, Straus and Giroux, 1979), 216.

10. Seamus Heaney, "Sixth Sense, Seventh Heaven," *Dublin Review*, no. 8 (Autumn 2002): 115–26.

11. For biographical works that examine the interconnection between Maritain's thought and his life—his varied political stances, his role in the development of Catholic ecclesiology, his friendships with artists, etc.—see Jean-Luc Barre, *Jacques and Raïssa Maritain: Beggars for Heaven*, trans. Bernard Doering

(Notre Dame, IN: University of Notre Dame Press, 2005); and McInerny, *The Very Rich Hours of Jacques Maritain*.

12. For the impact of this war on intellectual and artistic culture, especially in the Parisian circles in which Maritain moved, see Schloesser, *Jazz Age Catholicism*. See also Paul Fussell, *The Great War and Modern Memory* (Oxford: Oxford University Press, 1970).

13. Jacques Maritain, *Education at the Crossroads* (New Haven, CT: Yale University Press, 1960). The book is, to borrow a title from C. S. Lewis, a defense of learning in wartime. See C. S. Lewis, "Learning in War-Time," in *The Weight of Glory* (New York: HarperOne, 2009), 20–32. In this sermon preached in 1939, Lewis responds to the accusation that the pursuit of liberal education in time of war is frivolous. Lewis retorts that war is not exceptional; rather, it simply "aggravates the permanent human situation." He proceeds to argue on behalf of the nonutilitarian goods of education.

14. An examination of how broadly shared are the concerns, how similar are the analyses of the root causes, and how common are the proposed remedies is found in Alan Jacobs, *The Year of Our Lord 1943: Christian Humanism in an Age of Crisis* (Oxford: Oxford University Press, 2018).

15. Ibid., 129–31.

16. Maritain, *Education at the Crossroads*, 114.

17. Francis traces the deterioration of human and natural ecology to what he calls throughout *LS* the "anthropocentric model" of human thought and ethics. Maritain uses these very words in *The Twilight of Civilization*, 4; see n. 18, below.

18. Jacques Maritain, *The Twilight of Civilization*, trans. Lionel Landry (New York: Sheed & Ward, 1943), viii. The book is based on lectures delivered in 1939.

19. Maritain, *We Have Been Friends Together*, 57. On Maritain, see Bernard Doering, *Jacques Maritain and the French Catholic Intellectuals* (Notre Dame, IN: University of Notre Dame Press, 1983); McInerny, *The Very Rich Hours of Jacques Maritain*; Schloesser, *Jazz Age Catholicism*; Barre, *Jacques and Raïssa Maritain*. On his aesthetics, see Ralph McInerny, *Art and Prudence: Studies in the Thought of Jacques Maritain* (Notre Dame, IN: University of Notre Dame Press, 1988): and Trapani, *Poetry, Beauty, and Contemplation*.

20. Maritain, *We Have Been Friends Together*, 60.

21. Ibid., 61.

22. Ibid., 62. Before Nazism, World War I would shake the foundations of the Ameliorist myth dominant in the modern Western world. See Fussell, *The Great War and Modern Memory*.

23. Maritain, *We Have Been Friends Together*, 66.

24. Ibid., 68.

25. There are quite a few different versions of this thesis in modern philosophy. For a powerful contemporary version, see Robert Pippin, *Idealism as Modernism: Hegelian Variations* (Cambridge: Cambridge University Press, 1997). In *The Persistence of Subjectivity: On the Kantian Aftermath* (Cambridge: Cambridge University Press, 2005), Pippin argues that a coherent account of modern thought and civilization rests on the affirmation of the "autonomy of the normative domain, the claim that the only thing that bears on the sufficiency of a reason is another reason, never a mere state of affairs or cause on its own" (115). As he puts it in *Idealism as Modernism*, there is a "necessary discontinuity between the receptivity of sensation and the activity of thinking about sensory matter" (33).

26. Jacques Maritain, *Creative Intuition* (New York: Meridian Books, 1954), 53.

27. Ibid., 159, 152.

28. David Walsh, *Politics of the Person and the Politics of Being* (Notre Dame, IN: University of Notre Dame Press, 2016), 163.

29. Hobbes, *Leviathan*, 25.

30. Ibid., 41.

31. Walsh, *Politics of the Person*, 160.

32. Ibid., 163.

33. See, e.g., David Nye, *American Technological Sublime* (Cambridge, MA: MIT Press, 1994).

34. David Lachterman, *Ethics of Geometry* (London: Routledge, 1989), 172.

35. Ibid., 151.

36. Maritain, *Art and Scholasticism*, 7.

37. Jacques Maritain, *The Responsibility of the Artist* (New York: Scribner, 1960), 43.

38. Ibid., 63.

39. Ibid.

40. Ibid., 43.

41. Maritain, *Art and Scholasticism*, 36–37.

42. Natalie Carnes, *Image and Presence: A Christological Reflection on Iconoclasm* (Stanford, CA: Stanford University Press, 2017), 41. On museums, see Natalie Carnes, *Beauty: A Theological Engagement with Gregory of Nyssa* (Eugene, OR: Cascade Books, 2014), 25.

43. Carnes, *Image and Presence*, 248.

44. Ibid., 40.

45. Jacques Maritain, *Approaches to God* (New York: Paulist Press, 2015), 45–53. Maritain is famous, or infamous, for holding that metaphysics can be accessed through an intuition of being. I think that Maritain is wrong about this point as a reading of Saint Thomas's texts. But it seems to me that this is relevant to his account of beauty. Whatever may be the case about the starting point of metaphysics, we can certainly experience the contingency of things and gain some sense of the difference

between essence—what something is—and its existence—the fact that it exists. These ordinary insights of experience can certainly ground the experience of the givenness, even the gratuitousness, of what is. Indeed, it is precisely when being is encountered through the mode of the beautiful that these notions come to the fore most dramatically. See Matthew Pugh, "Maritain, Critical Realism, and the Intuition of Being," in *The Wisdom of Youth*, ed. Travis Dumsday (Washington, DC: Catholic University of America Press, 2016), 101–19; and John F. Wippel, "Maritain and Aquinas on Our Discovery of Being," in Dumsday, *The Wisdom of Youth*, 120–46.

46. Jacques Maritain, *Untrammeled Approaches* (Notre Dame, IN: University of Notre Dame Press, 2017), 213; emphasis in the original.

47. Maritain, *Art and Scholasticism*, 28.

48. See Eco, *The Aesthetics of Thomas Aquinas*; see also Gerald Phelan, "The Concept of Beauty in St. Thomas Aquinas," in *Aspects of the Neo-Scholastic Philosophy*, ed. C. A. Hardt (New York: Benzinger Brothers, 1932), 139. For a defense of form as the basis of the experience of the beautiful, see Hanke, *Maritain's Ontology of the Work of Art*.

49. C. A. Tsakiridou, *Icons in Time, Persons in Eternity: Orthodox Theology and the Aesthetics of the Christian Image* (Farnham: Ashgate, 2013), 145.

50. Ibid., 137.

51. Ibid., 142.

52. Ibid.

53. For a detailed study of Maritain's account of ontology, see Hanke, *Maritain's Ontology of the Work of Art*.

54. Tsakiridou, *Icons in Time*, 143.

55. Ibid.

56. On Maritain's relationship to Romanticism, see Dolan, "Being Laden with Love," 136–210. Dolan traces the development of Romanticism and the ways in which its emphasis on (infinite) longing, which seems to open up the subject to transcendence, closes it off because the fulfillment of the longing is in a constant state of deferral. Thus desire is a longing for that which is unattainable. As she notes, Maritain engages this longing (eros) for the beautiful by reference to the infinite richness of being and a metaphysics of participation.

57. Maritain, *The Responsibility of the Artist*, 51–52.

58. Maritain, *Creative Intuition*, 151.

59. Ibid., 161.

60. Ibid., 83.

61. Ibid., 9.

62. Jacques Maritain, *Rouault* (New York: Henry N. Abrams, 1954), no pagination.

63. Maritain argues strongly in favor of images of Christ as suffering servant rather than the types of images prominent in the tradition of Orthodox iconography.

He prefers depictions that involve the beholder in the suffering and passion of Christ. See C. A. Tsikiridou, "*Vera Icona*: Reflections on the Mystical Aesthetics of Jacques Maritain and the Byzantine Icon," in *Truth Matters: Essays in Honor of Jacques Maritain*, ed. John G. Trapani Jr. (Washington, DC: American Maritain Association/Catholic University of America Press, 2004), 224–46. I should add that Tsikirdou's reflections on Rouault's depictions of Christ in comparison to the Orthodox iconographic tradition are more detailed than what Maritain himself provides.

64. Maritain, *The Responsibility of the Artist*, 72.

65. Ibid.

66. Ibid., 70–71.

67. In *The Invisible Hand in Popular Culture: Liberty vs. Authority in American Film and TV* (Lexington: University Press of Kentucky, 2012), Paul Cantor argues against the view that artists stand alone in splendid isolation creating their artistic products, free from the influence of politics, audiences, and commercial concerns. Cantor, who is especially focused on works of popular art, notes numerous examples in which not only commercial interests but also audience feedback has altered works of art. Moreover, art is often the result of a complex set of contributors even if one person is credited, above all, for the final product.

68. Maritain, *Creative Intuition*, 134.

69. See Tsakiridou, "*Vera Icona*," 228.

70. Flannery O'Connor, *Mystery and Manners* (New York: Farrar, Straus & Giroux, 1962), 34.

71. Maritain's work on the creative intuition of artists and on the deeply valuable contributions of those who have followed Baudelaire's descent into the hell of modern life cuts against the supposition he advocates, in an uncomplicated way, that the standard neo-Thomist genealogy of modernity is a history of decline beginning with the repudiation of the thought of Aquinas in the fourteenth century. Connected to this supposition is another, namely, that Maritain's anthropology is thoroughly rationalist, focusing almost exclusively on the defense of reason as understood by Thomas Aquinas and on modernity as a series of philosophical errors. But the anthropology that undergirds the account of poetic creativity, the very account that modern artists have found so compelling, is hardly rationalist. It is true that Maritain's work exhibits in some places rationalist tendencies and contains in some places a neo-Thomist view of the history of the West. A critique of Maritain on this matter can be had in the writings of Simon Weil, who called the Gothic period "totalitarian" and promoted instead what she called the Romanesque Renaissance. For her essay on the latter, see "The Romanesque Renaissance," in *Selected Essays, 1934–1943: Historical, Political, and Moral Writings*, ed. and trans. Richard Rees (Oxford: Oxford University Press, 1962), 44–54.

72. Maritain, *Creative Intuition*, 283–84.

THREE. Nihilism and Modernity in Endless Crisis

1. Maritain, *Twilight*, 4.
2. Ibid., 6.
3. Ibid.
4. Maritain, *Creative Intuition*, 80, 87.
5. Friedrich Nietzsche, *The Birth of Tragedy and the Case of Wagner*, trans. with commentary Walter Kaufmann (New York: Random House, 1967). In this early work, the view of the artist or even the philosopher-artist, an appellation we are obliged to apply to Nietzsche as author of a philosophical work on the origins of art, is hardly that of an autonomous self-creator. The notion of will to power emerges as a dominant theme in later work. It is, as we shall see, problematic not only on its own but also in relation to other themes in Nietzsche's writings.
6. Friedrich Nietzsche, *The Will to Power*, trans. Walter Kaufmann (New York: Vintage Books, 1968), #12.
7. Ibid., #2.
8. Ibid., #4.
9. Ibid., #12.
10. Friedrich Nietzsche, *On the Genealogy of Morals*, trans. Walter Kaufmann (New York: Vintage Books, 1989), 97–166.
11. Nietzsche, *The Will to Power*, #9.
12. Ibid., #36.
13. Ibid., #5.
14. Ibid., #35.
15. Ibid., #32.
16. Friedrich Nietzsche, *Beyond Good and Evil*, trans. Walter Kaufmann (New York: Vintage Books, 1966), #201.
17. Friedrich Nietzsche, *Thus Spake Zarathustra: A Book for All and None*, The Portable Nietzsche, trans. Walter Kaufmann (New York: Viking Press, 1954), 129–30.
18. Robert Pippin, *Nietzsche, Psychology, and First Philosophy* (Chicago: University of Chicago Press, 2010), 54.
19. Robert Pippin, *Modernism as a Philosophical Problem: On the Dissatisfactions of European High Culture* (Oxford: Blackwell, 1991), 157.
20. Ibid., 158.
21. Ibid., 13.
22. Ibid., 13–14.
23. One of the questions for this position concerns the relationship between prelinguistic and linguistic modes of knowing and interacting with the world. This is connected to the question of how embodiment and animality ought to figure in

our accounts of rationality. On an Aristotelian view, there is continuity between nonhuman animals and humans, and this continuity helps explain how the growth in the use of language in human children arises naturally out of antecedent prelinguistic skills. As part of his defense of the analogies between nonhuman and human reasoning, Alasdair MacIntyre observes the way the young human child, not yet having the power of language but already actively investigating the environment, attends, recognizes, reidentifies, distinguishes, and classifies and, as a result of these investigations, acts on beliefs and from time to time changes its beliefs. He adds, "The child of course in acquiring language replaces many of its indeterminate beliefs with determinate beliefs.... But its beliefs, determinate and indeterminate alike, continue to depend for their content on its stock of recognitions, identifications and discriminatory classifications. And these are shared to a remarkable extent by members of different species, both language-using and non-language using." Alisdair McIntyre, *Dependent Rational Animals: Why Human Beings Need the Virtues*, Paul Carus Lectures 20 (Chicago: Open Court, 1999), 39. If we begin from within the circle of spontaneous reasons, it is hard to see how we make sense of these dependencies on prelinguistic capacities or of the close, evolutionary connection between nonhuman and human animals.

24. Jean-Luc Marion, *The Crossing of the Visible*, trans. James K. A. Smith (Stanford, CA: Stanford University Press, 2004), 81.

25. Stanley Rosen, *The Question of Being: A Reversal of Heidegger* (New Haven, CT: Yale University Press, 1993), 59.

26. Ibid., 74.

27. Ibid., 43. For a cogent and vigorous defense of an alternative to idealism and naive realism in the texts of Thomas Aquinas, see John O'Callaghan, *Thomist Realism and the Linguistic Turn: Toward a More Perfect Form of Existence* (Notre Dame, IN: University of Notre Dame Press, 2016).

28. Rosen, *The Question of Being*, 159.

29. See Kevin Hart's introduction to *Counter-Experiences: Reading Jean-Luc Marion*, ed. Kevin Hart (Notre Dame, IN: University of Notre Dame Press, 2007).

30. See Thomas Carlson, "Blindness and Decision to See: On Revelation and Reception in Jean-Luc Marion," in Hart, *Counter-Experiences*, 153–80.

31. Christina Gschwandtner, *Degrees of Givenness: On Saturation in Jean-Luc Marion* (Bloomington: Indiana University Press, 2014), 56.

32. Ibid.

33. Ibid., 77; emphasis in original. She also notes that the easing of the gap between extraordinary experiences, of the sort highlighted by Marion, and the more "mundane gifts of daily life" could engender an appreciation of, and care for, the environment in a way that would contribute to ongoing ecological dialogue (194–95).

34. Maritain, *Degrees of Knowledge*, 1.

35. Ibid., 7.

36. I have made this argument at much greater length and with more detailed attention to the texts of Thomas Aquinas and Marion in Thomas S. Hibbs, *Aquinas, Ethics, and Philosophy of Religion* (Bloominton: Indiana University Press, 2014).

37. Maritain, *Degrees of Knowledge*, 240.

38. Ibid., 247.

39. Ibid., 260.

40. Trapani, *Poetry, Beauty, and Contemplation*, 52.

41. Maritain, *Creative Intuition*, 94.

42. Hanke, *Maritain's Ontology of the Work of Art*, 92.

43. Aquinas, *Summa Theologiae*, I, 22, 2.

44. Of course, the challenge for the traditional understanding of the human person and of divine creation is not just the early modern contest between dualists and materialists or even the larger scale contest between enlightenment and Romanticism. The biggest challenge comes from Darwinian evolution, but Darwin's challenge is not the impossibility of a six-day creationist view. Very early on in the Christian interpretation of Genesis what we would call nonliteral readings of the creation narrative were defended, as, for example, in Augustine's famous book-length exegesis of *Genesis*. In what seems ironic from our perspective, Augustine calls his own interpretation, which rejects the six-day reading, a "literal" interpretation of the creation narrative; that shows how cramped our modern vocabulary is. See Augustine, *De Genesi ad Litteram: The Literal Meaning of Genesis*, Ancient Christian Writers (New York: Paulist Press, 1982).

45. William Desmond, *God and the Between* (Malden, MA: Blackwell, 2008), 250. Like Marion, Desmond refuses to work with any clear distinction between philosophy and theology. This makes his accentuation of creation ex nihilo problematic, for it is never clear on his view whether this is a philosophical or a revealed teaching. That, of course, is one of the difficulties of Desmond's election to pursue his inquiry at the intersection of, or *between*, philosophy and religion. Religion cannot escape philosophical perplexity, and philosophy cannot foreclose religion's question of God. Desmond refuses to draw the lines in this peremptory way, of course. But he must distinguish them in some way in order for the term *between* to have any meaning, and until he does, his source for the evidence of creation ex nihilo—is it philosophical reason or biblical revelation?—remains unclear.

46. Desmond, *God and the Between*, 28.

47. Ibid., 31.

48. Ibid.

49. Ibid., 33.

50. Ibid., 12.

51. Deane-Drummond, "*Laudato Si'* and the Natural Sciences."

52. Ibid., 398.

53. Ibid., 412.

54. Charles De Koninck, *The Cosmos*, in *The Writings of Charles De Koninck*, ed. and trans. Ralph McInerny (Notre Dame, IN: University of Notre Dame Press, 2008), 246.

55. Ibid., 246. See Luke A. Barnes and Geraint Lewis, *A Fortunate Universe: Life in a Finely Tuned Cosmos* (Cambridge: Cambridge University Press, 2016).

56. De Koninck, *The Cosmos*, 270.

57. Ibid., 292.

58. McIntyre, *Dependent Rational Animal*, 57.

59. De Koninck, *The Cosmos*, 246.

60. Pat Byrne, "The Integral Visions of Teilhard and Lonergan: Science, the Universe, Humanity and God," in *From Teilhard to Omega: Co-creating an Unfinished Universe*, ed. Ilia Delio (Maryknoll, NY: Orbis Books, 2014), 83–110. See Teilhard de Chardin, *Phenomenon of Man* (New York: Harper & Row, 1959), passim. For one account of the significance of the symbolism of return, see Mircea Eliade, *The Myth of the Eternal Return: Or Cosmos and History* (Princeton, NJ: Princeton University Press, 1971).

61. See Byrne, "The Integral Visions of Teilhard and Lonergan."

62. Teilhard, *Phenomenon of Man*, 165; emphasis in original.

63. De Koninck, *The Cosmos*, 297.

64. Ibid., 292.

65. Ted Benton, "Naturalism in Social Science," in *Routledge Encyclopedia of Philosophy*, ed. E. Craig (London: Routledge, 1998); retrieved from https://www.rep.routledge.com/articles/thematic/naturalism-in-social-science/v-1.

66. De Koninck, *The Cosmos*, 295.

67. Ibid., 274.

68. Blaise Pascal, *Pensées*, rev. ed., trans. A. J. Krailsheimer (London: Penguin Classics, 1995), #113.

69. Johnson, *Ask the Beasts*, 269.

70. Ibid., 268.

71. De Koninck, *The Cosmos*, 301.

72. Ibid. While *The Cosmos* takes seriously the cosmic conditions of tragedy, suffering, and violent death, it does not go in the direction of claiming that sin is inevitable, with the implication that God would be responsible for evil. De Koninck is not attempting to resolve the problem of evil in this text. As noted, his account of the cosmos takes seriously the varied contributions of distinct and relatively autonomous sciences. His theoretical account is underdetermined. Although De Koninck does not develop a Christocentric position, what he does say might be seen as a propaedeutic to such an account, one that would have as its centerpiece the suffering servant, the Cross as the transfiguration of all flesh through divine redemption.

73. De Koninck, *The Cosmos*, 311.
74. Leslie Armour, "Charles De Koninck, the Common Good, and the Human Environment," *Laval Théologique et Philosophique* 43 (1987): 67–80.
75. Edwards, *The Natural World and God*, 132.
76. De Koninck, *The Cosmos*, 256.

FOUR. The Ecological Poetics of Robinson Jeffers

1. Friedrich Nietzsche, *The Gay Science*, trans. Walter Kaufmann (New York: Vintage Books, 1974), 168–69.
2. Friedrich Nietzsche, *Beyond Good and Evil*, trans. Walter Kaufmann (New York: Vintage Books, 1989), Aphorism #161. The passage, standing alone, is a bit misleading. Nietzsche does not think that a return to a pristine nature, as that is understood in certain forms of Romanticism, is possible.
3. Max Hallman, "Nietzsche's Environmental Ethics," *Environmental Ethics* 13 (1991): 99–125.
4. Ibid., 123.
5. Michael Zimmerman, "Nietzsche and Ecology: A Skeptical Look," in *Reading Nietzsche at the Margins*, ed. Steven V. Hicks and Alan Rosenberg (Lafayette, IN: Purdue University Press, 2008). Other scholars, focusing on Nietzsche's claim that there is no nature, only interpretations of nature, are skeptical that Nietzsche's thought could underwrite an ecological ethics, or any ethics at all. See Martin Drenthen, "The Paradox of Environmental Ethics: Nietzsche's View of Nature and the Wild," *Environmental Ethics* 21 (1999): 163–75.
6. Nietzsche, *Thus Spake Zarathustra*, 125.
7. Ralph Acampora, "Using and Abusing Nietzsche for Environmental Ethics," *Environmental Ethics* 16 (1994): 187–94, at 189. Also see Ralph Acampora, "Nietzsche's Feral Philosophy," in *A Nietzschean Bestiary: Becoming Animal beyond Docile and Brutal*, ed. Christa Davis Acampora and Ralph R. Acampora (Lanham, MD: Rowman & Littlefield, 2003).
8. Sean Esbjorn-Hargens and Michael Zimmerman, *Integral Ecology* (London: Integral Books, 2009), 1: "Environmentalists value the natural world but typically subscribe to a conception of nature that either excludes value (subjective and intersubjective perspectives) or regards it as a conventional fiction for enhancing human survival.... Environmentalists often speak of nature as a complex dynamic system in which humans, like other animals and plants, are merely strands in a cosmic web that lacks any hierarchy or direction. Yet, if humans are merely raw material in a complex state of affairs—the *is*—they are in no way capable of calling for alternative actions based on moral obligation—the *ought*."

9. Erazim Kohak, *The Embers and the Stars: A Philosophical Inquiry into the Moral Sense of Nature* (Chicago: University of Chicago Press, 1984), 170.

10. There are other potential sources of discord between Nietzsche and contemporary environmentalism. Graham Parkes sees a tension between a constructivist view of nature, which surfaces in numerous places in Nietzsche's writings, and one that is "based on a reverence for the ultimately enigmatic nature of things," the latter of which fosters "loyalty to the earth and a reverence for and affirmation of the innocence of natural phenomena in all their transience." See Graham Parkes, "Staying Loyal to the Earth: Nietzsche as an Ecological Thinker," in *Nietzsche's Futures*, ed. John Lippitt (London: Macmillan, 1999), 167–88.

11. Everson, *Dark God of Eros*, 234.

12. On the influence of Nietzsche on Jeffers, see Coffin, *Robinson Jeffers*, 60–190. Coffin's comparison is marred by a rather crude reading of Nietzsche.

13. Letter to Sister Mary James Power, October 1, 1934, in Robinson Jeffers, *The Wild God of the World: An Anthology of Robinson Jeffers*, selected, with introd. Albert Gelpi (Stanford, CA: Stanford University Press, 2003), 189.

14. Quoted in Jeffers, *Wild God of the World*, 11.

15. Robinson Jeffers, *Road Stallion, Tamar and Other Poems* (New York: Modern Library, 1935), viii.

16. Ibid., ix.

17. Jeffers, *Wild God of the World*, 10.

18. Ibid., 48.

19. Robinson Jeffers, *Selected Letters of Robinson Jeffers: 1897–1962*, ed. Ann D. Ridgeway (Baltimore: Johns Hopkins University Press, 1968), 342.

20. Jeffers, *Wild God of the World*, 182.

21. Walsh, *The Modern Philosophical Revolution*, 13.

22. Ibid., 128.

23. Ibid., 129. This might well seem not so much a development of Hegel as the undoing of Hegel. Hegel looks to be the principal opponent of what Walsh commends as the revolutionary thrust of modern thought. If this is so, then how can modern thought, even the limited strain that Walsh examines, be considered a "consistent" development?

24. I attend below to the account of the philosophy of modern art in Jean-Marie Schaefer's *Art of the Modern Age: Philosophy of Art from Kant to Hegel*, trans. Steven Rendall (Princeton, NJ: Princeton University Press, 2000). One of Schaeffer's central claims concerns the development in the nineteenth century of theories of art, which replace the study of various concrete arts and to which future art is thought to need to conform.

25. Jeffers, *Wild God of the World*, 175.

26. Stephen Mulhall, *Philosophical Myths of the Fall* (Princeton, NJ: Princeton University Press, 2005), 11.

27. Everson, *Dark God of Eros*, 261.

28. Brody, *The Sublime in Modern Philosophy*, 3.

29. Ibid., 193. As Gelpi notes, Jeffers, unlike modernist poets, was not suspicious of rhetoric. He saw it as a vehicle for the "encounter between the human and inhuman" (*Wild God of the World*, 18).

30. Jeffers, *Wild God of the World*, 14.

31. One strain flowing from this dissolution gives rise, according to Gelpi, to modernism, with its "fracturing of form, the impersonal submersion or splintering of the poetic voce, the choice of abstraction and incoherence and indeterminacy" (Jeffers, *Wild God of the World*, 2).

32. Ibid., 175.

33. Albert Gelpi, "Robinson Jeffers and the Sublime," in Jeffers, *Wild God of the World*, 17.

34. Jeffers, *Wild God of the World*, 23.

35. Ibid.

36. I have in mind the critique of Romanticism as continuing the dualism by supposing that we need to move from the human, over here, to the natural, over there. See Timothy Morton's *Ecology without Nature* (Cambridge, MA: Harvard University Press, 2009).

37. Jeffers, *Selected Letters*, 262–63.

FIVE. The Sacramental Poetics of William Everson

1. William Everson, "Dionysius and the Beat Generation: The Reemergence of the Dionysian Spirit in Contemporary Life," in *Beat Down to Your Soul* (London: Penguin Books, 2001), 152.

2. Ibid.

3. Gelpi, Introduction to Everson, *Dark God of Eros*, xxxv. Also see Gioia, "In Memoriam: William Everson."

4. Thomas McDonell, "The Poetry of Brother Antoninus," in *Benchmark and Blaze: The Emergence of William Everson*, ed. Lee Bartlett (London: Scarecrow Press, 1979), 22.

5. Albert Gelpi, "Contending with the Shadows," in Bartlett, *Benchmark and Blaze*, 184.

6. Charles Taylor, *A Secular Age* (Cambridge, MA: Harvard University Press, 2007), 539.

7. McDonell, "The Poetry of Brother Antoninus," 19.

8. Everson's work bears some resemblance, in the order of artistic practice, to the theoretical project of Jacques Maritain. The epigraph to Everson's autobiography is a passage from Maritain's correspondence with the filmmaker Cocteau: "Maritain to Cocteau: 'God gave you no rest. You found yourself in that state where the inner self is shackled, which is like an agony of the mind, and with which Jesus is accustomed to being preceded.'" See William Everson, *Prodigious Thrust* (Santa Barbara, CA: Black Sparrow Press, 1996), 178.

9. Everson, "Dionysius and the Beat Generation," 155.

10. Nietzsche, *The Birth of Tragedy*, 112.

11. Ibid., 97.

12. Ibid.

13. Peter Berkowitz, *Nietzsche: The Ethics of an Immoralist* (Cambridge, MA: Harvard University Press, 1995), 44–66.

14. Nietzsche, *The Birth of Tragedy*, 37.

15. Ibid., 52.

16. Everson, "Dionysius and the Beat Generation," 153.

17. Ibid., 154.

18. Josef Pieper, *Divine Madness: Plato's Case against Secular Humanism* (San Francisco: Ignatius Press, 1995).

19. Maritain, *Creative Intuition*, 3. Maritain identifies this intercommunication as an operation of poetry, which is "another name for what Plato called *mousikè*."

20. Maritain and Cocteau, *Art and Faith*.

21. For all his attention to aesthetics, Nietzsche ignores the erotic elements in Plato, found especially in the *Symposium* and the *Phaedrus*. In his short book *Divine Madness*, Pieper focuses particularly on the positive role of *mania*, or madness, in the dialogues. There are two types: one undermines reason and renders us beasts; the other, a divine madness (*theia mania*), comes from above and elevates the human soul. Pieper writes, "the present time especially cries out for a keener awareness of the Socratic-Platonic wisdom." He continues, "It cries out for resistance to the attempt and the temptation to establish the autocratic rule of man, who deludes himself that he possesses sovereign power over the world and over himself." We have here yet another critique of the anthropocentric model. Pieper, *Divine Madness*, 58.

22. Everson, "Dionysius and the Beat Generation," 155.

23. Gelpi, Introduction to Everson, *Dark God of Eros*, xxxv.

24. T. S. Eliot, *The Complete Poems and Plays, 1909–1950* (San Diego, CA: Harcourt Brace Jovanovich, 1971), 68.

25. William Everson, *The Veritable Years* (Santa Barbara, CA: Black Sparrow Press, 1999), 25.

26. Ibid., 27.

27. John Paul II, *The Lord and Giver of Life* (50). All quotations are from the official English-language version of *Dominum et Vivificantem: On the Holy Spirit in the Life of the Church and the World* (Vatican City: Libreria Editrice Vaticana, 1986).
28. Everson, *The Veritable Years*, 27.
29. Ibid., 28.
30. Ibid.
31. Ibid.
32. Everson, *Prodigious Thrust*, 262.
33. Everson, *The Veritable Years*, 86.
34. Ibid.
35. Paul Griffiths, *Song of Songs: Brazos Theological Commentary on the Bible* (Grand Rapids, MI: Brazos Press, 2011), 5.
36. Everson, *The Veritable Years*, 86.
37. Ibid., 165.
38. Desmond, *God and the Between*, 29.
39. Ibid., 236.
40. Marion, *The Crossing of the Visible*, 33.
41. Ibid.
42. Maritain, *Creative Intuition*, 173.
43. Ibid., 86.
44. Everson, *The Veritable Years*, 11.
45. Gary Snyder, *The Practice of the Wild* (San Francisco: North Point, 1990), 39.
46. Neil Evernden, "Beyond Ecology: Self, Place, and the Pathetic Fallacy," in *The Ecocriticism Reader*, ed. Cheryll Glotfelty and Harold Fromm (Athens: University of Georgia Press, 1996), 101.
47. Everson, *Prodigious Thrust*, 200.
48. Ibid., 197.
49. Everson, *Dark God of Eros*, 199, 198.
50. Ibid., 228.
51. Everson, *The Veritable Years*, 121.
52. Johnson, *Ask the Beasts*, 149.
53. Desmond, *God and the Between*, 335.
54. Ibid., 339.
55. Everson, *Dark God of Eros*, 246–47.
56. Everson, *The Veritable Years*, 168.
57. René Girard, *I See Satan Fall Like Lightning*, trans. James G. Williams (Maryknoll, NY: Orbis Books, 2001), 9.
58. René Girard, *Violence and the Sacred*, trans. Patrick Gregory (Baltimore: Johns Hopkins University Press, 1979), 7.
59. Ibid.

60. Everson, "Dionysius and the Beat Generation," 155.

61. By contrast to the operation of the scapegoat in mythic orders, in the Jewish and Christian Scriptures, the accused scapegoat is often revealed to be innocent, as in the case of the false accusation against Joseph in Genesis and most dramatically of course in the trial and crucifixion of Christ in the Gospels. See Girard, *I See Satan Fall Like Lightning*, 13.

62. Roger Scruton, *The Death-Devoted Heart: Sex and the Sacred in Wagner's "Tristan and Isolde"* (Oxford: Oxford University Press, 2004), 10.

63. Ibid., 11.

64. Ibid.

65. Bernard Williams, *Truth and Truthfulness* (Princeton, NJ: Princeton University Press, 2002), 91.

66. Everson, *Dark God of Eros*, 311.

67. Maritain, *Creative Intuition*, 103.

68. Everson, *The Veritable Years*, 200.

69. Ibid., 201.

70. Everson, *Dark God of Eros*, 207–8.

71. Amans quodammodo penetrat in amatum, et secundum hoc amor dicitur acutus; acuti enim est dividendo ad intima rei devenire; et similiter amatum penetrat amantem, ad interiora eius perveniens; et propter hoc dicitur quod amor vulnerate, et quod transfigit iecur (Sent. III. D. 27, q. 1, a. 1, ad 4). Translation mine.

72. Maritain, *Creative Intuition*, 128.

73. Everson, *The Veritable Years*, 201.

74. William Everson, *The Naked Heart: Talking on Poetry, Mysticism, and the Erotic* (Albuquerque: University of New Mexico Press, 1992), 136.

75. William Everson, *Birth of a Poet* (Santa Barbara, CA: Black Sparrow Press, 1982).

76. See Lee Bartlett, *William Everson: The Life of Brother Antoninus* (New York: New Directions Books, 1988), 169. In his public presentations and in the very structuring of his poetry, his work is as much an "ordering of silences" as of words. Everson, *Dark God of the World*, 318.

77. Everson's association with another Dominican, Victor White, a scholar of the unconscious as interpreted according to Carl Jung's theory of archetypes, had a tremendous influence on his poetry. Here the polarities of male and female complement one another. See Bartlett, *William Everson: The Life of Brother Antoninus*, 153ff.

78. Wendell Berry, *Sex, Economy, Freedom, and Community* (New York: Pantheon, 1993), 143.

79. Roger Scruton, *Beauty: A Very Short Introduction* (Oxford: Oxford University Press, 2011). Despite his insistence on the connection, in this book, between beauty and the sacred and, in the Wagner book, on the connection between

the sacred and death, Scruton remains beholden to a Kantian vision of dignity and beauty. For reservations about this element in Scruton's work, see the review of *Beauty* by Sebastian Smee in the *Guardian*, March 21, 2009.

80. Everson, *The Veritable Years*, 141.
81. Ibid., 128.
82. Ibid., 129.
83. Ibid., 131.
84. Ibid., 140.
85. See, e.g., the myth about human desire in Aristophanes's tale in Plato's *Symposium*.
86. David O'Connor, *In Plato's Bedroom* (South Bend, IN: St. Augustine's Press, 2015), 157–58.
87. Everson, *The Veritable Years*, 142.
88. Ibid., 146.
89. Ibid., 150.
90. William Everson, *The Masks of Drought* (Santa Barbara, CA: Black Sparrow Press, 1980), 49.
91. Ibid.
92. Ibid.
93. Ibid., 50.
94. Ibid., 51.
95. Everson, *The Veritable Years*, 128.

SIX. Georges Rouault: Artist of Alienation and Transfiguration

1. James Davison Hunter, *To Change the World: The Irony, Tragedy, and Possibility of Christianity in the Late Modern World* (Oxford: Oxford University Press, 2010), 205.
2. Ibid., 220.
3. Courthion, *Rouault*, 188.
4. Quoted in Courthion, *Rouault*, 246.
5. Lionello Venturi, *Georges Rouault* (Paris: Skira, 1948), 60.
6. Fujimura, *Refractions*, 125.
7. See the following contributions in Stephen Schloesser, ed., *Mystic Masque: Semblance and Reality in Georges Rouault, 1871–1958* (Chestnut Hill, MA: McMullen Museum of Art, Boston College, 2008): Susan Michalczyk, "The Aesthetics of Shock: Baudelaire, Benjamin, Rouault," 193–204; Stephen Schloesser, "Rouault, 1921–1929: Jazz Age Graphic Shock," 133–56; and Margaret Miles, "Rouault and the Dynamics of Self-Deception," 109–16.

8. Courthion, *Rouault*, 240.

9. See Nicholas Wolterstorff, *Thomas Reid and the Story of Epistemology* (Cambridge: Cambridge University Press, 2001), 23–44.

10. Marion, *Crossing the Visible*, 51. Marion writes, "The authentic painting would not give itself to be seen in such glory if it had not taken and surprised our scope of expectation."

11. See the excellent discussion in the chapter "Art and the Artist," in Marion, *Degrees of Givenness*, 51–77.

12. Marion, *Crossing the Visible*, 27.

13. Ibid., 42.

14. The major monographs that survey Rouault's entire work are Courthion, *Rouault*; and Venturi, *Rouault*. For a catalog of works, see François Chapon and Isabelle Rouault, *Rouault: L'Oeuvre gravé*, 2 vols. (Monte Carlo: Sauret, 1978); and Bernard Dorival and Isabelle Rouault, *Rouault: L'Oeuvre peint*, 2 vols. (Monte Carlo: Sauret, 1988). For recent in-depth studies on his early work, see Fabrice Hergott, ed., *Rouault: 1903–1920*, exh. cat. (Paris: Museé National d'Art Moderne, Centre Georges Pompidou, 1992); and Soo Yun Kang, *Rouault in Perspective: Contextual and Theoretical Study of His Art* (Lanham, MD: International Scholars, 2000).

15. The best interpretive study is Stephen Schloesser, "Notes on the *Miserere* Plates Exhibited in *Mystic Masque*," in Schloesser, *Mystic Masque*, 157–80. Although the focus is on the specific set of plates for the *Mystic Masque* exhibition, Schloesser offers a unified account of the whole series.

16. Hunter, *To Change the World*, 203.

17. Ibid., 234.

18. John McCoy, "Technique and Space in the *Miserere*," in Schloesser, *Mystic Masque*, 279.

19. Ibid., 280.

20. On the process of making the prints for the *Miserere*, see Dolores DeStefano, "Never Satisfied: The Making of *Miserere et Guerre*," in *This Anguished World of Shadows: Georges Rouault's Miserere et Guerre*, ed. Holly Flora and Soo Yun Kang (New York: Museum of Biblical Art, 2006), 19–24.

21. Desmond, *God and the Between*, 333.

22. Schloesser, "Notes on the *Miserere* Plates," 171–72.

23. Ibid., 172.

24. Ibid., 163.

25. Marion, *Crossing the Visible*, 21.

26. Flora and Kang, *The Anguished World of Shadows*, 44.

27. Kang, *Rouault in Perspective*, 3. Venturi observes that these types were established quite early in Rouault's career, during the first two decades of the twentieth century. See Venturi, *Rouault*, 65. There is no real consensus on how to char-

acterize Rouault as a painter, or even on the question of which schools of art his painting most fully represents. See Kang on Moreau's influence on Rouault, *Rouault in Perspective*, 20–28; and Schloesser on his training in medieval stained glass and numerous other early influences, in *Mystic Masque*, 31–72.

28. Quoted in Schloesser, *Jazz Age Catholicism*, 218–19. The accusations were especially painful because Rouault had great admiration for Bloy, whose books he had discovered in the home of his deceased mentor Moreau; moreover, the themes of destitution and prostitution were central to the plots of Bloy's own books.

29. Mary Roberts, "Tears at the Heart of Spectacular Paris: Rouault's Prostitutes," in Schloesser, *Mystic Masque*, 117–24. For other discussions, see Kang, *Rouault in Perspective*, 41–55; Courthion, *Rouault*, 99–100; and Stephen Schloesser, "Rouault 1902–1920: The Hard Metier of Unmasking," in Schloesser, *Mystic Masque*, 90–92.

30. Quoted in Courthion, *Rouault*, 100.

31. The most important artistic influence for these early paintings may well be Baudelaire. Although she does not draw the connection between Baudelaire and Rouault's paintings of prostitutes, Soo Yung Kang spells out the influence, especially concerning the obsession with suffering, in her essay "Spleen and Ideal in Strife: Rouault's Baudelaire: 1918–1927," in Schloesser, *Mystic Masque*, 181–92.

32. Georges Rouault, *Souvenirs intimes* (Paris: Frapier, 1926), 14.

33. Jean Grenier, "Georges Rouault and the Bible," *Preuves* (April 1958). Quoted in Courthion, *Rouault*, 352.

34. Comments about the widespread influence of Pascal on French artists and especially on Rouault abound in the essays collected in *Mystic Masque*, which unfortunately does not have an index; see, e.g., 48–49, 57, 110, 175–76. See also the recent book by Bernard Grasset, *Pascal et Rouault* (Nice: Ovadia, 2016).

35. Maritain, *Creative Intuition*, 127.

36. Ibid., 283–84.

37. Desmond, *God and the Between*, 333.

38. Ibid.

39. Maritain, *Creative Intuition*, 152.

40. Nora Pessenti Ghiglia, "Rouault's Faces of Christ: Notes for a Pictorial Contemplation," in Schloesser, *Mystic Masque*, 423–30.

41. John Conley, "Imitating Nature: Maritain's Reservations Concerning Artistic Mimesis," in *Reading the Cosmos: Nature, Science, and Wisdom*, ed. Giuseppe Butera, American Maritain Association Publications (Washington, DC: Catholic University of America Press, 2012).

42. Maritain, *Art and Scholasticism*, 59.

43. Ibid., 60.

44. Maritain, *Creative Intuition*, 153.

45. Courthion, *Rouault*, 240. In words that mirror Maritain's observation that the artist has an alert receptivity to the surrounding world, Rouault comments that he kept his "eyes open night and day to the visible world." The result is palpable, "a whole world of thoughts and feelings awaken in me when I am in the presence of life and nature. I try to express this world as best I can" (244).

46. Kang, *Rouault in Perspective*, 245ff.

47. Ibid., 245.

48. The influence of Rembrandt is evident in the early period, for example, in *Night Landscape* (1897).

49. Courthion, *Rouault*, 193.

50. Maritain, *Creative Intuition*, 92.

51. Ibid., 146.

52. Courthion, *Rouault*, 294.

53. Ibid., 236, quoting an unpublished essay of Georges Chabot.

54. Rouault's accent on the Eucharist calls to mind the statement of Hopkins about the Catholic teaching on the Real Presence. In a letter to E. H. Coleridge (June 1, 1864), Hopkins writes, "The great aid to belief and object of belief is the doctrine of the Real Presence in the Blessed Sacrament of the Altar. Religion without it is somber, dangerous, illogical, with that it is—not to speak of its grand consistency and certainty—loveable. Hold that and you will gain all Catholic truth." C. C. Abbott, ed., *Further Letters of Gerard Manley Hopkins: Including His Correspondence with Coventry Patmore*, 2nd ed. (London: Oxford University Press, 1956), 17.

55. Bernard Dorival, *Cinq etudes sur Georges Rouault*, Temoins du Xxe siècle (Paris: Editions Universitaires, 1956).

56. Stephen Dahme, "'Pilgrim of Art': Artistic Autonomy and Christian Commitment in Rouault's Late Work," in Schloesser, *Mystic Masque*, 379–87.

57. Georges Rouault, *Stella Vespertina* (Paris: Drouin, 1947).

58. Jacques Maritain, *Ransoming the Time* (n.p.: Gordian Press, 1972). In *Creative Intuition*, Maritain writes, "It is through history that the union of nature and man is accomplished. As a result, nature radiates with signs and significance, which make her beauty blossom forth" (7).

59. Nora Possenti Ghiglia, "Rouault's Faces of Christ: Notes for a Pictorial Contemplation," in Schloesser, *Mystique Mask*, 417.

60. Rouault, *Stella Vespertina*, no pagination; translation mine.

61. Kang, *Rouault in Perspective*, 253.

62. Courthion, *Rouault*, 294. In Robert Bretell's *Modern Art 1851–1929* (Oxford: Oxford University Press, 1999), Rouault receives only passing mention as a student of Moreau, and Jopseh-Emile Muller's *Fauvism* (New York: Prager, 1967) justifies excluding Rouault for the following reason: "his moral preoccupations, his dominating expressionist tendencies, and especially his continuing attachment to chiaroscuro, exclude him from the ranks of the fauves properly speaking" (20).

63. Courthion, *Rouault*, 294.
64. Friedrich Nietzsche, *On the Advantage and Disadvantage of History for Life* (Indianapolis: Hackett, 1980), 8.
65. Ibid., 24.
66. There are interesting parallels here between Nietzsche's thinking and that of the main character in Dostoevsky's *Notes from Underground*.
67. Nietzsche, *Advantage and Disadvantage*, 57.
68. Ibid., 21.
69. As Bowie notes, Nietzsche here remains under the influence of Schopenhauer. Andrew Bowie, *Aesthetics and Subjectivity: From Kant to Nietzsche* (Oxford: Oxford University Press, 2003), 184.
70. Nietzsche, *Advantage and Disadvantage*, 39.
71. As Anthony Jensen notes in his study of the text, the study of the past is important not so much for emulation as for providing exemplars in relation to which those aspiring to greatness in the present can find worthy rivals. The past feeds present-day agonistic competition. Thus does Nietzsche turn back to an anthropocentric model. See Anthony K. Jensen, *An Interpretation of Nietzsche's "On the Uses and Disadvantage of History for Life"* (New York: Routledge, 2016), 145. For all his criticisms of Nietzsche's aesthetics, Marion's accentuation of the authentic artist as an isolated genius and on the inexplicable gap between the few who can experience authentic art and the many who do not echoes Nietzsche. On these matters, see Marion, *Degrees of Givenness*, 75–77.
72. See James Thrall Soby, *Georges Rouault: Paintings and Prints* (New York: Museum of Modern Art, 1945), 131.
73. Rouault, *Stella Vespertina*, no pagination; translation mine.
74. T. S. Eliot, "Tradition and the Individual Talent," in *Selected Prose of T. S. Eliot*, ed. with intro. Frank Kermode (New York: Farrar, Straus and Giroux, 1975), 38.
75. By contrast, Alasdair MacIntyre argues, living traditions are sites of development, intelligible novelty, and ongoing debates about standards. See his *Whose Justice? Which Rationality?*, 349–88.
76. Jean Cocteau, *The Cock and the Harlequin*, trans. Rollo Myers (London: Egoist Press, 1921), 28.
77. Courthion, quoting Rouault, *Stella Vespertina*, 48.
78. Nietzsche, *Advantage and Disadvantage*, 21.
79. Maritain, *Creative Intuition*, 283.
80. Ibid., 276.
81. Ibid., 283.
82. Ibid., 284.
83. Jenkins, *Ecologies of Grace*, 149.
84. T. S. Eliot, "Ash Wednesday," in *The Complete Poems and Plays* (London: Faber & Faber, 2004), 64.

SEVEN. Culture Care, Generativity, and the Calling of the Artist

1. Makoto Fujimura, "Fra Angelico and the Five-Hundred Year Question," in *Refractions*, 141.
2. Ibid., 144.
3. Maritain, *Creative Intuition*, 40.
4. Makoto Fujimura, "Why Art?," in *Refractions*, 111.
5. Ibid., 113.
6. James Breslin, *Mark Rothko: A Biography* (Chicago: University of Chicago Press, 1993), 265.
7. Ibid., 266.
8. Miguel Lopez-Remiro, ed., *Mark Rothko: Writings on Art* (New Haven, CT: Yale University Press, 2006), 39, 125.
9. Breslin, *Mark Rothko: A Biography*, 357. Breslin is quoting from an unpublished draft of a Rothko lecture on Nietzsche. For Breslin's understanding of the role of Nietzsche in Rothko, see 173–76, 357–59, 499–500.
10. Jonathan Har, "The Development of American Modernism, 1938–1948," *Oxford Art Journal* 11 (1988): 40–50.
11. Dore Ashton, *About Rothko* (Oxford: Oxford University Press, 1983), 112–13.
12. Breslin, *Mark Rothko: A Biography*, 278; original emphasis.
13. Ibid., 279.
14. Ibid., 268.
15. Jacob Ball-Teshuva, *Mark Rothko, 1903–1970: Pictures as Drama* (New York: Taschen, 2003), 50.
16. Maritain, *Crossing the Visible*, 26.
17. For a religious interpretation of Rothko that relies heavily on his Jewish roots, see Annie Cohen-Solal, *Mark Rothko: Toward the Light in the Chapel* (New Haven, CT: Yale University Press, 2013).
18. See Jean-Luc Marion, *In Excess: Studies of Saturated Phenomena*, trans. Robyn Horner and Vincent Beraud (New York: Fordham University Press, 2004), 72.
19. Ibid., 73.
20. Barbara Hess, *Abstract Expressionism* (New York: Taschen, 2005), 42.
21. Matali Kosoi, "Nothingness Made Visible: The Case of Rothko's Paintings," *Art Journal* 64 (2005): 20–31. See also Leo Bersani and Ulysse Dutoit, *The Arts of Impoverishment: Beckett, Rothko, Resnais* (Cambridge, MA: Harvard University Press, 1993).
22. David Gelernter, "Master in Depth," *Weekly Standard*, February 15, 2010.

23. "A Refraction by Makoto Fujimura," in Thomas Hibbs, *Rouault Fujimura: Soliloquies* (Baltimore, MD: Square Halo Books, 2009), 57.

24. Hibbs, *Rouault Fujimura: Soliloquies*, 54.

25. This is particularly true of the way in which he draws attention to the surface of the painting itself. As Courthion notes, Rouault "spreads the paint on the canvas like modeling clay, working it with palette knife, brush, and fingers, the marks of which remain on the finished pictures. Sometimes the paint is as sleek and as brilliant as freshly applied enamel. More often, however, it gives the impression of a battlefield: piled up, kneaded and rekneaded, touched and retoughed, pounded mercilessly. The result is an agglomeration of tone upon tone, a thick, warm integument of the richest texture." *Rouault*, 236.

26. See "Splendor," in Fujimura, *Refractions*, 22. As Fujimura points out, Rouault is greatly admired in Japan, where Fujimura himself first encountered his work.

27. Breslin, *Mark Rothko: A Biography*, 276.

28. Ibid., 278. According to Breslin, there is indeed a destruction but one that preserves in memory what has been left behind. Rothko operates by "pulverizing the familiar world of recognizable, stable objects—by grinding them to the point of dissolution—his works free us from the weight, solidity, and definition of a material existence, *whose* constricting pressures we still feel" (279).

29. On Buddhist thought and Hindu texts, specifically, the Bhagavad Gita, in Eliot's reflections in *Four Quartets*, see, e.g., Narsingh Srivastava, "The Ideas of the *Bhagavad Gita* in *Four Quartets*," *Comparative Literature* 29, no. 2 (1977): 97–108; Beryl Rosay McLeod, "Buddhism, T. S. Eliot and the *Four Quartets*," *Journal for the Study of Religion* 5, no. 1 (1992): 3–16; Tim Bruno, "Buddhist Conceptual Rhyming and T. S. Eliot's Crisis of Connection in 'The Waste Land' and 'Burnt Norton,'" *Asian Philosophy* 23, no. 4 (2013): 365–78. For a long footnote on the implications of the missing definite article in "Incarnation," see G. Douglas Atkins, *Reading T. S. Eliot: Four Quartets and the Journey toward Understanding* (New York: Palgrave Macmillan, 2012), 151–58.

30. For the catalog of a later Fujimura engagement with Eliot's *Quaretets*, see *QU4RTETS* (Princeton, NJ: Fujimura Institute, 2012).

31. Eliot, *Complete Poems and Plays*, 119.

32. Iris Murdoch, *Existentialists and Mystics: Writings on Philosophy and Literature* (London: Penguin Books, 1999), 216.

33. Ibid., 202.

34. Insisting on the distinction between ethics and aesthetics, Murdoch nonetheless proposes that "art is the great guide to morals." *Existentialists and Mystics*, 202.

35. Murdoch, *Existentialists and Mystics*, 217.

36. Brague, *The Kingdom of Man*, 214; original emphasis.

INDEX

anthropocentrism, xi–xiv, 1, 4, 8, 12–15, 17, 19–20, 22–23, 25–29, 40, 43, 48, 51–52, 59, 69–70, 72, 76, 78, 80, 84, 87–88, 105, 111, 128, 136, 154, 163n17, 174n21, 181n71
Aquinas, Thomas, x, xii, 2, 5–10, 16, 18–19, 21–22, 32, 39, 42–44, 52, 60, 62–65, 67–69, 100–101, 122, 132, 156n3, 156n10, 158n49, 159n54, 162n4, 164n45, 166n71, 168n27, 169n36
Arendt, Hannah, 34
Aristotle, 8–9, 25, 38–39, 41, 61, 65–68, 88, 125–26
   Aristotelian aspects, 8, 37, 167n23
art
   as abstract, 11, 28, 51, 60, 119, 125, 140, 143–44, 147
   as imitation, 98, 112, 125–126, 135
Augustine of Hippo, 16, 43, 67, 157n38, 169n44
autonomy, 1, 14, 19, 40, 44, 46, 49, 70, 86, 88, 107, 112, 164n25

Baudelaire, Charles, 49–50, 88, 110, 119, 122–24, 136, 151, 166n71, 179n31

beauty, 21, 40–41, 43–45, 48–49, 61
Benedict XVI, 1, 3, 13
Benton, Ted, 67
Bergson, Henri, 35–36
Berkeley, George, 111
Berkowitz, Peter, 86
Berry, Wendell, 103, 159n54
biocentrism, xi, xiii, 1, 4, 14, 17, 19–20, 22, 25–28, 48, 52, 70, 72–73, 75–76, 84, 87–88, 111, 128, 150, 154
Blake, William, 32, 159n58
Bloy, Léon, 121, 179n28
Boff, Leonardo, 21
Brague, Rémi, 20, 153
Breslin, James, 142, 144, 150, 182n9, 183n28
Brody, Emily, 79–80
Brother Antoninus, xiii, 26, 83
Byrne, Pat, 66

Carnes, Natalie, 41
Cavell, Stanley, 79
Cézanne, Paul, 120, 128, 147
Chagall, Marc, xii, 125, 161n1
Chesterton, G. K., x, 5–11, 32

Cocteau, Jean, xii, 31, 88, 135, 161n1, 162n3, 174n8
Courthion, Pierre, 110, 121, 126, 128, 183n25
creation, ix–xi, 1–3, 5–7, 9–10, 13, 16–22, 26, 33, 46–47, 54–55, 61–64, 67–70, 87, 90, 94, 96–97, 100, 104, 114, 130, 136, 140, 149, 153, 169n36, 169nn44–45
crisis of the visible, 109–12, 119
Croasmun, Matthew, 17
Cronon, William, 20–21, 158n52, 159n53, 159n60
culture care, xiii, 11–12, 140–41

Dante, 49–50, 88, 105, 110, 123, 135–36
De Koninck, Charles, ix, 52, 65–70, 81, 105, 161n69, 170n72
Deane-Drummond, Celia, 64, 156n1, 156n3
Derrida, Jacques, 59, 77–78
Descartes, René, 57, 59
Desmond, William, 52, 62–64, 68, 94, 114, 124, 169n45
Donne, John, 88, 102–3
Dorival, Bernard, 130, 178n14

ecological virtue, 3, 21, 140, 148, 156n3
ecology, natural and human, xi, 4, 8–9, 11–13, 19, 21, 28, 111, 126, 159n54, 163n17
Edwards, Dennis, 9, 15, 26, 70, 156n1
El Greco, 126
Eliot, T. S., xiii, 26, 84–85, 88–92, 135–37, 151–52, 183n30
Ellison, Ralph, 4
Enlightenment, xi, 4, 14, 20, 22–24, 28, 73, 78, 86, 95, 134, 169n44

Esbjorn-Hargens, Sean, 73, 171n8
Everson, William, xiii, 26–28, 73, 79, 83–85, 87–107, 109, 142, 148, 151, 174n8, 176n77
evolution in *LS*, in cosmos, x, xiv, 2–3, 13–14, 15–16, 52, 62–70, 79, 154, 167n23, 169n44

Fra Angelico, 139–40
Francis, x–xii, 1–11, 13–14, 19–22, 28, 31, 34, 62, 64, 73, 141, 156n2, 156n10, 163n17
Francis of Assisi, x, 5–8, 10, 17–19, 21
Freud, Sigmund, 21, 101
Fujimura, Makoto, xiii, 11–13, 28, 32, 139–142, 146–52, 183n26, 183n30

Gelernter, David, 147
Gelpi, Albert, xiii, 26, 79–80, 83–84, 88, 92, 173n29, 173n31
genealogy
  Maritain, xii, 28
  Nietzsche, 24–25, 52, 62, 86
  standard Catholic version, xiv, 2, 19, 22, 29, 50, 166n71
generativity, 12, 25, 133, 140, 147
Gill, Eric, 32, 47–48
Gilson, Etienne, 65
Gioia, Dana, 32, 155n7
Girard, René, 98, 176n61
givenness (gift), 42, 57–58, 64, 164n45
Grenier, Jean, 122
Griffiths, Paul, 93–94
Gschwandtner, Christina, 58–59
Guardini, Romano, 4

Hanby, Michael, 4
Hanke, J. W., 61, 162n4, 165n48
Hart, Kevin, 57
Heaney, Seamus, xiii, 33

Hegel, G. W. F., 59, 78, 172n23
Heidegger, Martin, 45, 57, 59, 79
Hobbes, Thomas, 14, 16, 37
Homer, 74
Hopkins, Gerard Manley, 10, 96, 102, 159n58, 180n54
Hume, David, 59
Hunter, James Davison, 109, 112–13
Husserl, Edmund, 57–59

icon, the, 94, 112–13, 116, 120, 124, 130, 136, 149, 165n63
idealism, 21, 36, 40, 45, 59, 64, 76, 111, 168n27
idol, the, 94, 111–12
idolatry, 26, 77, 124
inhumanism, 25, 74–76, 81–82

Jager, Colin, 23
Jeffers, Robinson, xiii, 25–26, 28, 64, 71, 73–82, 84–85, 95–97, 102, 109, 142, 150, 161n66, 172n12, 173n29
Jeffrey, David, 23
Jenkins, Willis, 7, 18–19, 159n54
Job, ix, 69
John of St. Thomas, 141
John of the Cross, 15
John Paul II, 3, 13, 90
Johnson, Elizabeth, 6–7, 69, 96
Jones, David, 32

Kang, Soo Yun, 120, 126, 178n27, 179n31
Kant, 23, 77, 79, 160n61
 Kantian aspects, 55–57, 64, 100, 160n61, 176n79
Kierkegaard, Søren, 59, 78
Kohak, Erazim, 73
Kosoi, Matali, 146

Lachterman, David, 38
landscapes, 27, 111, 115, 126, 128–32, 136, 159n53, 159n58
Levinas, Emmanuel, 78
Lewis, C. S., 34, 163n13
Locke, John, 20, 158n49
Lubezki, Emmanuel, ix
Luther, Martin, 8

MacIntyre, Alasdair, 66, 167n23, 181n75
Malick, Terrence, ix, x, 155n1
Mallarmé, Stéphane, 76
Manent, Pierre, xiv, 14
Marion, Jean-Luc, xii, 33, 52, 56–60, 77, 94, 109, 111–12, 145, 168n33, 169n36, 169n45, 178nn10–11, 181n71, 182n18
Maritain, Jacques, xii–xiii, 4, 11, 17–18, 21–23, 25–28, 31–51, 58–61, 64, 68, 76, 87–88, 94–95, 100–101, 110, 121–23, 125–26, 128, 135–36, 139–41, 143–44, 147, 150, 159n58, 160nn61–62, 161n1, 162nn3–4, 162n11, 163n12, 163n17, 164n45, 165n56, 165n63, 166n71, 174n8, 174n19, 180n45
Maritain, Raïssa, xii, 32, 35–36, 56
Mary Magdalen, 101
Matisse, Henri, 143–44
McCoy, John, 113–14
McDonell, Thomas, 84
McInerny, Ralph, 32
Merton, Thomas, 32, 159n58
Mondrian, Piet, 144
Moreau, Gustave, 134, 178nn27–28, 180n62
Mulhall, Stephen, 79
Murdoch, Iris, 153, 183n34

nature, x–xiv, 1–29, 36, 42, 45, 51,
  62, 65, 67, 69–72, 75–77, 79–82,
  84–87, 89–91, 94–97, 100–101,
  104, 106–7, 110, 112, 123–25,
  128–32, 141, 143, 151, 153,
  156n2, 157n41, 158n49, 158n52,
  159nn53–54, 160n61, 171n2,
  171n5, 171n8, 172n10, 180n45,
  180n58
Nichols, Aidan, 32
Nietzsche, Friedrich, 12, 24–25, 28,
  51–57, 59, 71–75, 77–81, 83,
  85–87, 92, 99–100, 111–12,
  133–35, 142–45, 161n66, 167n5,
  171n2, 171n5, 172n10, 172n12,
  174n21, 181n66, 181n69,
  181n71, 182n9
  Nietzschean aspects, 24–25, 28,
    56, 63, 73, 76, 92, 111–12, 142,
    144–46, 153

O'Connor, David, 104
O'Connor, Flannery, xiii, 32, 49
O'Connor, John, 32
Oreskes, Naomi, 3–4

pantheism, 20, 79–80, 95–96, 130
Pascal, Blaise, x, 59, 69, 95, 97, 115,
  120–24, 155n2, 157n38, 160n61,
  179n34
Paul, 17, 34, 103, 113
Percy, Walker, 4, 8, 157n38
Pippin, Robert, 54–57, 64, 160n61,
  164n25
Plato, 38, 57, 111, 174n19, 174n21
  Platonism, 8, 72, 88, 174n21
Poe, Edgar Allan, 123

Reid, Thomas, 111
Rembrandt, 27, 120, 128, 134, 180n48

Roberts, Mary, 121
Romanticism, xi–xii, 14–15, 18,
  20–25, 45, 48, 72, 80, 86, 88,
  134, 153, 159n58, 159n60,
  160n61, 165n56, 169n44,
  171n2, 173n36
Rosen, Stanley, 56–57
Rothko, Mark, 11, 28, 140, 142–150,
  153, 182n9, 182n17, 182n19,
  183n28
Rouault, Georges, xii–xiii, 11, 26–28,
  31–32, 45–46, 49, 109–37, 140,
  146, 149–50, 165n63, 178n14,
  178n27, 179n29, 179n31,
  179n34, 180n45, 180n54,
  180n62, 183nn25–26
Rousseau, Jean-Jacques, 72

Schloesser, Stephen, 116, 122, 161n74,
  163n12, 177n7, 178n15, 178n27
Scotus, xii
Scruton, Roger, 99, 100, 103, 176n79
Simon, Yves, 31, 161n1
Snyder, Gary, 95
Socrates, 56–57, 87, 97
  Socratic, 55, 57, 67, 86, 174n21
  pre-Socratic, 85
Steiner, George, 109
Stravinsky, Igor, 31, 161n1
Suares, Andre, 128
sublime, 15–16, 20–21, 23, 58, 62, 80,
  85, 96, 119, 141, 148, 152–53,
  160n61

Taylor, Charles, 84, 159n58
technocracy, 1, 4, 13, 33–34, 82, 132,
  153
Teilhard de Chardin, Pierre, 66,
  161n69, 170n60
Toulouse-Lautrec, Henri, 121

tradition, xii–xiii, 2, 5, 11–12, 16–18, 23–24, 27–28, 31–33, 39, 50, 53–54, 61, 64–65, 77–78, 85, 93, 120, 125, 130, 134–35, 137, 140–42, 149–51, 159n58, 165n63, 169n44, 181n75
tragedy, 62, 69, 74, 85–87, 101, 125, 128, 145, 161n69, 170n72
Trapani, John, 60, 162n4
Tsakiridou, C. A., 44–46, 58

van Gogh, Vincent, 147
Venturi, Lionello, 110, 178n27
Vergil, 124
Veronica, 113, 116, 118–20, 126–27, 132

violence, xiv, 2–3, 14–16, 18, 26, 70, 85, 87–88, 91, 97–102, 106–7, 142, 148, 151
Volf, Miroslav, 17

Wagner, Richard, 99–101, 176n79
Walsh, David, 25, 36–39, 62, 77–78, 172n23
Warhol, Andy, 139
White, Lynn, 19, 24
Williams, Bernard, 100
Wittgenstein, Ludwig, 79

Zimmerman, Michael, 72–73, 171n5, 171n8

THOMAS S. HIBBS

is the J. Newton Rayzor Sr. Professor of Philosophy at Baylor University, where he is also dean emeritus, having served sixteen years as dean of the Honors College and distinguished professor of ethics and culture. He is the author and editor of eight books, including *Wagering on an Ironic God: Pascal on Faith and Philosophy*.

www.ingramcontent.com/pod-product-compliance
Lightning Source LLC
Chambersburg PA
CBHW070401240426
43661CB00056B/2495